Environmental Decay

LITTLE, BROWN SERIES IN ECONOMICS

Richard E. Caves, CONSULTING EDITOR

Bain	*Environmental Decay: Economic Causes and Remedies*
Caves and Jones	*World Trade and Payments*
Eckaus	*Basic Economics*
Grossack and Martin	*Managerial Economics: Microtheory and the Firm's Decisions*
Hodgman	*National Monetary Policies and International Monetary Cooperation*
Sherman, H.	*The Soviet Economy*
Sherman, R.	*Economics of Industry*
Singer	*Public Microeconomics*
Thompson	*Statistics for Decisions*

Environmental Decay
Economic Causes and Remedies

JOE S. BAIN
University of California, Berkeley

Little, Brown and Company
Boston

This book is printed on recycled paper.

Preface

This book presents, primarily for advanced undergraduate students in college, a discussion of "environmental economics" — of the economic sources and effects of degradation of our environment, and of public policies designed to arrest, control, and reverse environmental deterioration.

As organized, it is a volume of both "text" and "readings." The first two chapters contain a relatively simplified abstract theoretical analysis of environmental degradation and its control, incorporating some brief illustrative factual examples. Some emphasis is placed on the distinction between two main categories of deterioration of the environment — i.e., "pollution" generated by production and consumption, and misallocations of land and water resources among uses and users.

The third chapter is an article analyzing the economic, sociological, and political sources of the recent environmental preservation movement, and appraising its prospects for survival as a popular political cause.

In each of Chapters 4 through 8 a particular environmental problem is dealt with, with emphasis on the facts of the case, and on their relation to theoretical generalities earlier developed. These chapters consider in turn water pollution, automotive air pollution, allocation of rural land and water resources between commercial uses and recreation, the deteriorating environment of our central cities, and the adverse environmental impacts of freeways and commercial airline travel. The "case study" approach embodied in these chapters seems appropriate in view of the widely variegated and complex character of individual environmental issues, and of the tendency of abstract theoretical analysis to miss much of the empirical detail that is such an essential part of these issues.

The concluding chapter is a summary of the findings of the preceding five chapters, relating them to each other and to the opening theoretical discussion in Chapters 1 and 2.

The content of the book should be readily understood by a reader who has had a strong course in elementary economics, or an elementary course plus a semester of intermediate price theory. Its uses may be various. As a whole it may be basic reading in a course in environmental economics. Or all or parts of it may supply supplementary reading in such a course, or selectively in environment-oriented courses in departments of engineering, city and regional planning, and so forth.

I should like to acknowledge numerous valuable criticisms of the original manuscript offered by Professor Richard E. Caves of Harvard University, and the prodigious labors of Mr. Richard Schwindt in collecting and organizing research materials that are the underpinning of Chapters 6 through 8. The final work-product, of course, is solely my responsibility.

Contents

Introduction

In the last decade there has been a rapidly rising tide of public concern in the United States over the degradation of our human environment, expressed in demands for measures to ameliorate, control, or
reverse this deterioration. A political movement has been built around
this attitude and common cause. The upsurge of public anxiety was
initially encouraged by — and subsequently itself has encouraged —
publications of every sort dealing with the perils of many types of
environmental deterioration.

This book, written primarily for college students, presents in Chapter 1 an analytical overview of the nature and working of the economic sources of environmental degradation, and in Chapter 2 a
discussion of the economic merits of various types of public measures
for controlling it. Five of the six subsequent chapters are individual
essays, each dealing with the economics of a specific environmental
degradation and control problem; one is generally concerned with the
social, political, and economic dynamics of the recent "environmental
movement." The concluding chapter attempts some synthesis of the
contents of these essays and relates them to our general analytical
framework.

THE SCOPE OF HUMAN ENVIRONMENT

First, however, we offer a brief discussion of what human environment includes; how it varies among individuals, groups, and regions;
and means of measuring changes in its quality.

Two things about human environment should be emphasized initially. First, it has a multiplicity of different aspects, and this is the

1

source of considerable elasticity in its definition. Second, human environment is far from uniform within a large country, and even more variegated among countries and continents. Many different localities, areas, and regions differ distinctly with respect to numerous aspects of environment. It is thus more appropriate to refer to the attributes of *an* environment (any one of many) than to those of *the* environment of a very large geographical area.

The social or human environment of an area, most broadly considered, embraces all the "external" or nonpersonal conditions and influences that affect the welfare of people in the area. A prime group of such environmental influences are physical and inorganic, and include — as measured in available quality or quantity or both — air, water, and climate. They also include many characteristics of land that are of direct or indirect importance to the population of an area, including for example its topography, the quantity and fertility of arable and related lands, and the relative proximities and qualities of natural resources that are available for outdoor recreational activities. Comparably important are natural biological attributes of an environment, embracing the type, quantity, and quality of wild vegetation, wild mammals, birds, and fish — as are the quantity and character of domesticated plants and animals upon which the population of an area draws for sustenance or other satisfactions.

Many significant aspects of environments — especially of urban ones — are man made (physiosocial). Among them are the supply and quality of streets and highways and of public transit systems, and the availability and dependability of domestic public utility services. They include the incidence and distribution of residential areas of various degrees of population density, and of low-rise and high-rise commercial and industrial buildings. Human environments embrace too the quantities and types of a multiplicity of manufactured devices (certainly not excluding airliners, trucks, and passenger automobiles) that alter the surroundings or living conditions of individuals in an area's populace.

A human environment in these many aspects clearly not only exists at any time, but is changing continually, and generally there are complex interactions among changes in many of the aspects of such an environment. For example, the massive introduction of freeways into countrysides surrounding major cities has, by promoting suburbanization, been crucial to very significant changes in the environments, first of those who became suburbanites, and second of the revised populations of the central cities.

A TYPICAL INDIVIDUAL'S VIEW
OF HIS ENVIRONMENT

The foregoing outline of the scope of a human environment may be brought into focus if we consider briefly the environment of a male individual of the most common type in this country today — an adult, employed urban dweller — as he may view it, beginning at his residence and extending outward. A central aspect of his environment is the interior of his dwelling, measured as to quality in numerous obvious dimensions. Proximate to this is what he steps into as he leaves his front door — whether an apartment hallway, a paved sidewalk abutting a paved street, a front yard garden with grass and greenery, or whatever. Once he is outdoors, an important environmental consideration involves the density or congestion, horizontal and vertical, of the buildings on his street, which determines how much light, air, and space he can enjoy in his own neighborhood and perhaps also how much street noise he is exposed to. Similarly important is the degree of maintenance of other dwellings on his street, which may range from slum-decrepit to highly maintained. And exceptionally important is the quality of the air he breathes in his home neighborhood, which may range from pure and clear to smog-laden with a surface concentration of carbon monoxide. The climate will also of course make a difference, as it may feature anything from frigid winters and hot summers to tolerably temperate weather the year round.

The next environmental consideration for this urban dweller concerns how long, at what expense, and with what comparative degree of comfort he can reach and return from his place of employment — all affected by numerous generally familiar factors. When at work, some important considerations include the adequacy of work space, the level of noise exposure, and whether or not there is satisfactory ventilation plus adequate heating or air conditioning as required. Also significant will be the quality of the outside air proximate to his place of work, the outdoor noise level, the extent to which the surrounding building pattern limits light, air, and space, and the extent of human congestion.

So much for conditions surrounding his work-day routine. The rest of his family, if he is married, will find all of the environmental conditions of his neighborhood at least as important as he does. In addition, reasonable proximity and accessibility to varied shopping facilities will be important to his wife. For his children, both the readiness of access to schools, on foot or by public transporation, and the relative proximity and adequacy of local parks and playgrounds will be significant.

The distance from home and quality of, as well as the extent of or conditions of access to, various types of recreational lands or waters (and also specialized recreational facilities) further comprise significant aspects of his and his family's environment. Are there fairly spacious developed city parks, and perhaps also regional parks embracing large tracts of undeveloped land, open to the public and close enough for a day's or afternoon's visit? And if so, are they in sufficient supply that on weekends human congestion does not greatly reduce their psychic satisfactions? If there are golf courses, to what extent respectively are they accessible at a cost he can afford, and to what extent inaccessible because of the high cost of their use? If rivers or lakes or ocean bays are located nearby, are their waters pure enough for general water sports, or sufficiently polluted to make anything but boating hazardous to health, or so contaminated as to bar all recreational uses? Further, if these waters are sufficiently unpolluted to permit appreciable recreational use, is there fairly widespread public access to their reasonably clean and attractive shores, or has public access to their shorelines been substantially preempted by industrial plants or other private developments?

So far as recreation may potentially involve summer or winter vacations, as well as long-weekend trips, some very important environmental considerations to urban residents include the distances (and travel times) to recreational resources and facilities in the distinctly nonurban "great outdoors." To reach comparatively "wild" forests and mountains and streams of various satisfaction-providing qualities, is the travel distance 50 or 250 miles by car (or, for those who can afford air travel, what is the travel time and cost)?

Moreover, what is the quality of these variously distant recreation areas, as determined, for example, by whether forests have been or are in the process of being heavily used for cutting lumber, or by whether streams run free or are noticeably impaired for recreational use by damming for the production of hydropower or by depletion through diversions for irrigation? And to what extent is access to the use of potentially available recreational resources blocked by private ownership, either absolutely or by high prices for use? Further, are recreational resources of the types mentioned reasonably accessible in sufficient supply that their quality is not greatly reduced by an appreciable congestion of vacationers?

More indirectly, and much less commonly perceived, an important aspect of the environment of an urban or other populace composes the extent and productivity of agricultural crop and range land in its region and in the country generally, the extent of available timber resources for cropping, the natural endowment of mineral resources, and so forth. In agriculture, moreover, various productive techniques — such as those involving the widespread use of certain long-lived pesticides and other chemicals — have more or less recently been recognized as having cumulative effects on environments. They intrude upon the natural "food chain" in various ways which tend both to lead to the deterioration of certain domestic food products and to endanger the survival of wild species of fish, birds, and land animals.

DIFFERENCES AMONG THE ENVIRONMENTS
OF DIFFERENT GROUPS AND THEIR SOURCES

It has been emphasized above that human environments in many of their aspects differ widely among geographic areas and regions. Most people can easily ascertain that the environment of residents in a large and densely populated urban steel-mill center is in numerous respects much different from that of the populace of an isolated village on New Mexico's high desert plateau.

What is perhaps less emphasized in many discussions of environmental problems is that within almost any large urban or metropolitan area, there are wide differences among many aspects of the environments of different socio-economic groups, as distinguished by ethnic identity, social background, and income and wealth. Significant intergroup differences are found in quality of housing and in dimensions of neighborhood quality: aesthetic quality of location; microclimate; extent of availability of light, air, and space; extent of exposure to regional smog; and degree of isolation from the noise and local air pollution associated with freeways and congested streets. Comparable differences among groups occur with respect to occupational habitat and surroundings. And, as regards recreational opportunities, there are wide differences among the types and qualities of recreation to which different groups have effective access. These intergroup differences in "effective environment" are primarily, though not exclusively, linked to differences in income and wealth and thus in power to purchase better housing in better locales, better recreation, etc. This leads us to a conclusion that is perhaps not intuitively obvious to all: quality of individual environment is in many aspects a purchasable commodity and is likely to improve with individual purchasing power. Therefore, personal income distribution is a potent factor in differentiating the individuals' environments.

Of course, money cannot buy for an affluent group high quality in every aspect of its environment. It is hard to live in the Los Angeles basin and find real or reasonably full escape from smog, and deterioration of common foods stemming ultimately from the use of long-lived chemicals in agricultural production is likely to affect nearly everyone. But individual income and individual environment are strongly linked — a fact which looms large in the discussion of urban blight and congestion in Chapter 7.

ENVIRONMENT AND ECOLOGY

So far we have contrived to describe the scope of human environment — and the principal aspects of it which have frequently deteriorated or are deteriorating because of human activity — without mentioning the associated term *ecology*. Yet words like *ecology* and *ecological* have become the key terms in the catch phrases that are most popularly used in referring to problems of degradation of the human environment.

Environment and ecology are certainly closely related concepts. A biological environment is the aggregate of all external conditions and influences affecting the life and development of an organism; a human environment embraces these things so far as they affect human beings. Ecology, in complementary fashion, deals with the mutual relationships among organisms, and between organisms (including humans) and their environments. Concern with degradations of human environments stems naturally, generically, from their ecological consequences — from observed or anticipated adverse changes in the relationships of humans to one another, or of humans to their evolving environments. Such changes are adverse if they result in a worsening of the physical well-being of human populations, or of the psychic satisfactions they enjoy.

Yet, as noted in Chapter 3 (pp. 78–80), ecology as a pivot for approaching problems of environmental change can be and has been used in an unfortunate and not particularly sensible way when "ecological balance" — a condition in which all species in a given system are able to interact in such a way that all survive and all maintain given relationships to relatively static current or preferred environments — is advanced as a goal of social policy.

There is really nothing sacred about a particular status quo in ecology or in environment. As noted in Chapter 3, natural forces, without the intervention or assistance of man, have wrought climatic and other environmental changes that have erased thousands of biological species from the earth. In historical time, man has been the primary agent in altering his environment in a multitude of ways — especially through progressive industrialization and the development and application of scientific knowledge (as, for example, in medicine). And these man-made changes have on balance greatly improved the state of well-being of men — in longevity, health, material wealth, and so forth. As man has progressively altered his environment, he has continually upset natural ecological systems — and this is far from all bad.

Some man-made alterations in human environment, however, appear to have been definitely bad. Man as the prime predator on earth has exterminated whole species of wildlife. And in a relentless and successful push for continued industrial progress, he began long ago to degrade many other aspects of his environment — proceeding in the last century to the point where his immediate material gains were more and more being offset by connected environmental degradations. It is this latter stage of human development that we presently observe. And at this stage we have become concerned with environmental degradation per se, with its specific as well as general sources, and with determining the point at which increases in material production are outweighed by adverse environmental consequences. In considering this latter issue, we are in a broad way primarily concerned with the adverse ecological consequences of further environmental deterioration.

But this does not imply that an optimal social policy should generally have as its broad aim freezing us in an environmental and ecological status quo, or rolling us back to some specified *status quo ante*. Our accumulation of knowledge of basic and applied science, and our very potent acquired ability to alter and develop our productive technologies — and in fact deliberately to alter our environments

— instead suggest that these powers should be much more strongly and systematically directed toward ameliorating, controlling, and improving the qualities of our environments — and thus toward averting and reversing generally adverse ecological changes. Thus, the essays on specific environmental issues in this book are at least as much concerned with public policies of environmental control as they are with the principal sources of ongoing degradation of human environments.

MEASURING THE COSTS OF ENVIRONMENTAL DETERIORATION

So much for a general description of the many facets of human environments, and the sources of their differences among regions and socio-economic groups. Let us now recall that the primary focus of this book is not so much on an evaluation of the quality of contemporary human environments as it is on environmental degradation and its control. In Chapters 1 and 2, as earlier indicated, we offer a general economic analysis:

1. of the sources of degradations of various aspects of human environments, and of their impacts on human welfare, and

2. of the economic merits of various types of public actions designed to ameliorate, control, or reverse various environmental degradations.

It is well to note at the outset that any satisfactorily rigorous, abstract analysis of these related matters must rest on the supposition that the costs to affected populations of degradations of environments are measurable essentially in monetary terms. This is necessary to enable us to measure their impacts on human populations in the same units as the costs of averting them, and thus to determine how much can justifiably be spent on environmental control. In the abstract analysis in Chapters 1 and 2, we will therefore assume that the social costs or values of environmental change are conveniently measurable in monetary terms.[1] Thereafter, as our analysis turns from the abstract to the practically applicable in Chapter 2, we alter our assumptions to

---

[1] Explicitly, this involves the assumption that the cost to every affected individual of any given degree of any particular environmental degradation is measurable in monetary terms, and that the aggregate cost of that degree of degradation to an affected populace can be arrived at by summing the individual costs of all members of the affected populace — assigning the same importance to anyone's dollar's worth of costs — to arrive at an aggregate social cost for each relevant degree of environmental degradation. From such aggregates, marginal and average social costs of successively greater degrees of degradation are then hypothetically calculable. The underlying assumption that the costs or dissatisfactions of different individuals are legitimately additive is in a degree arbitrary, but not implausible, and clearly necessary if we are to speak of measured costs of environmental change.

recognize that in fact the values of many environmental changes are not at all precisely measurable in monetary terms, and consider the difficult problems of formulating economically satisfactory environmental control policies when only physical properties rather than values of environmental changes can be measured.

1 General Economic Analysis of Environmental Degradation

In developing the general analysis described in the title of this chapter, we identify the general sources of environmental degradation and analyze their impacts on human welfare. In Chapter 2, we consider various alternative public policies of environmental control and analyze their comparative theoretical merits, finally turning to problems posed in selecting such policies in contexts wherein the monetary values of environmental changes are not readily measurable, and where expedient policies must be selected on an ad hoc basis.

We consider in this chapter two major sources of environmental degradation and their effects: (1) by-product wastes and side effects emanating from production and consumption, which generate "pollution" as it is broadly construed; and (2) environmentally degrading allocations of lands and waters among uses and users.

POLLUTION RESULTING FROM BY-PRODUCT WASTES AND SIDE EFFECTS OF PRODUCTION AND CONSUMPTION

A primary, general source of environmental degradation is the generation by the production or consumption of various goods or services of (1) by-product "waste" materials that are not productively used but are somehow disposed of, and (2) comparable tangible or intangible side effects. The by-product wastes in question are typically solid, fluid, or gaseous materials remaining after production or consumption is completed. They may range from the gases and particles emitted from the smokestacks of oil-burning factories to the discarded beer containers that consumers strew on roadsides and in parks and forests. Their effects generally constitute pollution of an environment.

9

In a number of instances, moreover, production or consumption degrades environments by simple or complex side effects not identifiable as residual wastes. One common side effect is the generation of noise. Another is the substantial impairment of the natural regulation of runoff from forested watersheds by indiscriminate lumbering practices. These side effects, like the effects of by-product wastes, may also be loosely designated as pollution.

By-product wastes are frequently discharged into "common property" resources like air and water, and this sort of pollution has received a large part of the attention of people concerned with our environments. But common-property pollution is not universally the case with such wastes, which may be disposed of on private lands in ways that damage the surrounding environment. And undesirable side effects of production and consumption may also either impinge on common-property resources (as does noise) or operate by damaging either privately owned or public lands.

The general effect of degrading an environment with pollution is to impose "gross costs" (otherwise referred to as losses or disbenefits) on members of the affected populace by lessening their physical well-being or the psychic satisfaction they derive from living. In many or most cases these gross costs are not matched by equivalent additional private or internal costs incurred by the producers or consumers that create them. Thus they are "external costs" imposed on the public but not internally borne by those responsible. Net losses in aggregate economic welfare then tend to ensue, because if their external costs are neglected by the responsible producers or consumers, the environmentally degrading supply and use of the culprit goods or services tend to be overextended — to amounts for which their marginal values to users are less than their full (internal plus external) marginal costs.

If the responsible parties are through some means forced by government to pay added private costs equal to the social costs of their contribution to environmental degradation, some degradation is likely still to occur. But it will occur in diminished degree because it has become privately expensive, thus leading to diminutions in the supply and use of the goods and services whose production and consumption add to environmental degradation. It is indeed possible in such cases that such supply and use and their connected degradation will be curtailed enough that the marginal increments to human satisfaction provided by the "culprit" goods and services are large enough to cover the full marginal costs (including those of environmental deterioration) that they generate, so that no net loss in aggregate economic welfare results.

Many economists, therefore, argue that there is such a thing as an optimal (socially most satisfactory) degree of environmental degradation that is economically preferable to lesser degrees. Their argument essentially states that, in order to maximize its total material welfare, society should seek and accept "tradeoffs" between increasing private production and consumption and avoiding added deteriorations of its environment to a point where the total human satisfaction obtained from private production and consumption, *minus* the social costs of environmental degradation stemming from such production and consumption, is maximized. An implication of this argument is that it is economically desirable to limit but not eliminate environmental degradations, because the cost of such elimination (in terms of private production and consumption foregone) would be too great.

How Pollution Generates Environmental Costs and Affects Aggregate Economic Welfare. The preceding general statements make clear the immediate need for a reasonably precise analysis of:

1. the determinants and determination of the gross environmental costs of pollution generated by the production or consumption of various "culprit" goods and services;

2. the reasons why, if such gross environmental costs are "external" to the producers and consumers that generate them, the "culprit" goods and services tend to be supplied in "excessive" amounts — with a resultant reduction in aggregate economic welfare; and

3. the general character of public policy measures by which such reductions in aggregate economic welfare can be averted.

ASSUMING COMPETITIVE OUTPUTS BY THOSE GENERATING POLLUTION. These matters are first analyzed in simplified form in Figure 1, which let us suppose first to refer to the pricing and supply of electric power to its users in a metropolitan area in any one year, when the power is generated by "steam plants" that burn fuel oil or coal to produce steam to drive electricity-generating turbines.

In Figure 1, the line DD' represents the aggregate annual demand curve of all users in the area for electric power, showing the alternative quantities of power per year they will purchase at alternative power prices. The price on DD' corresponding to each alternative quantity is a monetary measure of the marginal value (in consumption or further production) to all users of an added unit per year of power purchased at that price.

Supposing that all electric power in the area is supplied by a single public utility firm, the line MC_P represents its private or internal long-run marginal cost (inclusive of a normal interest return on investment) of providing successive increments to the annual electric power supply. (Since MC_P is represented as constant at all levels of output, it also measures the private average cost per unit of output at each output quantity.)

The line MC_E represents the firm's corresponding marginal external cost of providing successive increments of power per year (and again the average external cost per unit of output at each output quantity). These are the annual costs to the affected populace of

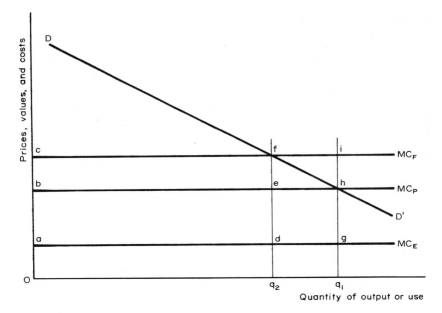

FIGURE 1

polluting the air mantle over them with sulfur dioxide, nitric oxide, particulate matter, and other pollutants emitted by steam plants. It is arbitrarily assumed (for purposes of initial simplification) that these costs are unaffected by the presence in the air mantle of air pollutants from other sources; that they are the same whether steam plants are the only regional source of air pollution or are only one of several sources. Under this assumption, the external environmental costs of supplying electricity can be analyzed independently.

The line MC_F represents the full marginal and average costs of supplying power in any year, and diagrammatically is simply the vertical summation of MC_P and MC_E.

Let us now suppose that a regulatory public utility commission requires the public utility firm to set the price per unit of electric power equal to its constant private average cost of supplying it, and to supply annually all power demanded at that price. Then, in Figure 1, the firm will supply the quantity oq_1 of electric power per annum at a price of ob. What are the resulting impacts on environmental costs and aggregate economic welfare?

First, there will be an annual gross environmental cost of, or loss from, air pollution measured by the area $bcih$ (equal to $oagq_1$). (This is alternatively the number of units of electric power provided annually multiplied by the average external cost per unit of power, or the summation of the marginal external costs of all units supplied.)

Second, there will be an annual net loss in aggregate economic welfare of fhi, this representing the excess of the total costs, fiq_1q_2, of supplying the power output increment q_2q_1, over the total value in use of that increment, fhq_1q_2.

If by some means the power producer could be induced to count MC_E as part of his private costs (e.g., by a tax per unit of power of bc, or by a ruling by a public utility commission that the producer should set the price per unit of electric power equal to the full average cost of supplying it), the producer would restrict his annual power output to oq_2. This would have the effect of reducing the gross environmental cost of air pollution per year by the amount of $efih$ to $bcfe$, but not by more, assuming the steam plant technology that determines the levels of MC_P and MC_E to be unchanged. It would also have the effect of eliminating any annual net loss in aggregate economic welfare, since at the output oq_2 all units of power supplied have marginal values in excess of, or (at f) equal to, their full marginal costs. Assuming steam plant technology given, the annual output oq_2 is in fact optimal from an aggregate welfare standpoint, even though it involves absorbing a substantial gross environmental cost.

Figure 1 has so far been employed to illustrate the case of external environmental costs generated by producers, and also that of supply of all output of a service by a single producer (albeit one forced by regulation to set price and output at competitive levels). It can also serve us to illustrate the case of environmental costs generated by a number of competitive producers of the same good or service, and the case of such costs generated by consumers.

Suppose in Figure 1 that DD' represents the aggregate annual demand curve of all users in a metropolitan area for taxicab service, as measured in vehicle miles. Suppose also that taxi service is provided by a considerable number of competitive firms, and that MC_P represents at each service output per year both the private or internal long-run average costs and long-run marginal costs of all firms supplying the service (it is thus the annual long-run average and marginal cost of service for the taxicab industry of the area). Further, MC_E represents at each annual output the marginal (and average) external costs of environmental degradation by the industry, due to the air pollution created by exhaust and evaporative emissions of air pollutants from its vehicles. MC_F is thus the full marginal and average cost of the annual supply of vehicle miles of taxi service, which is arbitrarily assumed not to vary with the length of individual taxicab trips.

If the industry has active price competition that drives price to the level of marginal and average costs — we will suppose that it does — this competition will induce the firms in the industry (the number of which may increase or diminish with service output) to supply oq_1 vehicle miles of service annually at a price of ob. The result in terms of gross environmental costs and welfare effects are then strictly comparable to those for a single supplier forced by regulation to follow competitive pricing rules. The annual gross environmental cost is $bcih$, and the net loss in aggregate welfare per year is fhi. Restricting annual output to the level where price equals full average and marginal costs (to oq_2) will reduce the annual gross environmental loss to $bcfe$ and eliminate any net loss in aggregate welfare.

CUMULATIVE EFFECTS OF SEVERAL SOURCES OF POLLUTION. So far we have supposed that the external environmental costs generated by the production or consumption of various goods in a region increases proportionately with annual output and use, as is depicted by the level of MC_E remaining constant as output and use increase. Where the pollution of common-property resources like air and water is involved, this may not be the case. After some point is reached in the increasing pollution of an air mantle, or of a stream, lake, or bay, environmental costs begin to increase more than proportionately with additions of pollutants. Or, in other terms, the value of air and water as assets for life support and aesthetics diminishes at a more rapid rate than that at which pollutants are increasingly discharged into the air and water. (See Chapter 4, p. 85.) Both overloading air and water with pollutants and accelerated chemical reactions among pollutants are responsible for this.

The result for any one regional industry which is a major polluter (let us say of water) is depicted in Figure 2. Suppose that a number of paperboard mills, owned by different firms, are all located on the lower reaches of the same river, all discharging pollutant chemical and other effluents into its waters. In Figure 2, MC_p has the same significance as it had in Figure 1, representing the long-run marginal and average private or internal production costs of all firms in the industry at various levels of annual industry output.

The demand curve DD' also has the same significance, representing the aggregate of the annual demands of paperboard buyers in the region, whom we will suppose to be solely supplied by the producers in question. This may be because the local paperboard market is geographically isolated from other sources of supply by distance and shipping costs, or because several regional groups of paperboard producers have agreed to divide the national market, each having a regional market immune from outside competition. The line DD' is thus a fraction of the national annual demand curve for paperboard, and the prices corresponding to various annual quantities on it measure the marginal values of paperboard to users in this regional market.

The major difference from the situation depicted in Figure 1 is that the marginal external cost per year of environmental degradation — pollution of the river water — of the regional industry increases more than proportionately with annual industry output, as is illustrated by the up-curving MC_E and MC_F curves for the industry. These curves register the annual marginal external costs of pollution of the river by the regional paperboard industry alone, as they would emerge if there were no other polluters of the river — its solo effects.

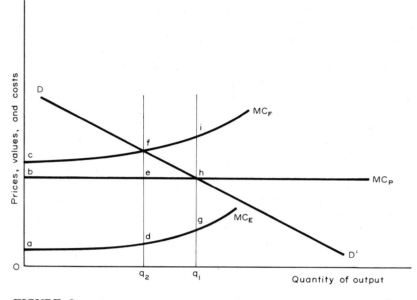

FIGURE 2

Viewing the regional paperboard industry in isolation, active competition in pricing will induce its firms to supply a total annual output of oq_1 at a price of ob. The resulting impacts will be a gross environmental loss from pollution per year of $bcih$, and an annual net loss in aggregate welfare of fhi. Taxation which raised the marginal internal costs of the industry to MC_F would tend to reduce annual output to oq_2 and gross environmental loss per year to $bcfe$, and to eliminate any net loss in aggregate welfare. The tendency of the external marginal costs of environmental degradation to increase more than proportionately with output is to increase gross environmental losses and net welfare losses at outputs such as oq_1. For future reference let us designate the gross environmental loss per year generated by the paperboard industry when it is disregarding external costs and annually producing oq_1, and when it is the only polluter of the river in question, as $_BC_E$ ($= bcih$).

Let us now assume that in the same area and located on the same river are three other regional industries, each of which is composed of a number of firms and produces a single good — for example, a petroleum refining industry producing only gasoline, a cane-sugar refining industry producing only sugar, and a steel industry producing only hot-rolled strip steel of a given grade. Let us assume also that each industry is the sole supplier of a protected regional market and thus faces an annual demand curve for its output that is simply a fraction of the national annual demand curve for the product it supplies. If each industry is analyzed on the assumption that it is the only polluter of the river on which all four industries are located, Figure 2 may be used to depict its annual individual environmental costs and aggregate welfare losses, provided we imagine that in Figure 2 for each industry the levels of demand (DD'), marginal private cost (MP_C), and external marginal environmental cost (MC_E) are different, and also possibly that the degree of upward curvature of MC_E differs among industries. Then, if there is active price competition in each industry and its sellers disregard their external costs, each of the additional three industries will produce an annual output oq_1 (at which MC_P intersects its annual demand curve) and will also generate a gross environmental cost per year of $bcih$, equal to its aggregate external costs (as determined by its output and the excesses of its MC_F over its MC_P).

Each industry thus generates its own solo annual gross environmental cost (some area $bcih$) if it is the only polluter of the river. Let us designate (at outputs oq_1) this solo environmental cost of river pollution by the petroleum industry alone as $_PC_E$, by the regional sugar refining industry alone as $_RC_E$, and by the regional steel industry alone as $_SC_E$.

If we now calculate the arithmetical sum of the solo gross environmental costs per year of the four industries — each computed on the assumption that it is the only polluter of the same river — as $(_BC_E + _PC_E + _RC_E + _SC_E)$, have we arrived at the total annual environmental costs of river pollution generated by the four industries when they are all producing outputs of oq_1 simultaneously? If we follow the argument developed above to the effect that increasing the pollution of a stream (or lake or air mantle) after a point causes environmental costs to increase more than proportionately with additions of pollutants, the answer to this question is no. The aggregated annual additions to the river of pollutants that the four industries will generate when each produces an output oq_1 will impose a gross total environmental cost per year greater than the arithmetical sum of their solo environmental costs per year. If we designate the total environmental cost per year generated by the four industries operating simultaneously as TC_E, then $TC_E > (_BC_E + _PC_E + _RC_E + _SC_E)$. Thus, gross environmental costs are elevated by the excess of TC_E over the summation of the four solo costs, and the total annual net loss in welfare is correspondingly increased.[1]

---

[1] These effects of the excess can be analyzed diagrammatically by adding shares of it to the gross solo costs of the individual industries in amounts proportionate to the sizes of their solo gross costs. Then the solo marginal external cost and marginal full cost curves of each industry would be elevated at each output by their similarly determined shares of the excess of total marginal external costs per year over the arithmetical sum of the "isolated" marginal external costs. For the sake of brevity, we will not perform such a diagrammatic exercise here.

ASSUMING MONOPOLISTIC OUTPUTS BY THOSE GENERATING POLLU-
TION. In the preceding analysis of the gross environmental costs and
reduction of aggregate economic welfare caused by producers whose
processes or products generate environment-degrading by-products or
side effects, we have assumed throughout that they arrived at purely
competitive prices and outputs of their products. That is, we have assumed that industries of suppliers of the same product, if they disregard the environmental costs they generate as external to their
operations, are engaged in sufficiently active price competition to
induce them to extend their combined output to a level at which the
selling price of their product equals the marginal and average private
costs of production of the industry members. If they did so, the resulting gross environmental cost and the net loss in aggregate welfare
that resulted from supplying such a good would tend to be maximized,
subject to the constraint that the revenues from its sales cannot remain below its private costs of production.

In contemporary Western economies, however, a major fraction of
the many industries supplying different goods or services are able to
suppress or restrain price competition sufficiently to set their selling
prices above their marginal and average costs of production and to
produce the correspondingly smaller outputs demanded at these
higher prices. This generally occurs when all or most of the output
of an industry is supplied by a few large producers and when as a
consequence they are able to arrive at agreements or tacit understand-
ings as to what price they will charge, or what corresponding combined output they will produce, in order to earn profits in excess of a
normal interest return on investment. In so raising prices and restricting outputs they are exercising some degree of monopoly power. And,
if their production generates pollution, their monopolistic output
restriction reduces the gross environmental costs of their production
below the level associated with competitive price-output determination, and also reduces and may eliminate the loss in aggregate welfare that is due to their disregard of external environmental costs.

These effects of monopolistic pricing and output restriction reach
an extreme if the member firms of an industry agree or move con-
certedly to establish a "joint monopoly" price and output, at which
their combined profits in excess of a normal interest return on investment (excess profits) are maximized. This development is depicted
in Figure 3, which we may suppose to refer to the combined operations in a single area of a few large smelters and refiners of lead, who
together are the sole suppliers of an isolated market of lead buyers.

In Figure 3, DD' is the annual demand curve for refined lead of the
collection of buyers for which they are the exclusive suppliers, the
price at each quantity on DD' representing the marginal value of lead
to all buyers. The line MC_P represents the long-run marginal and
average private costs in any year of the production of refined lead by
the combination of its producers, and MC_F their full annual marginal

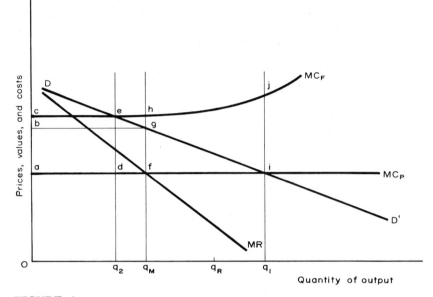

FIGURE 3

costs inclusive of their external environmental costs of air pollution. DD', MC_P, and MC_F have the same meanings that they did in Figure 2.

Included also in Figure 3 is the line MR, representing marginal revenue to the combination of refined lead producers resulting from successive increments to their combined annual lead output. That is, if we read downward from left to right on MR, the value (vertical height) of each successive point on MR represents the addition to the total revenue per year of the lead producers that results from the addition of one unit of output per year. MR lies below DD' because as output is extended by any unit increment, the addition to total revenue resulting from the sale of that increment is reduced by the small decline in the price of all units of output sold (as indicated by DD', which shows that selling price drops as output is increased). The line MR greatly simplifies the determination of the industry output at which the joint excess profits of the member firms of an industry are maximized.

In Figure 3, if the lead producers (neglecting external costs), pursued competitive pricing, they would produce a combined annual output of oq_1, and sell it at the unit price oa, generating gross environmental costs per year of $acji$, and reducing annual aggregate material welfare by eij, which is the excess of the total cost (ejq_1q_2) over the total value (eiq_1q_2) of an output increment q_2q_1. Alternatively, if they were forced by taxation to include their external costs in their private costs, and still priced competitively, they would produce the combined annual output oq_2, generate gross environmental costs per year of $aced$, and not reduce aggregate material welfare. oq_2 is the optimal output at which marginal full (social) cost equals marginal value of output.

If, however, neglecting external costs, they set a price to maximize their joint profits, they would produce the annual output of oq_M, at which the marginal private cost of increasing output becomes equal to the marginal revenue realized from increasing it, and charge a corresponding selling price ob. Then they would generate gross environmental costs per year of $achf$, and reduce annual aggregate economic welfare by only egh. Their combined excess profits per year would be maximized at $abgf$.

The tendency of monopolistic output restriction when external environmental costs are disregarded by producers is clear: it tends to reduce gross environmental costs below the level associated with competitive pricing, and possibly to reduce or eliminate losses in aggregate welfare due to the disregard of external costs.

The magnitude of these effects if a joint profit-maximizing elevation of price and restriction of output are imposed will of course depend on the position and price elasticity of the demand curve (DD') for the output in question, on the level of marginal private costs (MC_P), and on the comparative level and extent of nonproportionality to output of marginal full costs (MC_F). With a different relationship of these determinants of joint monopoly price and environmental losses, for example, oq_M might coincidentally equal oq_2, in which case gross environmental losses per year would be somewhat smaller and aggregate economic welfare would not be reduced. And with another relationship, oq_M might be smaller than oq_2, in which case annual gross environmental costs would be smaller yet, and reductions in aggregate material welfare per year would result *from monopolistic output restriction*, since the marginal value of annual output would then exceed its full marginal costs.[2]

Finally, it is quite possible — indeed probable — that a group of producers possessing some joint monopoly power will be unable, because of only partly suppressed rivalry, or unwilling, because of the fear of attracting additional producers into the industry, to restrict output and raise price fully to the joint-profit-maximizing level identified with the annual output oq_M. Then they may end up producing some annual output, oq_R on Figure 3, less than the competitive output oq_1, but greater than the joint-profit-maximizing output oq_m. In this case, the monopolistic output restriction they accomplish will reduce gross environmental costs by less than if they had restricted ouput to oq_M.

[2] A reduction in losses in aggregate welfare through monopolistic output restriction will generally occur unless the optimal competitive output, oq_2, lies between oq_M and oq_1 (in Figure 3), and also close enough to oq_1 that the welfare loss involved in producing oq_1 instead of oq_2 is smaller than the welfare loss *now due the deficiency of monopolistic output*. Such a placement of oq_2 is possible with certain combinations of demand elasticity and ratio of environmental to private costs.

The section running from page 11 to this point has presented a simplified analysis of the gross environmental costs and aggregate economic welfare losses that may be generated by pollution under various circumstances. We will refer to this analysis in Chapter 2 when we turn to the evaluation of alternative control measures designed to mitigate or eliminate the adverse effects of pollution. In this connection, it is pertinent to note that throughout the foregoing analyses we have assumed the production technologies (or consumer habits) from which these adverse effects emanate to be fixed and unchanging, implying unchanging relations to output and use of marginal private costs and marginal external costs. When we consider control measures, considerable emphasis will be placed on means of inducing changes in technologies (or consumer habits) which will reduce the external costs of environmental degradation.

Meanwhile, let us turn to a second source of environmental degradation — misallocation of lands and waters among uses and users.

DEGRADING ALLOCATIONS OF LANDS AND WATERS AMONG USES AND USERS

A second general source of environmental degradation comprises privately or publicly determined allocations of lands and waters among uses, and also among individual users, which lead to the deterioration of various environments. Regarding allocations among uses, two matters are involved: first, what shares of various types of lands and waters are assigned to or captured exclusively for different competing uses; and second, what shares are captured or assigned to be put simultaneously to two or more uses which are appreciably incompatible, in the sense that exploitation of the land or water for a second use reduces its value to those putting it to a first use. Regarding allocations among users, the matter involved is primarily the areas of urban land allotted to individual structures of various different horizontal areas, different vertical heights, and different cubic "bulks." This sort of allocation strongly influences, if it does not effectively determine, the density of resident population per unit of land area in residential areas and of work-day population in areas where employment is centered — and with it the degree of congestion of human beings, motor vehicle traffic, and so forth.

Some examples of allocations of land and water among uses that may degrade environments and the reasons for degradation, include:

1. In urban or metropolitan areas, allocations to industrial and commercial uses, beyond some threshold, of lands and waters potentially valuable for recreation, with the result of depriving citizens of the areas of potentially available environmental benefits.[3]

---

[3] Allocations of given lands to commercial instead of recreational uses generally involve their allocation to private rather than public ownership.

2. Also in metropolitan areas (including their suburbs), preponderant allocation of available lands to building sites, with negligible or inadequate reservation of "greenbelts," extensive public parks, and so on, with a resultant degradation of the environment because of lack of easy access to preserves of light, air, and space.

3. Specific public allocations of rights-of-way for urban freeways which, by their presence, deteriorate local environments by creating aesthetic nuisances, and in use do the same by spilling externalities of noise and noxious automotive exhaust emissions over adjoining areas.

4. Allocation of out-of-town forest and water resources to commercial uses (lumbering, hydro-power production, irrigation) sufficiently to deteriorate the environment of urban residents by limiting the quantity, quality, and accessibility of open-country recreational resources.

Examples of environment-degrading allocations of lands among individual users include, as already suggested: (1) urban land area allocation per residential dwelling unit or per urban resident which degrades the environment by depriving residents of desirable amounts of light, air, and space around their dwelling places, producing traffic congestion in residential areas, etc.; and (2) land area allocations per occupant of commercial and industrial buildings (as affected by heights and bulks of such buildings that are publicly permitted) which have comparable environmental effects.

In appraising allocations of land and water resources among uses and users, most economists would be guided by the welfare-maximizing rule mentioned above in discussing the idea of an "optimal" degree of environmental degradation resulting from pollution. That is, in the case of allocations of local or out-of-town lands and water suitable for environment-enhancing recreational use, they would argue that these resources should be allocated between commercial and recreational uses in such proportions that the marginal or incremental additions to overall welfare resulting from the last incremental allocation of such resources to commercial use should be equal to the marginal or incremental loss of welfare resulting from the consequent reduction of the value of the recreational environment. Similarly, most economists would approve the dispersion of residential building in a tract by increasing the minimum allowable area of a single residential lot progressively from 2,500 to 20,000 square feet only to the point where the increments to environmental benefits of greater

---

With commercial uses of privately owned land, private net revenues gained from land rentals and from the profits of commercial occupants may greatly exceed any private or public net revenues collectible for recreational use of the lands — for familiar institutional reasons — even though the value of unreimbursed benefits of recreational use substantially exceeds the largely reimbursed benefits of commercial use. Thus, commercial interests and private landowners have strong economic incentives to oppose allocation of much recreationally valuable lands to recreational uses.

dispersion and of increased light, air, and space were greater than the incremental losses of the value of the other productivity of the land thereby incurred. The rules of economically optimal allocation would determine the optimal tradeoff between environmental benefits and other competing benefits and suggest the wisdom of settling for less than environmentally ideal allocations of lands and waters. Some would not agree with this rule because they assign special "bonus" benefits to higher environmental quality.

How Environmentally Degrading Misallocations of Lands and Water Generate Environmental Costs and Affect Aggregate Economic Welfare. Like pollution, allocations of lands and waters that deteriorate environments impose gross environmental costs on members of the population affected and may reduce aggregate economic welfare. The major sorts of imposition of environmental costs and net welfare losses by such allocations may be illustrated by a short sequence of examples.

ALLOCATION OF WILD RESOURCES SUITABLE FOR RECREATION. Let us first consider the allocation of land and water among competing uses, taking as our first example the allocation of a remaining "wild river" (heretofore undeveloped for commercial uses) between recreational use and use for the production of hydroelectric power. The simplest allocative choice here would be between preserving the river exclusively for recreational use (with no commercial development) and devoting it exclusively to intensive use for producing electric power (with no recreational use). Common sense tells us that if the aggregate net value per annum of the use of the river to recreationists enjoying its exclusive use (V_R) exceeded the aggregate net value per annum of the river flow in contributing to the production of electric power (V_P), allocation of the river exclusively to recreational use would maximize its addition to aggregate welfare (in the form of environmental benefits). Its allocation exclusively to electric power production would result in a gross environmental cost equal to V_R, and in a loss of aggregate economic welfare of $(V_R - V_P)$.

These and related outcomes are depicted in Figure 4, which for each alternative use relates the intensity of use of the river to the net marginal values of that use at successively greater use intensities. In this figure, the intensity of use or "output" respectively in recreational use and power production is measured in different terms. Intensity of use for recreational purposes is measured in terms of man-days per year of use; for power production, use intensity is measured in terms of megawatt hours of electric power produced per annum. Moreover, the scales on the horizontal axis on which these two outputs are measured are coordinated, so that any quantity on the horizontal axis of Figure 4 designates the same number of units of each of the two alternative outputs. For example, the distance oq_{100} designates both 100 man-days per year of recreational use and 100 megawatt hours per year of electric power production. (This coordination is necessary to facilitate further graphical analysis.)

On Figure 4, the line MV_R shows the net marginal value per man-day per year of recreational use at each successive quantity of man-days used. Any net marginal value per unit of use is equal to a corresponding gross marginal value of use minus connected marginal costs of use (for travel, equipment, shelter, sanitary facilities, litter cleanup, etc.), but not minus any payment for use of the river. The line MV_R is thus a sort of market demand curve for recreational use of the river, showing the numbers of man hours per year of use which would be demanded at various prices or net user charges per unit for use of the river, equal to various marginal values shown on the line. It is the horizontal sum of the individual demand curves for recreational use of the river of all the many individual demand curves of individual users, unless its level is reduced below this sum by congested use of the river.[4] The value of MV_R at any intensity or quantity of use is the net marginal value to all users of an additional man-day per year of recreational use of the river.

On the same figure, the line MV_C shows the net value of the marginal product of the commercial use of the river flow per megawatt hour per year of electric power (and should at each output represent the sales price of an added megawatt hour per annum minus the associated marginal costs of dams, pipes, turbines, and related equipment, but not minus any payment for use of the river).

Since all connected costs of using the river either for recreational purposes or for generating electric power have been deducted in arriving at MV_R and MC_C, both welfare-maximizing recreationists and profit-maximizing power producers (if there is no monopolistic restriction of power output) should, as exclusive users, extend their annual intensity of use of the river to the point where MV_R or MV_C is equal to zero. Thus, recreational users would spend ob man-days per year on or at the river, and power producers would produce od megawatt hours per year of power.

If the river is allocated exclusively to recreational use, therefore,

---

[4] This reduction would result from the fact that the marginal value of any given quantity of use by every individual user, i, would be lessened because the quality of the units he used would be reduced by the negative external effects of concurrent, "interfering" use by many other individuals. In this respect, the line MV_R differs from the usual demand curve for a private good, in the use of which no such external effects are encountered. Formally for such a private good, the marginal value in use of the good to any individual is primarily a function of the quantity of it he uses — i.e., $mv_i = f(q_i)$ for the specified good. In the case of recreational use of the river, however, the marginal value of any quantity of the use of the river to an individual is also a function of the total quantity (Q) of use of the river by all users — i.e., $mv_i = f(q_i, Q)$, with increases in Q beyond some critical point reducing mv_i at all values of q_i, and progressively as Q becomes greater.

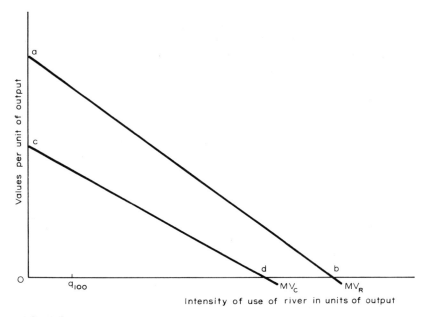

FIGURE 4

annual environmental benefits of recreation with a value measured by the area *oab* should be created or preserved, and the use of the river for recreation would make the larger of the two possible additions to aggregate economic welfare. If instead the river is allocated exclusively to power production, the annual aggregate net value of the use of the river would be measured by the area *ocd*. There would be a gross environmental cost of lost recreation per year, *oab*, and an annual loss in aggregate economic welfare (due to shifting from recreational to power-producing use of the river), *abdc*.

Suppose that the positions of the two MV lines in Figure 4 were reversed, so that *ab* represented MV_C and *cd* represented MV_R. Then allocating the river exclusively to power production would make the larger of the two possible additions to annual aggregate economic welfare, and there would be a gross environmental cost per year of *ocd*. Alternatively, allocation of the river exclusively to recreation would generate annual environmental benefits valued at *ocd*, but result in a reduction of aggregate economic welfare per year of *abdc*.

In making allocative decisions concerning the use of rivers (or forest lands), the more usual choice is between (1) allocation exclusively to a single use and (2) allocation to dual or multiple uses. The comparative merits of allocation to dual or multiple uses as distinct from single uses deserves some attention. This is because two or more uses, although in a degree complementary in that one use does not preclude the other, are also mutually incompatible in some degree, in the sense that devotion of the river to one of the uses lessens its value for the other use or uses.

The problem may be illustrated by considering the effect of devoting a previously wild river (let us say the same river referred to in Figure 4) jointly to recreational use and to intensive hydroelectric power production. In this case, the essential phenomenon is that development of the river for power production distinctly reduces the marginal value of any quantity of recreational use, the total quantity of such use demanded, and thus the total net value realized from recreational use, *perhaps* sufficiently to make the combined total values of the two uses less than the value of exclusive recreational use. The external effects of using the river for power production on its value for recreational use would result generally from several dams converting flowing stretches of river into still-water reservoirs with fluctuating levels; from altering the pattern of daily rates of streamflow below dams so that the flow was periodically too small to sustain much if any fish life (or water-oriented recreational activity in general); from elevated water temperatures in reservoirs or in reduced streamflows above the level where more highly prized fish like trout can survive; and from the blockage of the migration of anadromous fish like salmon and steelhead trout through the river, thus eliminating them or greatly reducing their numbers in the river.

These possible consequences of dual use of a river for recreation and power production are depicted in Figure 5, in which the horizontal scales measuring the intensities of the two uses are the same as in Figure 4, and the significance of the net marginal value lines is the same. In Figure 5, then, MV_R shows the net marginal values per man-day at each successive annual quantity of man-days of recreational use of the river exclusively for recreation; and MV_C shows the net marginal value of the use of the river flow per megawatt hour of electric power per year at each successive rate of annual output of electric power, when the river is used exclusively for power generation.

What happens if the river is used dually for recreation and for power generation? Unless power-generation operations are altered to benefit fishermen, the net marginal value of river use for power generation will, in any year, remain unchanged at MV_C. The interferences of power generation, however, will lower the marginal value of use of the river for recreation at every quantity by some amount — let us say to MV'_R (*ef*). Then the aggregate net marginal value of the use of the river for both purposes in any year will be the vertical sum of MV'_R and MV_C, represented by the dashed line ΣMV (*ghd*).

With the value of recreational use of the river so reduced by its simultaneous use for power, the total net annual value of the dual use of the river will be measured by the area *oghd*, smaller than the value of using it for recreation alone (*oab*). The addition of power-generation use to recreation use will result in a net annual loss of aggregate

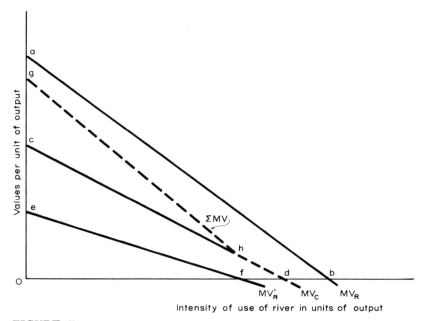

FIGURE 5

economic welfare *abdhg*. The gross environmental cost per year of dual use will be *abfe*.

It is quite possible, of course, that using the river for power generation will not reduce its value for recreation as severely as Figure 5 indicates, and that ΣMV might lie above MV_R, indicating an annual net value of dual-purpose river use greater than the annual net value of recreational use alone, though still showing some gross environmental loss from shifting from exclusive recreational to dual use.

So far we have been centering our attention on a single wild river viewed in isolation — on its comparative net annual values when used alternatively for recreation alone or electric power production alone and on the effect on its total net recreational value and on aggregate economic welfare of using it dually for recreation and power production. A general conclusion is that allocation of the river to electric power production alone will result in a loss of its total net recreational value, and that its allocation dually to electric power production and recreation will significantly reduce its total recreational value. However, a population in a given region — most of which is concentrated in one or more metropolitan areas — may in many cases have feasible access (at travel costs they are able and willing to afford) to a number of rivers which provide roughly the same mix of recreational opportunities.

Assuming that river developments for electric power production generally allocate any river to dual use for power production and recreation, developing any one of the several rivers economically accessible to a given population will induce some (probably few) people who previously used the river for recreation to abandon river-oriented recreation altogether. The development will also induce some, but not all, of the remaining previous recreational users of the river to shift their river-oriented recreation activities to other, "second-choice" rivers. As more of the several available rivers are allocated to joint use for electric power production and recreation, the intensity of recreational use of the remaining wild rivers (as long as there is at least one left) will proceed in a cumulative fashion.

Four results of this process are worth noting. First, the total recreational value of the remaining wild river or rivers will increase as the intensity of their recreational use increases, and this will tend to put them nearer to, into, or further into the category of rivers which can make their greatest contribution to aggregate economic welfare by being preserved for recreational use alone. Second, the additions to the total recreational value of the remaining wild rivers will not be as great as the losses in recreational values of the rivers newly developed for power production for two reasons: Intensity of use of "second-choice" rivers by those who have shifted to them from "first-choice," previously wild, rivers will be smaller than their previous intensity of use of the latter rivers, and the marginal values to them of given quantities of use will be smaller. Thus, the total net recreational value they realize now will be smaller than that derived from using the rivers from which they have been displaced. Third, the total net recreational values realized by those who continue to use the developed rivers will be reduced. Therefore, the total net recreational value realized from the several rivers combined will be reduced by the development for electric power production of each wild river in turn, though by less than the gross loss of recreational values on that river alone, because part of these losses are recouped by recreational river users by shifting to "second-choice" wild rivers, as long as any remain. In typical actual situations in recreational areas near the major population centers of the country, the gross environmental cost of developing a large fraction of all rivers for commercial uses very probably also results in a substantial loss in aggregate economic welfare. Fourth, if in a region the process of developing ever larger proportions of wild rivers proceeds beyond a certain point, the total net recreational value of the remaining wild rivers is reduced by the congestion created by very intensive use, and the average value per man hour of river use declines for all their users. This results in an added gross recreational loss and reduction in aggregate economic welfare.

Tendencies comparable to those associated with use of rivers as recreational resources apply to and are observed in the progressive allocation to joint commercial and recreational use of other recreational resources — of forests, for example. Suppose that a tract of several square miles of prime forest land in an attractive mountainous area (complete with brooks, meadows, and so forth) may be allocated exclusively to recreational use by making it a recreational preserve; or may be allocated exclusively to lumbering restricted to a rate of tree removal consistent with a constant annual yield of lumber; or allocated to dual use for lumbering of this sort and for recreation. Suppose further that the total net value of exclusive recreational use (at whatever level of intensity of use develops) is $10 million per year; that the total net value of the land for lumbering use (with or without joint recreational use) is $4 million per year; and that the total recreational value of the tract if lumbering operations are regularly being carried out is reduced to $5 million per year. (This reduction would be attributable to the general impairment of the wilderness characteristics of the forest land, to the invasion of the tract by lumberers' access roads, to impairment of parts of the forest floor by dragging out cut trees and subsequent erosion, to some impairment of brooks, and so forth.) In the situation described, exclusive recreational use would provide the largest annual addition ($10 million) to aggregate material welfare, all in the form of environmental benefits. Exclusive use for lumbering would impose a net loss in aggregate welfare of $6 million per year, and a gross environmental cost of $10 million. Dual use for recreation and lumbering would result in an annual loss in aggregate net welfare of $1 million per year and a gross environmental cost of $5 million. We leave it to the reader to calculate the results of various allocations with different relative values of different uses — for example, if the total net value of the forest land for lumbering exceeds $5 million per year, recreational value under dual use remaining unchanged, dual use adds to economic welfare. In the case of forest land, the cumulative effects of converting more and more timber lands from exclusive recreational use to dual recreational and commercial use (even with tight restrictions on lumbering practices) are comparable to those analyzed with respect to the progressive development for commercial use of larger proportions of available wild rivers — effects which are enlarged if populations seeking the recreational use of these resources are increased.

ALLOCATION OF URBAN RECREATIONAL RESOURCES. The same sort of analysis can be "brought to town" to evaluate the allocation of various urban lands with high recreational potential as between recreational and commercial use. A stretch of ten miles of the shore of a very large lake (let us say one of the Great Lakes) that is really within an urban area will do nicely as an example. Suppose that the net total values of the shore land as sites for industrial plants of a mixture of types is $15 million per year, whereas its net total value as an area devoted exclusively to recreation is $20 million annually. Its contribution to aggregate economic welfare will be greatest ($20 million per year) if it is reserved exclusively for recreational use. If in the history of the development of the metropolitan area, however, the land has been fully occupied by industrial plants, and will remain so occupied, this allocation would impose a net loss in aggregate economic welfare of $5 million annually, and a gross environmental loss, primarily to the residents of the metropolitan area, of $20 million.

Staying within a metropolitan area, let us consider another device of land allocation among uses, namely that of potential residential land as between residential building lots and "greenbelts" of open country within a residential area. Suppose that a number of realtors (sufficiently numerous that they will not attempt to practice monopolistic withholding of land supply from the market) are about to subdivide for residential use a twelve-square-mile tract of land, on the fringe of the built-up area of the city, hitherto devoted to pasturage and consisting of open grassland and lightly forested land. Under the persuasion of a metropolitan planning authority, they consider two joint development alternatives: Plan I, allocation of all twelve square miles to residential development; and Plan II, allocation of five-sixths, or ten square miles of the land, to residential development, and one-sixth, or two square miles, to two municipally guaranteed greenbelts continuing in use for pasturage. The two greenbelts would cut through the twelve-square-mile tract so as to minimize the average distance of individual residential lots from a greenbelt.

Under Plan I (full residential development) the realtors will be able to carve out, after allowing for areas occupied by streets and stores (the values of which we will neglect), 48,000 building lots of 5,000 square feet each. This quantity of lots is measured by oq_I on Figure 6. Under Plan II (development with greenbelts) they will be able to offer only 40,000 building lots of 5,000 square feet each, plus two greenbelts with a total area of two square miles. The 40,000 quantity of building lots under Plan II is measured by oq_{II} on Figure 6.

To continue our diagrammatic analysis, we need to determine the market demand curves for lots in the tract, under Plans I and II respectively. Each market demand curve is drawn so that each price on it is also the marginal value of an added lot to its would-be purchaser when the corresponding quantity of lots has been sold to buyers who realize larger marginal values per lot. (Such a demand curve may represent the simple market demand curve for the twelve-square-mile tract if no comparable tracts are being offered, or its share of the total market demand curve for several such tracts, if several are being offered.)

Let us suppose that the market demand curve for lots in the tract under Plan I is represented by $D_I(MV_I)$, and that the market demand curve for lots under Plan II is represented by $D_{II}(MV_{II})$, on Figure 6 (the higher level of D_{II} reflecting greater value per lot under the greenbelt plan). Competitive selling of the lots under Plan I should then result in a selling price per lot of oa (determined at the intersection of D_I with the zero-elastic supply curve q_IS_I); similar selling

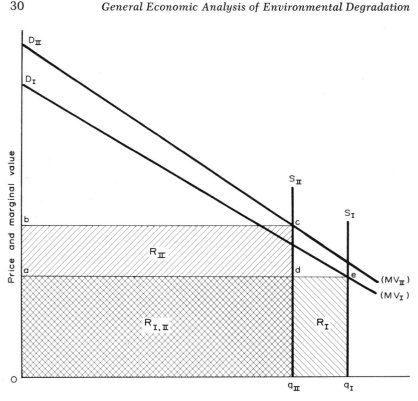

FIGURE 6

of lots under Plan II should result in a selling price per lot of *ob* (determined at the intersection of D_{II} with the zero-elastic supply curve $q_{II}S_{II}$).

Under Plan I, the total revenue received by the sellers of the lots is measured by the area $oaeq_I$, which is the sum of the cross-hatched area $oadq_{II}$ (the area $R_{I, II}$) and the single-hatched area $q_{II}deq_I$ (the area R_I). Thus under Plan I, total revenue is measured by the area $(R_{I, II} + R_I)$. Under Plan II, supposing that the set-aside greenbelt has zero net commercial value, the total revenue received by sellers is measured by the area $obcq_{II}$, which is the sum of the cross-hatched area $R_{I, II}$ and the single-hatched area R_{II}. Thus, under Plan II, total revenue is measured by the area $(R_{I, II} + R_{II})$. Because the total revenue areas under Plans I and II share in common the revenue indicated by the cross-hatched area $R_{I, II}$, the difference in the revenues under the two plans will be that between the areas R_I and R_{II}. With the comparative placement of the two demand curves, D_I and D_{II}, that we have supposed, it is clear from Figure 6 that R_{II} is greater than R_I and that Plan II will yield a revenue larger than that for Plan I, by the amount $(R_{II} - R_I)$.

We have indicated above that the number of given-sized lots available under Plan I would be 48,000 (oq_I) and that the number of lots of the same size available under Plan II would be 40,000 (oq_{II}). If we now suppose that the selling price per lot, oa, under Plan I would be $5,000, and the selling price per lot, ob, under Plan II would be $7,500, simple multiplication of corresponding prices and quantities will reveal that total revenue under Plan I would be $240 million, whereas total revenue under Plan II would be $300 million. Thus Plan II's revenue advantage of ($R_{II} - R_I$) would be $60 million (a difference consistent with the plotting on Figure 6).[5]

The revenues received for lots under Plan I and Plan II respectively are not full measures of their environmental values, because the total net values of lots under each plan should include not only sales price multiplied by the number of lots, but also the excess of the total amounts that inframarginal buyers would have been willing to pay for the lots, over and above their actual selling prices. Figure 7 refers to the Plans I and II just discussed and has the demand curve for lots and the quantity of lots sold under each plan identical to those in Figure 6. The total net value of lots under Plan I is measured by the area $0D_I cq_I$, which is equal to the cross-hatched area $0D_I aq_{II}$ (the area $T_{I,II}$) plus the single-hatched area $q_{II}acq_I$ (the area T_I). Thus, under Plan I, total net value is measured by the area ($T_{I,II} + T_I$). The total net value of lots under Plan II is measured by the area $0D_{II} bq_{II}$, which is equal to the cross-hatched area $T_{I,II}$, plus the single-hatched area T_{II}. Total net value under Plan II is measured by the area ($T_{I,II} + T_{II}$). Because the total net value areas under Plans I and II have in common the total value indicated by the cross-hatched area $T_{I,II}$, the difference in the total net values under the two plans will be that between the areas T_I and T_{II}. With the comparative placement of the two demand curves we have chosen (and the comparative price elasticities, which we have depicted as identical at any common output), T_{II} in Figure 7 is greater than T_I, and total net value under Plan II exceeds that under Plan I by the amount ($T_{II} - T_I$).

The discrepancy between revenue differences and total net value differences as between a dispersed residential land development (Plan II) and a compact land development (Plan I) is consistent with the generalizations, first, that such total value differences will only coincidentally be equal to corresponding revenue differences, and, second, that in a range of "extreme" cases in which R_2 is greater than R_1, T_1 may be greater than T_2, so that the development plan yielding the larger total revenue may yield the smaller total net value (and environmental advantage).

Suppose we are comparing dispersed and compact development

---

[5] The revenue difference would favor Plan I over Plan II if the price per lot under Plan I exceeded $6,250, lot prices under Plan II remaining at $7,500.

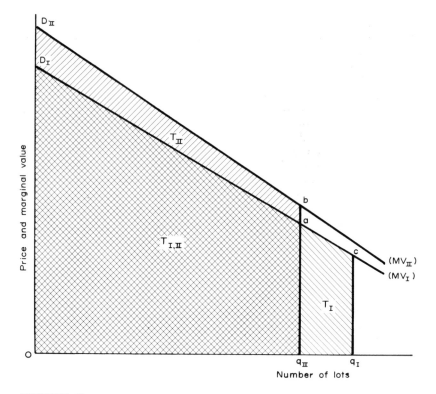

FIGURE 7

of a residential tract, where the total revenue from the dispersed development (Plan II) exceeds that from the compact development (Plan I) — where R_{II} exceeds R_I. Then the excess of T_{II} over T_I is decreased, erased, or reversed to where T_I exceeds T_{II}, as (1) the demand curve for land under Plan I becomes progressively less elastic compared to the demand curve for land under Plan II; (2) as the proportional difference in marginal value per square foot of land under the two plans becomes progressively smaller; and (3) as the total square footage of land sold under Plan I becomes progressively larger relative to the square footage of land sold under Plan II (and vice versa with respect to all three points).

A full diagrammatic exposition of this complex proposition is not warranted here. Using the example already depicted in Figures 6 and 7, however, we can illustrate the effect on the comparative total values of dispersed and compact developments of land of having a comparatively less elastic demand for land under the compact plan (our Plan I above).

Figure 8 is a replica of Figure 7 with one exception: the quantities and prices of lots sold under Plans I and II respectively are the same

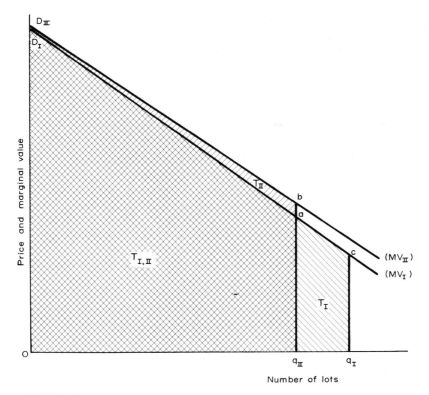

FIGURE 8

as in Figures 6 and 7, and the revenue advantage of Plan II is thus the same as shown in Figure 6. The exception is that whereas in Figure 7 the market demand curve for lots under Plan I (D_I) has the same price elasticity as the market demand for lots under Plan II (D_{II}) at every common quantity, in Figure 8 the price elasticity of demand of D_I is substantially lower than the price of elasticity of D_{II} at every common quantity. This change has the effect of increasing the excesses of the marginal values of inframarginal lots over their selling price under Plan I, and leaving such excesses unchanged under Plan II, for which demand elasticity has not been altered. This change is sufficient, given the other relevant values in the example, to make T_I greater than T_{II}, and thus to make the total net value under Plan I ($0D_I cq_I$) greater than the total net value under Plan II ($0D_{II} bq_{II}$) — even though total sales revenue under Plan II is the greater.

The foregoing exposition has explored in part the logically possible effects on the net total residential land value of more dispersed (e.g., with greenbelt) development in place of more compact (e.g., without greenbelt) development of a tract of land. We have seen that, depending on relationships of demand for land under the two types of development, and on the comparable relationships of area of land developed, a dispersed development may yield a total net value (and environmental benefit) that is greater than, equal to, or less than that realized from a more compact development — even though the revenue from selling land under the dispersed development plan may be consistently the greater.

So much for the logically possible environmental effects of more dispersed as compared to more compact land development. What of the more probable direction of environmental effects? There is a severe shortage of hard evidence which would permit us to give a factual answer to this question. However, we may offer a speculation concerning one.

First, it seems improbable that the market demand curve for lots offered under a compact (no-greenbelt) development plan will be less elastic at any common quantity of lots than the demand curve for lots offered under a dispersed (greenbelt) development plan. One main argument supporting this proposition is that purchasers who are willing to pay a substantial price premium for lots with dispersed development attach a premium to the connected acquisition of increased light, air, and space, and that inframarginal buyers of lots with dispersed development will be inclined to assign significantly higher marginal values (relative to selling price) to the lots they buy, as compared to purchasers who prefer to accept lots with compact development and a substantially lower price. If so then the demand for lots offered under dispersed development should probably have a less elastic demand at any common quantity than that for lots offered under compact development. This tendency for a lower price elasticity of demand for the higher-priced lots offered with dispersed development should be reinforced by the fact their purchasers on the average will tend to have higher incomes, and that therefore inframarginal buyers among them would be prepared to offer prices (equal to marginal values) comparatively higher than actual selling prices for lots, as compared to generally less affluent purchasers of lower-priced lots with compact development. The probable relationships of demand elasticities for lots offered under dispersed and compact development respectively are thus probably approximated in Figures 6 and 7 (though they may, if anything, understate the comparative inelasticity of demand for lots with dispersed development). Figure 8, in which the elasticity of demand at any common quantity is smaller under compact than under dispersed development, probably depicts an atypical comparative demand situation.

Second, if the predicted relationship of demand elasticities holds, and if (1) in addition the selling price per lot under dispersed development is substantially higher than under compact development (the price ratio in the preceding example was 1.5 to 1 in favor of dispersed development), and (2) the quantity of lots under compact development is only moderately greater than under dispersed development (the quantity ratio in the preceding example was only 6 to 5 in favor of compact development), the total value of land under dispersed development will tend to be the greater. In this event, dispersed development would yield larger environmental benefits than compact development. Subject to the specified qualifications concerning lot-price and lot-quantity differences under dispersed as opposed to compact development, this is our tentative conclusion.

THE DENSITY OF RESIDENTIAL BUILDING. The same sort of analysis applies to the effects of different allocations of lands *among users*, as typified in different amounts of residential land allotted per residence. Such a difference in allocation may be illustrated as follows: Suppose that a group of realtors sufficiently numerous that they will not individually or collectively practice monopolistic restriction of land supply are developing a residential tract of six square miles, which after allowance for streets, etc., make available 120 million square feet of land for building lots. They face the choice of subdividing this land either into 40,000 lots of 3,000 square feet each (Plan A), or into 24,000 larger lots of 5,000 square feet each (Plan B). If the competitive selling price of 3,000-square-foot lots is $2,100 ($0.70 per square foot), and the competitive selling price of 5,000-square-foot lots is $5,000 ($1 per square foot), it is evident that total sales revenue under Plan B will be $120 million, and total sales revenue under Plan A will be $84 million — giving Plan B a revenue advantage of $36 million.

This difference, however, as in the greenbelt example, will not be a reliable measure of the differences in net total values of the land under the two plans, since each total value includes, in addition to revenue, the excess of the total amounts that inframarginal lot buyers would have been willing to pay for lots, over and above their actual selling prices. With total revenue under Plan B exceeding that under Plan A, the relationship between net total values under the two plans will depend on the comparative elasticities of demand for lots under the two plans, and on the differences in the marginal values per square foot of land at various common quantities. (No difference in the square footage of land available for development enters into this example.)

The difference in net total values of the tract could be analyzed with diagrams substantially comparable to Figures 7 and 8, inserting demand curves for land under the two plans with specified relationships of their elasticities. It would be found in this example that if the elasticities of demand under Plans A and B were identical at any common quantity of lots (though decreasing as the number of lots increased) that the net total value of the tract under Plan B (dispersed development) would substantially exceed the net total value under Plan A (compact development) — as was the case under similar assumptions in the greenbelt case depicted in Figure 7. It would also be found that if the demand curve for lots under Plan A were sufficiently less elastic than the comparable demand curve under Plan B, the net total value of the tract under Plan A would exceed that under Plan B, even though Plan B has a revenue advantage — as was the case under similar assumptions in the greenbelt case depicted in Figure 8.

Again as in the greenbelt case, it is unlikely that the demand curve for lots under compact Plan A would be less elastic (probably it would be more elastic) than the demand curve for lots under dispersed Plan B. Therefore, Plan B will probably yield a greater net total value of the tract than Plan A, and the excess of net total value favoring Plan B will be a measure of the superiority of its environmental value.

In passing, it may be asked why, if total revenue under Plan B distinctly exceeds that under Plan A, realtors would ever rationally decide to subdivide the tract into 3,000-square-foot lots. A possible explanation is that the prices per square foot of land and the total revenues that we have assigned to Plans A and B are those that would prevail if the land were sold after the tract was fully built up under either plan, when the greater congestion under Plan A became entirely visible to all, depressing the relative price per square foot of land under Plan A to the stated level of $0.70 per square foot. But if all the land were originally sold partly before any residential building took place and partly when only a small proportion of it had been occupied by residences, the initial sales price per square foot of 3,000-square-foot lots might have been higher than the sales price per square foot of 5,000-square-foot lots — e.g., $1.20 per square foot under Plan A as opposed to $1.00 per square foot under Plan B. Then at the time of initial sale of the land, Plan A would yield $144 million in revenue as compared to $120 million under Plan B, and realtors would presumably subdivide into smaller lots according to Plan A. This initial revenue advantage to Plan A could occur because of purchasers' lack of foresight concerning the undesirable congestion of residential building that would occur under Plan A. After full occupancy of all lots with buildings, the price per square foot of land under Plan A could then drop below such a price under Plan B, and the eventual total revenue relationship of development under the two plans could become as we have originally depicted it.

HAVE WE NEGLECTED ANY RELEVANT VALUES OR COSTS? In our earlier analysis of the choices among allocating tracts of land or rivers either to exclusive recreational use, or to exclusive commercial use, or to joint use, we concluded that the unit of natural resources in question should be allocated to exclusive recreational use whenever this would increase aggregate economic welfare. Did we leave out any relevant value or cost in the calculation that led to this conclusion? We deliberately left out of the net value of any natural resource unit in commercial use that part of the value of the commercial goods and services that can be produced by using the natural resource which is or would be contributed by labor and capital used in exploiting the natural resource.

This value of the product of labor and capital, which is included in the market value of goods and services produced in exploiting the natural resource unit, has been omitted from the net value of the natural resource in commercial use for the following reason: We plausibly assume that in the long run the labor and capital that is not used in commercial exploitation of a natural resource unit because the unit is reserved for exclusive recreational use will contribute just as large an annual value of product elsewhere in the economy — either in producing the same good or service (e.g., lumber or electric power) from other resource units, or in producing any other good or service.

If, in the long run, labor and capital displaced from exploiting a natural resource unit will contribute a smaller annual value of product elsewhere, the resulting annual loss in the value of product of the labor and capital should be added to the net value of the natural resource unit in commercial use, for purposes of comparison with the net value of the resource in exclusive recreational use.[6]

Also, in our earlier analysis of the choice between denser and more dispersed development of a tract of urban residential land, we implied that a more dispersed development should be preferred to a denser development whenever the total net value per annum (including environmental values) of the land would be greater with dispersed rather than dense development. Have we omitted any relevant value or cost in this calculation?

The principal source of an omission could be the fact that more dispersed development of urban land reduces its capacity to provide residences for people, so that dispersed, as opposed to dense, development forces a substantial number of people to reside elsewhere — in the same urban or metropolitan area, or in some other city or town. Will this induced shift in places of residence impose any costs we have not counted? It will not if the persons who are induced to reside elsewhere will not thereby suffer any loss in the sum of the total annual value of the satisfaction-providing commercial goods and services they are able to purchase and the total annual value of their environment. For this to hold, the total annual value of their product in employment should not be reduced, or at any rate not reduced by more than the value of their environment is improved. In the long run, these provisos should be met, and there should be no net costs of

---

[6] No further qualifications are necessary unless the allocation of a resource unit to exclusive recreational use involves its reallocation from a previous commercial use. Then there would be added short- or medium-term losses because specialized capital goods previously used in the exploitation of the natural resource could not be transferred to other uses, and these losses should be included in any calculation of the alternative net values of natural resource units in alternative uses.

increased residential dispersion to be counted in evaluating dispersed as compared to dense residential development. If, of course, more dispersed residential development does not develop with the city, but is later imposed to replace an ongoing pattern of denser residential development, the short-term costs of relocating people may be substantial and should be counted in any calculation of an optimal degree of dispersion of residential development. We will neglect here attendant sociological problems of changes in the allocations of lands among users, but give them some attention in Chapter 7.

SUPPLEMENTARY READINGS

1. Robert U. Ayres, "Production, Consumption, and Externalities," *American Economic Review*, 59, June, 1969, pp. 282–297.
2. Ronald Coase, "The Problem of Social Costs," *Journal of Law and Economics*, 3, October, 1960, pp. 1–44,
3. F. Trenery Dolebar, Jr., "On the Theory of Optimal Externality," *American Economic Review*, 57, March, 1967, pp. 90–103.
4. Charles J. Goetz and James Buchanan, "External Diseconomies in Competitive Supply," *American Economic Review*, 61, December, 1971, pp. 833–890.
5. Henry Jarrett, ed., *Environmental Quality in a Growing Economy: Essays from the 1966 RFF Forum*, Baltimore, Johns Hopkins Press, 1966.
6. Allen V. Kneese, Robert U. Ayres, and Ralph C. D'Arge, *Economics and the Environment: A Materials Balance Approach*, Baltimore, Johns Hopkins Press, 1970.
7. E. J. Mishan, "The Postwar Literature on Externalities: An Interpretive Essay," *Journal of Economic Literature*, 9, March, 1971, pp. 1–28.
8. E. J. Mishan, "Reflections on Recent Developments in the Concept of External Effects," *Canadian Journal of Political Economy*, 31, February, 1965, pp. 3–34.
9. Robert Solow, "The Economist's Approach to Pollution and Its Control," *Science*, 173, August, 1971, pp. 498–503.

2 Public Policies for Control or Management of Our Environment

We have noticed above the degrading impacts on human environments of pollution generated by the production and consumption of various goods, and of certain misallocations of lands and waters among uses and users. As these impacts have increased, environments have been progressively deteriorating. Further deterioration is threatened.

These developments have inspired widespread public demands for governmental policies aimed at controlling and abating environmental pollution ("pollutants"), and also at allocating or reallocating land and water in ways which will preserve or improve environments. Some such public policies have been developed and applied — most of them relatively recently — but they are very frequently inadequate to their presumed purposes. Their failure to accomplish more is attributable in considerable part to the effective political opposition of various commercial interests to stiffer, more effective public controls and regulations, which they fear would adversely affect their profits.

Nevertheless, many natural scientists, economists, and others have studied and evaluated the designs of public policies which should, in dealing with various specific sources of environmental deterioration, accomplish the desired ends of preserving and improving environments.

The characteristics of the major types of the environmental control policies proposed which promise to be reasonably efficacious are reviewed in this chapter. Their comparative economic and other merits are evaluated. The problem of comparative evaluation of such policies is, of course, not simply ranking them from best to worst for all purposes, because numerous individual policies are practically applicable only to a limited range of environmental problems. Thus, each alternative environmental control policy should be evaluated with respect to its comparative merits in dealing with that certain range of problems of environmental degradation to which it is well suited.

PUBLIC POLICIES DESIGNED TO DEAL WITH POLLUTION

In this discussion, we will consider first public policies designed to deal with pollution generated by production and consumption, deferring for subsequent discussion public policies formulated to deal with the adverse environmental effects of misallocation of lands and waters. The public policies designed to deal with pollution control which we will consider include: (1) imposing taxes or charges upon the generators of pollutant by-products or side effects equal to all or part of the environmental costs that their pollutants impose on affected populations; (2) offering public subsidies to creators of pollution to pay for the cost of reducing or eliminating their output of pollutants (as, for example, by treatment of emissions of pollutants created by production processes to reduce their volume and potency); (3) setting legal limits on the quantities of various pollutants that a process or product may emit and prohibiting the use of processes or sale of products whose pollutant emissions exceed these limits; (4) governmental participation, with a controlling hand, in the development and introduction of production technologies or product designs that will generate less (or no) pollutant by-products or side effects; and (5) outright governmental banning of the production of certain products.

The Effects of Taxes on Pollution. The taxation policies envisaged would generally be designed to impose on a producer whose production process or product generates pollutant by-products or side effects (or on a consumer whose consumption does likewise) a tax or charge per unit of pollutant emitted. The tax would be equal to all or part of the environmental cost generated per unit of production or consumption. It could reasonably be constant per unit of output regardless of the level of output if environmental costs increased only proportionally with output, or increasing per unit of output as output increased, if environmental costs increased more than proportionally with output. If such a tax were equal at each output level to the total external environmental costs of production or consumption, it would have the effect of raising the marginal and average private costs of the producer or consumer to equality with the full average and marginal costs of production or consumption, inclusive of environmental costs.

There should be two principal effects of such a taxation policy.

First, in all cases it should tend (other things being unchanged) to reduce the volume of production or consumption of the taxed good, as resultant higher private costs should be reflected in higher prices. This should have the benefit of a corresponding reduction in gross environmental cost and of an elimination of any net loss in aggregate welfare due to the previous disregard of external costs, if monopolistic output restriction has not previously accomplished the same task.

A second probable effect is more important in those cases where the taxed producer is able to reduce his environmental costs of production by altering his production process or his product: The addition by tax to his private marginal and average production cost of his previously neglected external costs of environmental degradation tends to provide an incentive for him to make changes in his process or in the design of his product whenever these changes will increase his marginal and average private internal costs of production by less than they reduce his marginal and average costs of environmental degradation — and, thus, by less than these changes reduce his pollution taxes. This effect is highly desirable, because it tends to result in a reduction both of gross environmental costs and of the full marginal and average costs of production.

THE EFFECT OF POLLUTION TAXES ON JOINT-MONOPOLY INDUSTRIES. The incentive just described is most obviously operative when a pollution tax is imposed on a small group of producers who are the sole suppliers of an isolated market for their common product, who can and do pursue joint-monopoly output restriction and price-raising to maximize their joint excess profits (as illustrated in Figure 3 in Chapter 1). Any reduction of their marginal and average full costs — e.g., by increasing their private marginal and average production costs by less than they reduce their marginal and average environmental costs (and pollution taxes) — will enable them to increase their maximized joint excess profits.

The operation of this incentive is illustrated in Figure 1, where DD' is the demand curve for the combined output of the few sellers and MR shows the marginal addition to their total revenue of an added unit of output at each output quantity. Costs before any induced pollution-reducing changes in processes are shown by solid horizontal lines. MC_P shows the initial marginal and average internal private costs of production of the combined producers. MC_E shows their initial marginal and average environmental costs of water pollution and also their initial marginal and average pollution taxes (both assumed for simplicity to be invariant with increases in industry output). MC_F shows the initial full marginal and average costs of production (all borne by the producers because of pollution taxes) and is the vertical sum of MC_E and MC_P.

One initial impact on the producers of imposing pollution taxes equal to environmental costs of pollution — if they are to maximize

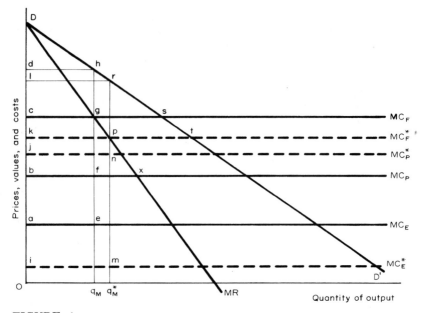

FIGURE 1

joint profits — is to induce them to produce the output oq_M (at which MC_F equals MR) and sell it at the corresponding price od. This output contrasts with larger monopolistic output bx that they would produce to maximize profits if not subject to the pollution tax and with the still larger competitive output, with pollution taxes, of cs. The gross environmental cost will be $bcgf$ ($= oaeq_M$). There will be a net loss in overall welfare of ghs,,due to monopolistic output restriction. And the sellers' combined excess profit will be $cdhg$.

Suppose now that the imposition of the pollution tax, together with the prospect of having it lowered by as much as environmental costs of pollution are lowered, induce the producers in question to seek for optimal process changes — those for which the decrease in MC_E will have the greatest excess over the increase in MC_P, thus minimizing the level of MC_F. Assuming that such process changes are possible, costs after the changes are shown by dashed horizontal lines. MC_P^* shows the new marginal and average internal private costs of production, somewhat elevated; MC_E^* shows the new marginal and average cost of pollution and the new marginal and average pollution taxes; MC_F^* shows the new full marginal and average costs of production (all of which are private costs because of the taxes) and is the vertical sum of MC_E^* and MC_P^*.

One impact of the induced pollution-reducing changes in processes will be to increase joint-profit-maximizing output to oq_M^* and reduce price correspondingly to ol. The gross environmental cost of pollution will be reduced from *bcgf* to *jkpn*. There will be an unabated net welfare loss of *prt* due to monopolistic output restriction, but overall welfare will have been increased by the expansion of output from q_M to q_M^*, and gross environmental costs beneficially reduced by a large fraction, without the expenditure of additional resources as large as the reduction in environmental costs. Finally, the producers will have had ample incentive to make the process change, since it has markedly increased their aggregate excess profits from *cdhg* to *klrp*. The same profit incentive for pollution-reducing product (as opposed to process) changes should be operative, provided that significant reductions in demand for the product do not result. The full potential effects of the pollution tax in this example are somewhat obscured by the large amount of monopolistic output restriction that is involved throughout.

THE EFFECT OF POLLUTION TAXES ON COMPETITIVE INDUSTRIES. The operation of the pollution tax incentive on a regional industry that is made up of a large number of small producers engaged in active price competition which always in the long run forces a reduction of selling price to the point where price is equal to average costs of production (inclusive of a normal interest return on capital) is illustrated in Figure 2. For comparability with Figure 1, each marginal and average cost of industry output is the same with many producers (in Figure 2) as it is with few (in Figure 1). Thus MC_E is

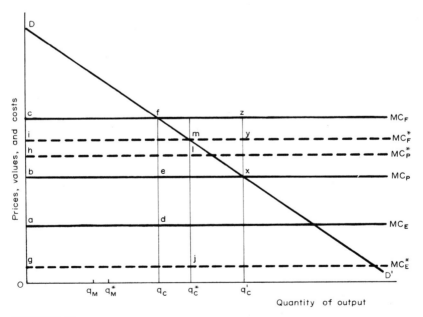

FIGURE 2

supposed to be at the same level in both figures, and the same applies to MC_P, and to all other relevant marginal costs.

In the competitive situation analyzed in Figure 2, the initial impact of imposing on producers a marginal and average pollution tax per unit of output equal to MC_E (elevating private marginal and average costs of output from MC_P to MC_F) will be to force a restriction of competitive output from oq'_C to oq_C (raising its price from ob to oc per unit) — though this reduced output is substantially larger than that secured from joint monopolists (oq_M from Figure 1). The gross environmental cost will then be $bcfe$ (reduced from $bczx$ by output restriction), and there will be an elimination of a net loss in aggregate economic welfare of fzx because of the induced restriction of competitive output.

Will the individual producers involved now have an incentive (as did the joint-profit-maximizing producers in Figure 1) to minimize their marginal and average full costs (at MC_F^*) by raising marginal and average private costs from MC_P to MC_P^* in order to reduce marginal and average environmental costs (and pollution taxes) from MC_E to MC_E^*? It may be argued that every individual producer, acting independently, would have an incentive to do just that, temporarily reaping an excess profit of yz per unit of his output (industry price c minus his new average cost i) until the rest of the producers had made the same adjustment. (After all producers made the same adjustment, industry price would fall to i, and none would make an excess profit.) Moreover, his probable apprenhension that each of the rest of the competing sellers in his industry will in due course make adjustments parallel to his — thus leading to a new no-profit industry equilibrium at price i — will not deter him from making the adjustment in question.

This is because, if he expects all others to make the same adjustment, thus lowering industry price, he must want to make that adjustment defensively, to bring his marginal full costs down to equality with the anticipated future price, i, for industry output. Thus, every producer has both an offensive motive (to earn temporary profits by being among the first to lower costs) and a defensive motive (to avoid incurring losses by being late in reducing his costs to the forthcoming level i) to make the adjustment in question (that is, minimize his marginal and average full costs at MC_F^* by raising MC_P to MC_P^* in order to reduce MC_E to MC_E^*).

After all producers have independently made the adjustment in question, in a new long-run competitive equilibrium (promoted by the pollution tax), the competitive industry output will be q_C^* instead of q_C, and price will be i instead of c. Gross environmental costs will be reduced from $bcfe$ to $himl$, even though output is larger. The output q_C^* will be optimal, involving no net welfare loss, since at that output the marginal value of output equals its full marginal cost (MC_F^*). The major advantage of the competitive over the monopolistic adjustment to the pollution tax is that losses of welfare due to monopolistic output restriction are avoided.

THE EFFECT OF POLLUTION TAXES ON THE "IN-BETWEEN" INDUSTRIES. So far we have discussed reactions to a pollution tax only for few-firm joint monopolies that can set joint profit-maximizing prices, and for atomistically competitive industries in which no concerted control of industry prices is possible. What of industries with relatively few firms that are able to set industry prices above the competitive level (above average costs) but not as high as the joint profit-maximizing level? They should generally have the same incentives to minimize their full marginal and average costs by raising their production costs (through technological change) by less than this change reduces their pollution taxes. The outcomes for them in reducing gross environmental costs and welfare losses and increasing industry outputs should roughly lie between the extremes illustrated in Figures 1 and 2.

The incentives for improving processes provided by pollution taxes to practically all industries in which an appreciable monopolistic restriction of output and raising of prices is practiced are especially pertinent to the actual world of industries. In this world, the extremes of full monopolistic output restriction and unrestricted competitive output are relatively rare. Most cases fall between those extremes, generally nearer the competitive than the monopolistic one. In this dominant range of "in-between" industries, pollution taxes should generally have the desired incentive effects. The results of their imposition may be expected to diverge from those depicted in Figure 2 in degrees responding to increases in the degrees of monopolistic output restriction and price raising practiced.

MAXIMIZING THE BENEFICIAL EFFECTS OF POLLUTION TAXES. Moreover, taxes equal to environmental pollution costs, as imposed on parties (principally producers) who are able to reduce these costs by changing their processes or products, provide incentives to reduce pollution costs that are desirably selective as among groups of producers supplying different products. Producers with relatively large environmental costs per unit of output, if taxed by an equal amount, will be willing to undertake larger increases in their unit costs of production that reduce their unit environmental costs by a given percentage than producers with substantially smaller environmental pollution costs. This is because of the larger absolute pollution-tax savings that the former producers will realize by achieving a given percentage reduction in their environmental pollution costs per unit of output. A pollution tax always set equal to a producer's unit pollution costs is thus likely to provide incentives for larger absolute reductions in pollution costs where these costs are higher, thus having a maximal impact in inducing the reduction of overall pollution costs. Further, such a pollution tax will tend, other things being equal, to induce larger reductions of pollution costs by those producers whose private costs of improving processes or products to reduce pollution costs by given percentages are smaller, and this tendency is consistent with the maximization of aggregate economic welfare.

The imposition of pollution taxes — especially at levels equal to the environmental pollution costs generated by taxed producers or consumers — thus tends to rate high among governmental policies aimed at controlling and reducing environmental degradation due to the pollutant by-products or side effects of private production and consumption. The high rating stems from the incentives that such taxes provide for private actions to curtail the generation of pollutants. This being so, several comments are in order.

First, for maximum effectiveness, such pollution taxes should be imposed directly on the parties responsible for a given pollution, rather than on the users of their products. For example, it will be generally more efficacious to tax directly the producers of a type of detergent which when used generates pollution, than to tax its users directly and let the effect of increased costs to the users "filter down" to the responsible producers in the form of a reduced sales volume at any price or a lower price at any sales volume.

Second, in the case of durable goods that provide services in different amounts to different users, where the environmental pollution costs generated are proportional to the amount of service the durable good provides to the user — as in the case of automobiles — a pollution tax levied either on the user or on the producer has its deficiencies. If the auto user is taxed for the pollution cost per mile of driving (for example, by raising the tax on gasoline), this may reduce his driving mileage somewhat but will not induce him to alter the design of his auto appreciably. He is unable to do so, except perhaps by adding pollution-inhibiting accessories to his car, and their cost, together with the fact that their installation will not reduce the gasoline tax he pays, may well deter him from installing them. Further, the resulting incentive for automotive producers to alter the designs of their autos will be indirect, diluted and weak. On the other hand, taxation of auto producers by an amount per auto equal to the costs of the environmental degradation (accumulated over years of use) generated on the average by its use would provide more direct and powerful incentives for altering automotive designs to reduce the pollutant emissions of autos, but as the tax was passed on to auto buyers by increased auto prices, it would be discriminatory between buyers who drove their cars, respectively, relatively few and relatively many miles per year.

Third, where the source of environmental degradation is found in the habits of consumers — as in the case of littering the landscape with discarded beverage containers — direct taxation of individual consumers is administratively impractical. And indirect consumer taxation by levying a tax on and raising the price of beverage containers would (in addition to having uncertain incentive effects) be insufficient; it would also be inequitable, because it would tax beverage use and not littering. It would probably need to be supplemented by banning other than reusable and returnable containers, the "refund" payment for the return of which would be substantial.

The pollution-tax approach to inducing the reduction by private producers or consumers of the generation of environmental pollutants is generally much more effective if taxes are levied on producers rather than on the consumers of their products. The approach encounters multiple difficulties if the producer and the consumer jointly contribute to the amount of environmental pollution cost that is generated. Finally, the administrative costs of a pollution tax are obviously less if the number of parties to be taxed is comparatively few rather than very many.

The Effects of Subsidizing Polluters to Reduce Pollution. An alternative public policy aimed at reducing the quantity and cost of the pollutant by-products of private production involves the public subsidization of producers for all or part of the costs of reducing their emissions or effluents of air or water pollutants. Although these reductions of pollutants may result from real technological alterations in basic production processes, they typically have been secured by adding "treatment plants" to reduce the quantity and potency of pollutant emissions of effluents before they reach the air or water.

The general merits of this sort of subsidization policy can best be evaluated if first we suppose that a governmental body pays the full original and operating cost of reducing pollutant emissions from the processes of a group of producers of the same good, when these producers are the sole suppliers of the product to an isolated market. We will suppose that the producers are in active competition and that the governmental body provides adequate incentives for their acceptance and indicated use of the subsidy (e.g., by making acceptance a condition for continuing production). In Figure 3, we depict the general effects of providing each producer in the competitive group with the same subsidy per unit of product output, to be spent for attaching to his facilities a treatment plant which will process the waste emissions or effluents of his production to reduce their volume and potency.

In Figure 3, DD' is the demand curve for the combined output of the group of producers. The marginal and average private costs of production of all firms in the industry are represented by MC_P. The corresponding marginal and average environmental costs that they generate before any subsidized treatment plants are added are at the level MC_E. They are costs external to the producers and are disre-

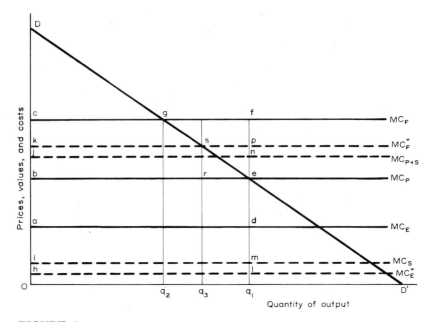

FIGURE 3

garded by them since they pay no taxes equivalent to any part of them. Their full marginal and average costs of production are MC_F (the vertical sum of MC_P and MC_E), and are disregarded by the producers because they pay no taxes equal to any part of the MC_E component of MC_F.

Before the addition of subsidized treatment plants, the group of producers — if active competition among them drives selling price to equality with their private average costs — will produce the competitive output oq_1 and sell it at the competitive unit price of ob. The gross environmental cost resulting will be $bcfe$ ($= oadq_1$). And there will be a net loss in aggregate economic welfare of efg, due to their producing an output which exceeds the optimal output by q_2q_1.

Suppose now that a governmental body grants subsidies for the installation and operation of waste treatment plants to all producers, these plants having marginal and average costs per unit of output of MC_S, and that the treatment plants, by reducing the quantity and potency of waste emissions or effluents from production, reduce the marginal and average environmental costs generated by the subsidized firms from MC_E to MC_E^*. (This is a saving in environmental costs greater than the costs of the subsidies, and thus increases overall welfare — as any economically justifiable subsidy should.) Then the marginal and average private costs of production of firms in the industry remain unchanged at MC_P; thus marginal and average private plus subsidized costs will be MC_{P+S}; and the full marginal and average costs of production (the vertical sum of MC_P, MC_S, and MC^*_E) will be reduced from MC_F to MC^*_F.

What are the results of the subsidy and the connected reduction in environmental costs? First, the producers of the industry will leave their output and price unchanged at oq_1 and ob respectively, not raising prices because of the addition to plant costs of MC_S, or lowering them because of the reduction of full costs to MC^*_F. This is because both of these cost changes are external to the producers (not paid for by them directly, or indirectly through corresponding taxes), and they therefore disregard them in arriving at their price and combined output. In brief, producers in the sort of situation described will be totally unresponsive in price and output determination either to subsidies for the treatment of waste products, or to reductions in the environmental costs of production which the subsidized activities bring about. This complete unresponsiveness is, in general, economically undesirable, since subsidy-induced cost changes have no influence on the producers' prices or outputs.

The desirable results of the subsidy in Figure 3 are to reduce gross environmental costs from *bcfe* to *jkpn* and to reduce them by more than the subsidy cost of *bjne*. One undesirable result is that the failure of the subsidized producers to react to the subsidy and its effects will result in their maintaining an output of oq_1, which, after the subsidization of waste treatment and its effects, will still result in a net loss in aggregate economic welfare of *eps* (though this is a smaller welfare loss than the presubsidy one of *efg*). An optimal adjustment to the subsidy would involve setting industry output at oq_3.

The most serious deficiency of the subsidy policy described, however, is that it provides absolutely no incentive for producers to adopt, or discover and adopt, internal changes in their processes which would further reduce environmental costs per unit of output by more than they increased private production costs. This, of course, is because of the fact that reductions in external environmental costs do not save them anything, so that there is no financial incentive (such as a reduction in pollution taxes) for them to spend their own money in reducing the environmental pollution they generate. This is true not only when the group of firms is so competitive as always to drive price to the level of average cost (as shown in Figure 3), but also when the group can exercise some degree of monopolistic output restriction and price raising above average costs. Therefore, the subsidy policy described provides no incentive at all for the subsidized producers to do other than remain technologically stagnant, not dealing themselves with the environmental pollution costs they generate. In this very essential respect, a policy of subsidizing to reduce pollution is distinctly inferior to the previously described policy of taxing producers in amounts equal to the environmental costs of pollution that they generate.

Legal Limits on Pollutant Emissions of Products or Processes Eligible for Production or Use. Among other governmental policies that have been used to control or decrease the environmental degradation wrought by the pollutant by-products and side effects of private production is that of imposing limits on the physical quantities of various pollutants that a type of product may generate when used and forbidding the manufacture of products whose emissions of pollutants exceed these limits. The policy is being most prominently applied to automobile manufacturers, who by government edict must by a given year (1975 or 1976) produce autos whose exhaust emissions per mile of driving do not exceed specified physical amounts of uncombusted hydrocarbons, nitric oxide, carbon monoxide, etc., in order to be permitted to continue production. Such a policy has seemed suitable for application to durable goods like autos, which cause air pollution in proportion to the amount of service (miles of driving) that their users get from them. But it is potentially applicable to nondurable goods that, although they also generate pollution as used, are fully used up in short order by their buyers (e.g., detergents) and also could be imposed on producers in the form of limits on the permissible physical amounts of pollutants that their production processes generate per unit of output.

Such a policy tends indeed to provide very powerful incentives for private producers to develop products or processes which will add less to the environmental costs of pollution. It does, however, have two significant deficiencies.

First, even if the reduction in environmental costs (as measured in dollars) which would be accomplished by conforming to the limits on physical pollutants that are imposed were accurately or even approximately measurable or measured, the extra production costs of conforming to these standards are frequently not accurately known, particularly if conforming involves the discovery or development of new technologies for production or new product designs. If this is the case, a governmental authority may very well impose physical limits on pollutant emissions the production costs of conforming to which exceed the reduction in environmental costs accomplished. In this event, conforming to the overly stringent physical limits will reduce overall economic welfare (causing us to pay excessive marginal costs for given marginal improvements in the environment). Alternatively, a governmental authority may impose insufficiently stringent physical limits on the emission of pollutants, in the sense that more stringent limits could have been conformed to with an increase in production costs less than the resulting reduction in environmental costs. Given a pervasive lack of knowledge about the production costs of conforming to various physical limits on the emission of pollutants, the policy of setting these limits is in serious danger of achieving nonoptimal results and causing appreciable sacrifices of overall economic welfare.

A pollution-tax policy of the sort previously described, on the other hand, has the comparative merit of providing incentives only for pollution-reducing processes or product changes which reduce estimated environmental costs by as much or more than the connected increase in production costs (which may be learned along the way) and of pushing toward the margin at which such increases in production costs equal the connected reduction of environmental costs.

Second, the imposition of physical limits on the pollutant effects of products or processes tends to induce producers to conform to these limits through product or process changes which are least unprofitable to them, and these may not be the changes that would maximize overall economic welfare. This is particularly true of changes in the design of products like automobiles. Unfortunately, the pollution-tax policy tends to suffer the same deficiency, at least in some measure.

Governmental Participation in Altering Products or Processes. The foregoing suggests that there are some hazards in providing private producers with incentives to accomplish reductions in environmental pollution costs (through physical limits or through pollution taxes) and then leaving the means of reducing these costs strictly up to the private concerns. These hazards become greater in the case of product changes as the product is increasingly complex and multidimensional in its design characteristics — thus creating multiple product-change alternatives which will achieve the same reduction in environmental costs. It has therefore been suggested that policies which provide incentives for private producers to reduce the environmental costs they generate should be coupled with the policy of having appropriate governmental agencies participate — with a controlling hand — with private producers in the development, choice, and introduction of environment-saving products and processes. Otherwise, the discretionary powers of the private producers may be unduly great.

Banning of Certain Products. There is one sort of environment-protecting policy which can be recommended for highly selective use because of its merits of simplicity and low administrative cost. This is the outright prohibition of the production or sale of certain products. It would seem to be appropriate only as applied to products which impose or are the bases for the imposition of very large environmental costs and which, if they perform substantially indispensable functions, can be replaced by substitute products which perform about the same functions at an acceptable private cost and are responsible for the imposition of substantially lesser environmental costs. Examples of candidates for this policy treatment include, for example, pesticides with long-lasting adverse effects on the environment (like DDT), non-reusable and "nonreturnable" beverage containers, and detergents containing components that inflict severe and prolonged environmental damage. The criteria for the designation of such products for prohibition are of course very important.

PUBLIC POLICIES AIMED AT AVERTING OR ARRESTING MISALLOCATIONS OF LAND AND WATER

Let us now consider public policies directed at arresting ongoing degradation of environments by misallocating lands and waters among uses and users.

We will consider first those affecting allocations among uses. Regarding the allocation among uses of out-of-town recreational resources like rivers and forests, federal public policies have, for several decades, supported their progressive developments for commercial purposes that have probably reduced their total net recreational values by more than they have increased their total net commercial values (see Chapter 6). Thus, these developments may have imposed both gross environmental costs and net losses in aggregate economic welfare in a manner illustrated earlier in Chapter 1 (Figure 5). A fundamental reversal in the major thrust of these federal policies seems indicated, as will be suggested in detail in Chapter 6.

Within metropolitan areas, policies aimed at securing better allocations of lands among uses should have similar broad purposes, but require different devices for implementation. Preserving or securing lands for environment-enhancing regional park areas of natural countryside, beachfronts, conventionally manicured parks, and greenbelts is undoubtedly best undertaken when land for these uses has not yet been developed for other urban uses. Appropriate zoning regulations that preserve both public and private lands for the uses mentioned by prohibiting their use for residential, commercial, or industrial purposes are indicated as instruments of public policy (see Chapter 7). If the land to be reserved for recreation has already been developed for other urban uses, and reallocation of the lands from such uses would be needed to create parks and greenbelts, numerous difficulties connected with the relocation of people, industrial plants, etc., are encountered.

Also, within large cities, misallocations of land among users that impose very crowded living conditions on a part of the population, as distinct from conditions of living that give reasonable amenities of light, air, and space to another part, should be remedied by various means. Such means include revised building codes for new urban construction, and dispersion of overcrowded central-city populations into smaller towns in outer suburban areas. The problem of remedies here is a complex one and will be discussed in detail in Chapter 7.

ENVIRONMENTAL CONTROL WHEN THE VALUES OF ENVIRONMENTAL CHANGES ARE NOT SATISFACTORILY MEASURABLE

In the preceding evaluation of alternative public policies of environmental control or management, we made the provisional assumption that monetary values could generally be placed on given physical changes in environments. For example, we assumed that adding to an urban air mantle given quantities of several air pollutants per day generates aggregate losses in the physical well-being and psychic satisfaction of the affected populace that can be measured in monetary terms. Or that the increase in the aggregate psychic satisfactions of people seeking river-oriented recreation which results from allocating a river exclusively to recreational use rather than to joint commercial and recreational use can also be assigned a measurable monetary value. This assumption is extremely convenient, since it implies that environmental losses or gains, and the costs of averting or creating them, are commensurable in the same dollar unit. Thus, assuming the measurability of an environmental loss in monetary terms, we can directly compare this loss with the monetary cost of averting it (to see if averting it will or won't increase aggregate economic welfare).

As long as we assumed that the values of environmental changes are measurable in monetary terms, we were led to emphasize the merits of environmental control policies the efficacy of which depends strongly on commensurability in dollar units of environmental changes and the costs of averting or attaining them. Thus, with respect to pollution control, major emphasis was placed on the imposition of pollution taxes equal to the monetary value of the external environmental costs of pollution, or on the granting of subsidies only in such quantities that will result in reducing environmental pollution costs by a dollar amount greater than the subsidies. In discussing the optimal allocation of lands or waters between environment-improving recreational use and commercial use, we leaned heavily on the assumption that the total net value of a resource in recreational use is measurable in the same monetary terms in which the net value of the same resource in commercial use is measurable.

It is unfortunate from the standpoint of our ability to design and apply optimal environmental control policies, which should depend on the commensurability in monetary terms of environmental and nonenvironmental values and costs, that the values or costs of most environmental changes are at present not practically measurable in monetary terms. No one is currently able to estimate with any reliability the dollar cost of an environmental degradation caused by raising the physical level of pollutants in air or water by a given physical amount, or the total net value of recreational use of a river — whether reserved for recreational use alone or devoted to joint commercial and recreational uses. And so it goes with related pollution and allocation problems. This does not mean that the values of environmental change are not *conceivably* measurable in monetary terms, as in general they are. But in the present state of knowledge — which fortunately is improving — these values are in general not practically measurable in such terms.

This lack of practical ability to place monetary values on environmental changes impedes the specification of environmental control policies that are likely to be approximately optimal from an economic standpoint. It also forces public agencies devoted to environmental controls to settle for generally inferior policies which rely very little on meaningful economic calculations of environmental gains and losses.

Instead, the public agencies tend to rely on intrinsically arbitrary physical goals supplied by natural scientists, public-health experts, engineers, urban planners, foresters, fish-and-wildlife experts — etc., ad infinitum. Thus, such experts will supply goals of "permissible" part per million of various pollutants in ambient air or in streams and derive from them proposed physical limitations on the quantity and quality of "permissible" pollutant emissions per unit of use of, or of output from, various sources into the air or into streams. Or they will devise physical goals for the amount and type of recreational resources to be preserved for recreation and the amount to be devoted to joint commercial and recreational use based on estimates of the "requirements" of various populations for recreational resources of various qualities.

Such "technical" physical goals are unlikely to correspond at all closely to the economic goals at which we would arrive in the same cases, given the practical measurability of the monetary values of various environmental changes. They may err, from an economic standpoint, in the direction of being set either too high or too low, the costs of attaining them being considered. And correlatively, the derived physical limitations on the emissions of pollutants, or prescriptions for the allocations of lands and waters among environment-enhancing and other uses, may, from an economic standpoint, range from distinctly insufficient to overly sufficient — in the latter case calling for environmental improvements the costs of attaining which will almost certainly reduce aggregate economic welfare. Yet the unwisdom of such technical goals and connected regulating policies is hard for the economist to disprove with hard figures, other than in exceptional cases.

In this context, the comparative efficacy of different public policies of environmental control requires some reevaluation. In the general area of pollution control, governmental imposition of precise physical limits on pollutant emissions from production or from the use of products — with conformity to such limits being a prerequisite for permission to produce — has an improved comparative advantage.

The limits imposed may not be economically optimal, but incentives for pollution-reducing technological and product changes by private producers are provided. And in the political tug of war between the regulators and the regulated, the limits arrived at are unlikely to be too stringent from an economic standpoint.

Connected policies of governmental participation with private industry in developing and introducing pollution-reducing technologies and products similarly rise on the preference scale among alternative policies.

Taxation for pollution becomes a weaker policy tool, because of the lack of monetary measurements of the environmental costs of pollution upon which the level of taxes should be based. Nevertheless, relatively low pollution taxes (probably well below the environmental costs of pollution) should provide significant incentives for private reduction of pollution, especially where such a reduction can be accomplished rather cheaply. Subsidization of private producers for reduction of their pollutant emissions is weakened as a policy tool for a similar reason — lack of knowledge of the environmental pollution cost that a subsidy eliminates. Since it would be a deficient tool even if environmental pollution costs were measurable, it appears to be more deficient when such costs are not measurable.

Outright banning of especially noxious products, when much less noxious ones are available to perform the same function, remains a viable tool of environmental control policy. And so do external public-enterprise activities designed to ameliorate massive environmental degradation problems.

Various policies designed to avert or correct misallocations of land and water between environment-improving and other uses, which were discussed in the previous section, largely retain the merits and demerits previously attributed to them when environmental values are not at all precisely measurable. But they may have to be implemented by — as substitutes for reasonably precise goals and regulatory measures — simply strong pushes in directions indicated by observations of environments and by common sense. The policy-maker in this area who lacks monetary measures of environmental gains and losses from various allocations or reallocations of lands and water lacks a powerful tool. But since actual decisions on allocations are in any event more strongly influenced by political processes than by gains or losses in environmental quality and in overall economic welfare, the political power to influence decisions in the evidently right direction may in any case be the most essential weapon for securing improvements in allocative policies affecting environment.

It may be added that in some policy contexts, such as that of determining an optimal density of residential building in an urban area, measures indicating the values of environmental changes are not totally lacking. Systematic comparative data on land values for example, can be used to infer the improvement in environmental values attributable to progressively more dispersed residential building.

PREVIEW OF THE ESSAYS
IN THE FOLLOWING SIX CHAPTERS

In Chapters 1 and 2 we have presented a general economic analysis of the sources of environmental degradation, their impacts on economic welfare, and public policies designed to avert further degradation and improve human environments. The analysis has of necessity been highly general in character and carried on at a level that largely abstracts from specific environmental problems — except so far as it has made synoptic reference to some of them for illustrative purposes.

Chapter 3 is an essay which supplements our general economic analysis by probing the economic and sociological causes of the recent upsurge of public interest in preserving and improving our environment, appraising the viability of environmental control as a significant political issue, and evaluating the comparative wisdom of some alternative broad attitudes concerning the proper goals of an environmental policy. In his essay, Anthony Downs introduces many relevant considerations that are not strictly "economic" in character.

Each of the succeeding five chapters (4 through 8) is devoted to a specific, actual type of environmental problem, with strong emphasis on the factual details and peculiarities of each problem (frequently peculiarities not expressly dealt with in the general analysis of Chapters 1 and 2) and on public policies either already employed or currently available for ameliorating or eliminating each problem. These essays deal in turn with water pollution; automotive air pollution; protection and preservation of rural recreational resources as environmental assets; the multiple sources of and possible remedies for the deterioration of the environments of our central cities; and the several environmental impacts of our freeway and airline transportation systems — and what to do about them.

Though in each of these essays economic analysis is applied to a particular problem of environmental deterioration, each essay is semiindependent of the abstract general analytical Chapters 1 and 2, in the sense that no endeavor is made in any of them formally to reintroduce the relevant analytical constructions of that first chapter. At the same time, each of the essays (in Chapters 4 through 8) provides real illustrations of some of the abstract generalizations developed in Chapters 1 and 2 (as well as some particularizations peculiar to the factual problem at hand) in manners that should be obvious to anyone who has read the first two chapters.

Chapters 4 and 5 are focused on the sources of and remedies for two sorts of pollution — of water and of air — and their dependence on the abstract analysis of the generation and the abatement of pollution in Chapters 1 and 2 will be obvious to all. The same applies preponderantly to Chapter 8 — concerning freeway and airline systems.

A large part of Chapter 6 (on rural recreational resources) is concerned with the allocation of land and water between commercial uses and environment-enhancing recreational uses. The application in this part of the related abstract analysis of Chapter 1 of the environmental impacts of allocations of lands among uses will be evident. In a shorter section of Chapter 6, the external environmental costs of the side effects of inferior logging methods and practices in forests are considered, and the application of the relevant abstract analysis of Chapter 1 clearly is involved in that consideration.

The substance of Chapter 7 is the finding that the environmental deterioration of central cities stems from a variety of sources. Misallocation of land among uses is analyzed — the discussion clearly drawing on the general analysis on pp. 28–35 of Chapter 1. More emphasis is placed on misallocations of land (and housing) among users — in an applied analysis directly related to the analytical constructs of pp. 35–38 of this chapter, though the sources of this misallocation of lands among users (largely racial prejudice and an unbalanced distribution of personal income) seem more or less peculiar to the contemporary central-city environmental problem. This latter misallocation in turn generates a special species of external environmental costs connected with crowded living conditions and with racial segregation in land allocation — not analyzed in Chapter 1. In addition, central cities are generally afflicted more severely than other areas with every common sort of external environmental costs of pollution, including those analyzed in Chapters 4, 5, and 8, as well as some others. The general analysis of such external costs on pp. 11–20 of Chapter 1 obviously supports an understanding of this phase of central-city environmental problems.

The last five essays comprise over half of this book because of our belief that only a limited amount can be learned about environmental problems and their management through abstract economic analysis and that, in addition, much more can be learned by reasonably detailed empirical studies of a number of actual environmental issues.

Chapter 9, the last in this volume, is a summary and comparison of the findings developed in Chapters 4 through 8, and briefly recapitulates their relationships to generalizations set forth in Chapters 1 and 2.

SUPPLEMENTARY READINGS

1. William J. Baumol, "On Taxation and the Control of Externalities," *American Economic Review*, 62, June, 1972, pp. 307–322.
2. James M. Buchanan, "External Diseconomies, Corrective Taxes, and Market Structures," *American Economic Review*, 59, March, 1969, pp. 174–177.

3. Comptroller General of the United States, *Examination into the Effectiveness of the Construction Program for Abating, Controlling, and Preventing Water Pollution,* Washington, D.C., 1969.
4. Otto A. Davis and Morton I. Kamien, "Externalities, Information, and Alternative Collective Action," in *Public Expenditures and Policy Analysis,* R. H. Haveman and J. Margolis, eds., Chicago, Markham Publishing Co., 1970.
5. H. A. J. Green, "The Social Optimum in the Presence of Monopoly and Taxation," *Review of Economic Studies,* 29, 1962, pp. 66–78.
6. C. Wright, "Some Aspects of the Use of Corrective Taxes for Controlling Air Pollution Emissions," *Natural Resources Journal,* 9, January, 1969, pp. 63–82.

3 The Political Economy of Improving Our Environment

ANTHONY DOWNS

American public interest in improving the quality of our environment has had a recent remarkable upsurge. The intensity of this interest has clearly changed much faster than the quality of the environment itself.

What has caused this relatively sudden shift in public attention?

Why did this issue suddenly become almost preeminent among our domestic concerns when so many other urgent, previously discovered domestic problems remain unresolved?

And how long will the American public sustain a high intensity of interest in ecological matters?

In this essay I seek to answer these questions by exploring certain key political and economic forces and structures in our society, plus their interactions with major aspects of environmental issues. I believe there is a systematic "issue-attention cycle" in American domestic affairs. This cycle causes certain individual problems to leap into sudden prominence, remain there for a short time, and then gradually fade from public attention — though still largely unresolved. This and other conclusions provide insights into how long, and to what extent, public attention in America will remain sufficiently

Reprinted from Downs, Kneese, Ogden, and Perloff, *The Political Economy of Environmental Control*, Berkeley, 1972, by permission of the publisher, Institute of Business and Economic Research, University of California, Berkeley. Acknowledgement is also due the Herman Royer Program in Political Economy, University of California, Berkeley, which sponsored the public lecture on which this essay is based, and to Dr. Downs.

focused upon environmental issues to generate effective changes concerning them.

CAUSES OF INCREASED INTEREST
IN THE ENVIRONMENT

The most obvious reason for our rising concern about the environment is the dramatic deterioration in the past few years of certain easily perceived environmental conditions. A whole catalog of now-well-known symptoms can be quickly arrayed. It includes ubiquitous urban smog, more littering and greater proliferation of solid waste, oceanic oil spills that gum up beaches and destroy oxygen-producing plankton, greater pollution of water supplies with DDT and other poisons, the incipient "death" of more large bodies of water like that of Lake Erie, the threatened disappearance of many wildlife species, widespread overcrowding of many facilities from local expressways to national parks, and even the suspension of more dust in the earth's upper atmosphere. As millions of citizens observe these highly visible or well-dramatized worsenings of conditions around them, they become increasingly convinced that *someone* ought to "do something" to counteract these trends.

Ironically, many of these negative developments are caused by positive changes in society which are highly valued by these same citizens. Hence, "doing something" to reduce environmental deterioration will not be easy. Three such positive developments are particularly important causes of "negative fallout" upon environmental quality.

First, as all thoughtful observers of pollution have pointed out, *the very richness of our material goods production and consumption is responsible for an immense amount of the environmental pollution which has alarmed so many citizens.* For example, electric power generation creates smoke and air pollution if it is based on fossil fuels or causes rising water temperatures if it is based on nuclear fuels. Thus, up to now, rapid increases in power generation inescapably imply greater environmental pollution. At the same time, a key foundation for escalating living standards in the United States during this century has been the doubling of electric power consumption every ten years. So more pollution is the obverse side — hence the price — we have paid for the tremendous advantages of being able to use electricity in more and more ways. Similarly, much of the litter which blights even our remotest landscapes stems from the convenience of our using throwaway packages for many goods. Thus, to regard environmental pollution as a purely negative aspect of modern life would be to ignore its direct linkage with many material advantages that most citizens enjoy.

A second positive aspect of American life related to rising environmental pollution is what I call the democratization of privilege. It is really another offshoot of our increased affluence. Many more Americans are now able to participate in certain activities and consume certain kinds of goods and services that were formerly the exclusive prerogatives of a small wealthy minority. Many members of that minority — which includes much of our highly vocal intellectual elite — are incensed, even outraged, by some of the consequences of having their formerly esoteric advantages spread to "the common man." The most frequent irritant caused by democratization of privilege is congestion of all kinds, particularly in public facilities.

For example, rising highway congestion is a frequent cause of complaint almost everywhere. Yet its main cause is the rapid spread of automobile ownership and usage throughout the nation. In 1950 about 59 percent of all families in the United States had at least one automobile, and 7 percent owned two or more. By 1968 the proportion of families owning at least one automobile had climbed to 79 percent, and 26 percent had two or more cars. In just the eight years from 1960 to 1968 the total number of registered automotive vehicles rose 27 million — or 38 percent — as compared to a rise in human population of 20.5 million — or only 11 percent. By now, motor vehicles cause approximately 60 percent of all air pollution. So the tremendous increase in smog levels in all metropolitan areas does not primarily result from larger population, as many ecological alarmists claim. Rather, it is caused by the democratization of mobility achieved by spreading single and multiple ownership of cars and greater use of trucks. In this and other respects, *changes in the behavior of those who are already alive are vastly more significant in causing pollution than increases in their number.*

The democratization of privilege is also directly responsible for elbow-to-elbow crowding in national park campsites, rising suburban housing density, expansion of new subdivisions into formerly picturesque farms and orchards, and the transformation of once-tranquil resort areas — like Hawaii's Waikiki Beach — into forests of high-rise buildings. It is now much more difficult than ever for the wealthy to flee from busy urban areas to places of quiet seclusion because so many more people can afford to go along with them. Thus *the elite's environmental deterioration is often the common man's improved standard of living.* But that does not stop members of the elite from emitting loud cries of anguish at the "desecration" of their favorite spots. The most striking instance of the resulting complaints involve those conservationists seeking to prevent the building of roads into wilderness areas. They want the tiny number of hardy souls who go there on foot to have the place all to themselves, so they vehemently oppose making it easy for the "masses" to join them. I can certainly understand their desire to preserve some untouched wilderness areas. But, at the same time, I believe every complaint about environmental deterioration caused by congestion should raise at least a suspicion in our minds that perhaps a few elitists are objecting to the extension of their formerly exclusive privileges to thousands, or even millions, of others who were never before able to share them.

A third positive factor underlying greater concern with environmental quality is a marked increase in our aspirations and desired standards concerning what our environment ought to be like. Rising dissatisfaction with the general performance of the "system" in the United States results, in my opinion, not primarily from poorer performance by that system, but rather from a rapid escalation of our aspirations concerning what its performance ought to be. Nowhere is this phenomenon more striking than concerning the quality of our environment. One hundred years ago white Americans were wiping out whole Indian tribes without a qualm. Today, in contrast, many serious-minded citizens are attempting to make important public issues out of the potential disappearance of the grizzly bear, the whooping crane, the timber wolf, and other exotic creatures. Only a tiny minority of Americans would ever see these beings under the most optimistic assumptions (except in zoos or motion pictures). Meanwhile, in Brazil thousands of Indians are still being murdered each year — but American conservationists are less interested in that human massacre than in what happens to rare breeds of animals no less remotely located. Similarly, urban aesthetes cry out about galloping sprawl in metropolitan fringe areas, while at the same time ignoring hundreds of thousands of slum dwellers who live in rat-infested housing a few miles away. Hence the escalation of our environmental aspirations is far more selective than might at first appear. Yet, regarding many forms of pollution, we are now becoming rightly upset at both practices and conditions we have largely ignored for decades. An example is the dumping of industrial wastes and sewage into our rivers and lakes. This increase in our environmental aspirations is part of a general cultural phenomenon stimulated both by our success in raising living standards and by certain aspects of the communications media discussed later herein.

This brings me to another factor responsible for rapidly rising interest in environmental pollution: an explosion of ridiculous and exaggerated rhetoric concerning this subject. According to some well-publicized alarmists, all life on earth is threatened by an environmental crisis. Some claim human life will probably end within three decades — or perhaps less — if we do not do something drastic about current behavior patterns.

Are things really that bad? Is the world about to end unless we totally reorganize our production and consumption processes? Frankly, I am not enough of an ecological expert to offer any certain answer. But I am highly skeptical concerning most extremely alarmist views because of the constant cacophony of Cassandras proclaiming that human doom and disaster will result from many other so-called crises in our society.

What is a crisis anyway? I believe there are two reasonable definitions. The first kind of crisis consists of a rapidly deteriorating situation moving toward a single disastrous event at some future moment. The second kind of crisis is a more gradually deteriorating situation that will eventually pass some subtle point of no return involving conditions which are equally disastrous in the long run, but less obvious and more gradual in effect.

Regarding most American domestic problems, I do not believe either of these definitions is applicable. Many intellectuals hate to admit it, but the American system actually serves the majority of citizens rather well in terms of most indicators of well-being. Regarding such things as real income, personal mobility, variety and choice of consumption patterns, longevity, health, leisure time, and quality of housing, most Americans are better off today than they have ever been — and extraordinarily better off than most of mankind is now or ever has been. True, and important, a significant numerical minority is suffering from each of a number of serious problems — a different minority for each problem. I am referring to such problems as hunger, poverty, racism, poor public transportation, low-quality education, crime, drug addiction, and unemployment. The number of persons suffering from each of these social ills is very large *absolutely* — often in the millions. But these numbers are small *relatively* — usually less than 15 percent of the entire population. Moreover, the absolute level of deprivation regarding many of these problems is probably shrinking as society improves its performance in attacking them. What is *not* improving is the gap between that performance and what most people — or at least highly vocal minorities — believe society *ought* to be doing to solve these problems. For a variety of reasons, our aspirations and standards have risen much faster than the actual output of our social system. Therefore, although most Americans, including most of the poor, are receiving more now, they are enjoying it less.

Yet this relationship between each of our major social problems, including environmental pollution, and our efforts to solve it certainly does not qualify as a genuine crisis. Why, then, do we keep hearing cries of "crisis" — of which those concerning the environment are among the most recent?

DYNAMICS OF THE "ISSUE-ATTENTION CYCLE"

Public perceptions of most crises in American domestic life do not reflect changes in real conditions as much as they reflect the operation of a definite and systematic cycle of heightening public interest and then boredom with major issues. This issue-attention cycle is rooted in both the nature of certain domestic problems and the way major communications media interact with the public.

The cycle itself has five clearly definable stages which occur in predictable sequence as follows:

1. *The Preproblem Stage.* This stage prevails whenever some highly undesirable social condition exists but has not yet captured much public attention. Many specialized experts or interest groups may already be alarmed about the issue. But somehow they have not succeeded in dramatizing it or otherwise bringing it to the center of the stage of public attention. *Usually, objective conditions regarding this problem are far worse during this preproblem stage than they are by the time the public becomes interested in the problem.* For example, the evil effects of racism, poverty, and hunger in the United States were vastly worse before these became major public-policy issues than afterward.

2. *Alarmed Discovery and Euphoric Enthusiasm.* As a result of some dramatic series of events (like the racial riots of 1965 to 1967) or for other less obvious reasons, the public at large suddenly becomes aware of and alarmed about the evils of a particular problem. This sudden alarmed discovery is invariably accompanied by euphoric enthusiasm about society's ability to "solve this problem" or "do something effective" within a relatively short time period. This combination of alarm and confidence results in part because of the strong public pressures in America for all political leaders to claim that every problem can be solved in some meaningful sense. This belief is part of the great American tradition of optimism. That tradition views most obstacles to social progress as *external* to the structure of society itself — like mountain ranges to be climbed by energetic frontiersmen. Therefore, every such obstacle can be eliminated and every problem solved without any fundamental reordering of society itself, if only we devote sufficient effort to it. This feeling is embodied in the motto of the Army Air Force during World War II: "The difficult we do immediately; the impossible takes a little longer." In older and perhaps wiser cultures, there is an underlying sense of irony about attacking certain problems. It springs from a widespread and often confirmed belief that not all problems can be solved *at all* in any complete sense. This irony has traditionally been absent from our optimistic culture and is only now beginning to develop. It is mockingly exemplified by the joke that confidence can be defined as that feeling of power and strength you experience before you understand the problem.

3. *Realizing the Cost of Significant Progress.* The third stage in the issue-attention cycle consists of a gradually spreading realization — first by responsible experts and later by the general public — that the costs of eliminating the evil associated with this problem (whatever it is) are very high indeed. Really moving toward a solution of the problem would not only take a great deal of money but would also require major sacrifices of power, energy, and institutional advantage by large groups in the population who now enjoy these benefits. The public thus begins to realize that the evil itself results in part from arrangements that are providing significant benefits to some-

one — often to a great many people. Examples have already been cited of how air pollution results from the benefits of electric power consumption and automobiles. In some cases the magically painless cure of technological progress and innovation can eliminate some of the undesirable results associated with this problem without causing any major restructuring of society or any loss of present benefits by others — except perhaps for higher money costs. Such a mainly technological solution to social problems is a consummation devoutly to be wished — and initially assumed to be possible regarding nearly every problem in the optimistic American tradition. But, in reality, the very nature of our most pressing social problems involves either deliberate or unconscious exploitation of one group in society by another or the prevention of one group from enjoying something which another wants to keep for itself. For example, upper-middle-class whites regard geographic separation from poor people and blacks of all income levels as providing definite benefits to themselves. Clearly, any equality of opportunities or access to the advantages of suburban living for the poor and for blacks cannot be achieved without at least some sacrifice of these "benefits" of separation by those who now enjoy them. The gradually spreading realization of this type of relationship constitutes an important part of the third stage.

4. *Gradual Decline of Intense Public Interest.* The above-described stage almost imperceptibly becomes transformed into the fourth stage: a gradual decline in the intensity with which public interest is focused upon the problem concerned. As more and more people realize how difficult and how costly to themselves it would be really to solve this problem, three reactions set in. Some people just get discouraged. Others feel positively threatened when thinking about the problem and its solutions, so they suppress such thoughts. Still others become bored by constant focus on this issue. Most people experience some combination of these feelings. Consequently, public desire to keep attention focused on this issue wanes. This result is encouraged by the fact that by this time some other issue is usually entering Stage Two. Hence it exerts a more novel and thus more powerful claim upon the center of the public-attention stage. (The specific mechanisms involved in Stage Four are discussed in detail later.)

5. *The Postproblem Stage.* In the final stage of the issue-attention cycle, an issue which has lost its position at the center of public attention moves into a sort of prolonged limbo — a twilight world of lesser attention or spasmodic recurrences of interest. However, the issue has a different relation to public attention in this final stage from that which initially prevailed even though it was also out of the spotlight in the preproblem stage. For one thing, during the period when public attention was sharply focused on this problem, a number of new institutions, programs, and policies may have been specifically created to help solve it. These new entities always persist and

often have some impact even after public attention has largely shifted to other problems. For example, during the early stages of the so-called War on Poverty, the Office of Economic Opportunity (OEO) was set up and initiated many new programs. Even though fighting poverty has by now faded as a central public issue, OEO still exists. Moreover, many of its programs have had significant successes, even though funded at a level far below that necessary really to ameliorate poverty.

A second difference between the first and last stages of the issue-attention cycle is that any major problem, once it has been elevated to national prominence, may sporadically recapture public interest. Or important aspects of it may become attached to some other problem which later surges to the center of the public stage. Therefore, problems that have "been discovered" and have made it through the cycle to this final stage almost always receive a higher average level of attention, public effort, and a general concern than those which are still in the prediscovery stage.

The duration of these five stages varies considerably from issue to issue. But their sequence almost always follows that described.

PROBLEMS THAT EXPERIENCE THE ISSUE-ATTENTION CYCLE

Not all major social problems go through this issue-attention cycle. Hence, I make no claim that this phenomenon is universally applicable in analyzing how our society perceives and deals with major problems. Nevertheless, I believe it is a useful device for understanding the way we treat problems that have three specific characteristics. The first is that the preponderant majority of persons in society are not suffering from the problem as much as a small minority which nevertheless contains millions of people. This is typical of many pressing urban and other social problems in America today. Most people are not strongly enough motivated by the severity of their own suffering from such problems to keep their attention riveted on them.

The second characteristic necessary to trigger the issue-attention cycle exists when the sufferings caused by a given social problem are generated by social arrangements which provide significant benefits to a majority or a powerful minority of citizens. For example, the majority of Americans who own cars — plus the powerful automobile and highway lobbies — receive short-run benefits from regulations that prohibit the use of motor-fuel tax revenues for financing public transportation systems, even though such systems are desperately needed by the urban poor and other relatively small groups in large cities.

The third characteristic likely to cause a specific problem to lose its grip on public attention is the absence — or cessation — of any intrinsically exciting qualities or dramatic events concerning it. When big-city racial riots were being shown nightly on the nation's television screens, public attention naturally focused upon their causes and consequences. But when they ceased occurring — or at least the media stopped reporting them so intensively — it was equally natural for public interest in them to decline in intensity. Similarly, as long as the National Aeronautics and Space Administration (NASA) was able to stage a series of ever-more-thrilling space shots, culminating in the worldwide dramatic television spectacular of Americans walking on the moon, it generated sufficient public interest to sustain high-level Congressional appropriations for its programs. But once the climactic moon landing was successfully accomplished, NASA could do nothing half as dramatic for an encore. Even repeating the same feat no longer seemed anywhere near as exciting (though a near-disaster on the third try did revive audience interest!). So NASA's Congressional appropriations soon plummeted. Some problems are very difficult to dramatize at all. Examples are poor housing, inadequate public transportation, and the rising costs of medical service. Other problems — particularly crime — have been so overdramatized by the media for so long that it is extremely difficult to intensify their coverage or alter it so as to generate public support for truly effective remedies.

The requirement that a problem be dramatic and exciting is important to the maintenance of public interest in it because *all news is in reality "consumed" by much of the American public (and by publics everywhere) largely as a form of entertainment.* As such, it competes with other types of entertainment for a share of each person's time. Hence, in the fierce struggle for space in the highly limited universe of television viewing time or newsprint, each issue must vie not only with all other social problems but also with a multitude of nonnews items that are often far more pleasant for the public to contemplate. These include sporting news, weather reports, crossword puzzles, comics, and daily horoscopes. Far more households watch television each day than obtain their news from television — presumably because other programs interest them more. Similarly, many well-educated businessmen turn to the sports page before they read the front page, as is well known in newspaper circles. In fact, the amount of television time and newspaper space devoted to sports coverage, as compared to international events, is a striking commentary on the relative value which much of the public places on knowing about these two subjects.

When all three of the above conditions exist concerning a given problem which has somehow captured public attention, the odds are very great that it will soon move through the entire issue-attention cycle — and therefore gradually fade from the center of the stage. The first condition means that most people will not be continually reminded of the importance of this problem by their own suffering from it. The second condition means that solving the problem requires sustained attention and effort, plus fundamental changes in social institutions or behavior. It also means that significant attempts to solve the problem are probably quite threatening to important groups in society. The third condition means that sustained focus upon this problem by the media quickly becomes rather boring to a majority of the public. As soon as the media realize that continued major emphasis upon this problem is threatening to many people and boring to even more, they will shift their focus to some "new" problem. They are particularly likely to do so in American society, because all our media are run for profit, and they make the most money by appealing to the largest possible audiences for their commercial messages. Thus, as Marshall McLuhan has pointed out, to a great extent it is the audience itself — the American public — which "manages the news" shown to it by maintaining or losing interest in a given subject. This circular influence is certainly not the only one determining what issues are brought before the public or kept there. Nevertheless, it is probably at least as significant as the personal views of the news commentators whose "managing the news" has been so castigated by Vice-President Agnew. In reality, the issue-attention cycle is but one aspect of a profound dilemma facing every democratic society in this age of instantaneous globe-spanning communications. The communications media now have the capability of reporting almost any event in the whole world within a few minutes — or at most a few hours — after it happens. Therefore, the amount of information that could conceivably be presented to the viewing and reading public colossally exceeds the time available in which to present it, given existing limits on the span of public attention. For example, there are 3.5 billion people in the world; if each of them carries out ten acts each day, then about 35 billion acts occur every 24 hours. Yet the average half-hour television newscast reports only from 15 to 35 separate events other than sports and weather information. (It could present almost three times as many if it eliminated sports and commercials, but even that would hardly be a large number.) Given the tiny fraction of all events that can conceivably be reported on each broadcast, it is totally impossible for newscasters to present a truly representative picture of the millions of events that took place that day. This is true regardless of how sincerely they want to select what is presented without any personal bias. Consequently, all news media tend to focus mainly upon the novel, the weird, the sensational, and the extremist occurrences and views in society — particularly because they are trying to sell commercial products by attracting maximum audiences. And the less total time or space they allot to news, the smaller is the percentage of *all* that has happened that they cover. (That is why television news is more distorted and less complete than newspaper reporting.)

Under these circumstances, the very idea that *anyone* could select a truly unbiased and objective report of each day's events is ludicrous. Yet that idea embodies nearly everyone's conception of the way news media ought to behave. Its persistence is a natural result of our inability to design or even conceive of any fundamentally more appropriate way of coping with our immense oversupply of news information in relation to the average man's capacity to absorb it. Admittedly, I have no easy remedies for this dilemma. I do believe society could significantly improve present policies regarding news dissemination (for example, by *requiring* longer TV newscasts with shorter commercials), but that is the subject of a different essay.

Until we find some entirely different way of coping with this dilemma, we are likely to continue being confronted by a stream of supposed crises involving individual social problems. Each will rise into public view, capture the center of the stage for a while, and then gradually fade away as it is replaced by more fashionable issues moving into their crisis phase.

THE PROSPECTIVE LONGEVITY
OF THE ENVIRONMENTAL ISSUE

Will improving the environment as an issue suffer an early decline in public interest resulting from the issue-attention cycle described above? In my opinion, it has certain characteristics which will protect it from the rapid decline in intensive public interest that has characterized many other recent issues.

In the first place, many kinds of environmental pollution are much more visible and clearly threatening to a majority of citizens than the evils associated with most other social problems. This is particularly true of smog and other forms of air pollution. The greater the apparent threat from these visible forms of pollution and the more vividly that threat can be dramatized, the more public support improving the environment will receive, and the longer it will sustain public interest. This places ecologists in the ironic position of potentially benefiting from some environmental disaster such as a "killer smog" that would choke thousands of people to death in one or two days. Actually, there is nothing new about this position — every cause benefits from having martyrs. This is clearly illustrated by the history of every issue from early Christianity to the Black Panthers. Yet even the most appealing symbols lose their impact after a while, or if they are constantly repeated. The piteous sight of an oil-soaked seagull — or even a dead person — pales after it has been viewed a hundred times, or even a dozen times. To quote an expression of the Vice-President, which was widely attacked, but which expresses an accurate insight into the nature of media, "If you've seen one slum, you've seen them all." Moreover, some of the most serious environmental threats are posed by forms of pollution which are invisible or at least not easily perceived by the senses. Thus, our propensity to focus attention on the most visible forms of pollution may cause us to clean up those we can easily perceive but ignore even worse hidden threats.

A second advantage possessed by environmental pollution as an issue is that it threatens almost everyone in society, rather than just a small percentage of the population. Consequently, it is not politically divisive, so politicians can safely devote major attention to it without fearing adverse repercussions. In this respect, attacking environmental pollution is unlike attacking racism or poverty. The latter inherently antagonize large and important blocs of voters who benefit from the sufferings of others or at least are not threatened enough by each problem itself to favor spending lots of money to solve it.

The third virtue of improving the environment as an issue is that much of the blame for pollution can be plausibly attributed to a small group of villains whose wealth and power make them excellent scapegoats. Proponents of improving the environment can therefore courageously attack these scapegoats without antagonizing the vast majority of citizens. Moreover, regarding air pollution, that small group actually has enough power to improve pollution seriously if it really seeks to do so. If the few leaders of the nation's top automobile manufacturing firms, power generating firms, and fuel supply firms could be persuaded to change their behavior significantly, a drastic improvement in the level of air pollution could be achieved in a relatively short time. Gathering widespread support for attacking any problem is always easier if the ills associated with it can be blamed on a small number of public enemies, as Ralph Nader's success shows. This tactic is especially effective if these enemies are susceptible to popular hostility because of their extreme wealth and power, or eccentric dress and manners, or obscene language, or some other trait that makes them different from the average person. Then society can aim its dissatisfaction or outrage about the problem itself at this small group without either feeling any personal identity with its members or having to face up to the need to alter its own behavior significantly. Such scapegoating is much easier regarding air pollution than water pollution. Nevertheless, it is easier to find scapegoats other than the public itself regarding almost all forms of pollution than it is with other major issues like attacking poverty, poor housing, hunger, or racism, because the solutions to those problems would require millions of Americans to change their own behavior patterns or accept higher taxes.

The fourth characteristic of the issue of improving the environment which may lengthen its center-stage tenure is the possibility that mainly technological solutions can be devised for most pollution problems. Then pollution could be greatly reduced without any need to alter the basic attitudes, desires, and behavior patterns of a large fraction of the population. The traumatic difficulties of achieving significant institutional change could thus be escaped through the magic of purely technical improvements in such things as automobile engines, water-purification devices, fuel composition, and sewage treatment facilities.

A fifth aspect of this issue which will vastly strengthen its political support is that most of the costs of reducing pollution can be passed on to the public through higher prices in product markets, rather than paid for by higher taxes. Consequently, politicians can demand strict adherence to costly environmental quality standards without having to pay the high political price of alienating taxpayers by raising the required costs through taxes. True, some types of pollution — particularly water pollution — are caused by the actions of public bodies, especially municipal sewer systems. Effective remedies for this pollution will require higher taxes or at least higher prices for public services. But the major costs of eliminating or reducing most forms of environmental pollution can be added to product prices and thereby passed forward to the ultimate consumers. This is a politically painless way to pay for attacking a major social problem. In contrast, effectively attacking most other important social problems requires major income redistributions attainable only through both higher taxes and higher transfer payments of subsidies. Examples of such politically costly problems are hunger, poverty, slum housing, low-quality health care for the poor, and poor public transportation.

Many ecologists oppose paying the cost of producing a cleaner environment through higher product prices. They would prefer to force the polluting firms themselves to bear these costs through lower profits. In a few highly oligopolistic industries, like petroleum and automobile production, that approach might be effective. But in the long run, I believe it could not pay much of the total cost without simply driving capital out of the industries concerned — and thereby eventually pushing up product prices anyway. Furthermore, it is economically just for those persons or firms who use any given product to pay the full costs of making it — including the costs of avoiding environmentally damaging pollution in the production process. Therefore, in most cases — including those involving pollution by public bodies which provide services — I believe the ultimate users of each product ought to pay for any costs required to produce it without badly harming the environment. Such payment is best made through higher product prices. After all, these consumers doubly benefit from such antipollution activities: they still get to use the product rather than having it banned, and they do not suffer from any pollution required to produce it.

In my opinion, it would be extremely unwise in most cases to try paying these costs by means of government subsidies in order to avoid passing them on to the consumers of the products concerned. I strongly believe we need to conserve our limited capabilities of raising money through taxation for attacking those problems which cannot be dealt with in any other way.

A sixth reason why the cleaner-environment issue may last longer and receive more financing than many others is that it could lead to the creation of a large private industry with a strong vested interest in continued public and private spending against pollution. Already dozens of new firms with "eco-" or "environ-" in their names have sprung up to exploit the supposedly burgeoning markets in anti-pollution equipment and services. If this industry grows large enough, we might even generate an environmental-industrial complex about which some outgoing future President could warn us in his departing speech — probably to no avail! Any major issue gains longevity if both its sources of political support and the programs related to it can be institutionalized in large bureaucratic organizations. Those organizations then develop a powerful desire to keep public attention focused on the problems that support them. However, I doubt if this new antipollution industry will ever even come close to the defense industry in size and power. The main reason is that the principal causes of pollution lie in the enormously decentralized behavior of the majority of American citizens. So effective antipollution activities cannot be carried out separately from society as a whole, but must involve behavior changes by millions of people. In contrast, weapons can be produced in an industry which imposes no behavioral changes on the average citizen (other than higher taxes) and expended in wars waged abroad by others or never used at all (though obviously this is not always the case). Moreover, the supposed national hazards used to justify large defense expenditures can be shrouded in secrecy difficult for the average citizen to penetrate. But the quality of our environment is both intrinsically more visible and harder to cover up in the name of national security.

The final reason I believe improving the environment may remain at center stage longer than most other domestic issues lies in the very ambiguity of this entire subject. "Improving the environment" is a tremendously broad and all-encompassing objective. Hence almost everyone can attach his or her particular cause to it, and claim — with some plausibility — that this cause is another way to make the quality of our life better. This ambiguity will make it easier to form a majority-sized coalition regarding problems which individually affect only minority-sized groups and hasten their exit from the center of public attention.

All seven of the factors mentioned imply that *political* forces are unusually favorable to both the launching and sustaining of a major public and private effort to improve the quality of our environment. Yet we should not underestimate the capacity of the American public to become bored with something that does not imminently threaten them, or promise huge benefits for a majority of citizens, or strongly appeal to their sense of injustice. Particularly in the present overall "up-tight" mood of the nation, I believe most citizens do not really want to confront the need for major social changes or pressing actions on any issues except those which seem to threaten them directly — such as urban violence and crime. Even concerning crime, the public does not yet seem to want to support much really effective change in our basic system of justice, as opposed to mainly rhetorical change in its superficial aspects. The present administration has apparently concluded that a relatively low-profile government — one which does not try to lead the public to accept significant institutional changes — is what the majority of Americans want at this point in history. If this view is correct, or if it remains dominant within the federal government regardless of its accuracy, then no really major environment-improving programs are likely to receive long-sustained public attention or support.

Some proponents of improving the environment are relying on student opinion or the sustained support of young people to keep this issue at the center of public attention. However, if that is its main foundation, it will almost surely fade very quickly from public attention. Young people form a highly unstable base for the support of any policy, since they have extremely short-lived staying power. For one thing, young people do not stay young very long — at least they do not long enjoy the large amount of free time and energy they possess while in college. Also, as new individuals enter the category of "young people," emphasis on particular issues changes. As older ones leave it, accumulated skills in marshalling opinion and support are dissipated. Moreover, the radicalism of the young has been immensely exaggerated by the media's tendency to focus attention mainly upon those few who espouse extremist views. Most young people are really not so different from their parents — at least regarding political issues — however much some observers like to deny this fact sentimentally.

Therefore, in spite of the relative advantages in retaining public attention which the bundle of issues called "improving the environment" enjoys, there is good reason to believe that it, too, will suffer the gradual loss of public attention inherent in the issue-attention cycle. However, it will undoubtedly be eclipsed at a much slower rate than other recent issues which have shot into prominence and then virtually disappeared within very short periods.

SOME ECONOMIC ASPECTS OF THIS ISSUE

Because the primary emphasis of this essay is upon the political aspects of improving the environment, I can deal only briefly with a few of its salient economic aspects. Hence the following sections present what are really suggestions for further thought, rather than fully reasoned explorations of the topics involved.

Decentralized Economic Decision Making and Pollution. In purely economic terms, one key cause of rising environmental pollution arises from the combined effect of the way we make most economic decisions and the nonmarket nature of many polluting actions. In most highly industralized, non-Communist nations, production and consumption involve intensively specialized activities carried out by millions of separate decision makers. Each of these specialists makes relatively little attempt to take account of all the potential spillover effects of his behavior upon other people before taking whatever actions he believes are desirable. Instead, each just goes ahead and acts to serve his own interest (in the private sector) or some combination of his own interest and his view of the public interest (in the public sector). Within the private sector, where most decisions concern voluntary transactions in markets, this type of decision making is called *free enterprise*. Within the public sector, it is called muddling through by most people, but *disjointed incrementalism* by decision theorists. It is *disjointed* because millions of individuals act separately without explicit coordination; it is *incremental* because each acts mainly to solve immediate problems rather than to carry out some long-range comprehensive plan.

This kind of decentralized decision making in the private sector can be very efficient at taking into account those interrelations among actors which flow through markets, assuming a reasonable degree of competition exists in those markets. When the fruits of one person's or group's behavior are bought and sold by others acting voluntarily, the willingness or unwillingness of those others to engage in such transactions causes the originator of that behavior to modify it in what is a socially rational manner in the long run. Thus, if consumers want more color TV sets or smaller cars, then these items will be produced, as long as competition among producers pressures them to respond to consumer desires. True, there are many imperfections in the market systems of a modern society. Moreover, producers themselves exert some influence on what consumers believe they want. Yet the market-oriented decision making still works far more effectively than any other system to allocate resources rationally in response to public desires, as long as the costs, benefits, and resources involved are handled in voluntary, buyer-seller transactions.

But in modern society, many costs and benefits of human action flow directly from one person or group to another without going through any explicit market transactions. For example, when passing motorists produce air pollution that burns the eyes of local residents, no voluntary sale or purchase is involved. The residents cannot signal their displeasure to the motorists by refusing to buy market-oriented services produced by the motorists, thereby pressuring the motorists to behave differently. Such direct effects of one actor upon another independent of voluntary market transactions are called externalities by economists. Market-oriented decision making normally ignores externalities, since they do not enter the usual calculus of profit and loss. Therefore, wherever significant externalities exist, the free-market decision process is ineffective at taking into account the welfare of all those affected by the decisions and actions concerned. This is particularly true where the externalities involve collective effects reaching large numbers of people simultaneously. Then each individual cannot usually alter the basic outcome himself, even through non-market actions, because he is such a small part of the total population concerned.

Thus, in any situation where both externalities and collective effects are important, markets alone are not capable of automatically generating corrective behavior for many actions of individuals or groups which adversely affect those around them. Instead, some type of nonmarket intervention or regulation is necessary to take proper account of these spillover effects. This is one of the basic causes of a great deal of governmental activity. Thousands of public programs, from combating crime to forecasting gross national product, are essentially designed to counteract or control human interrelations that do not flow through markets.

Clearly, many forms of environmental pollution are external effects with collective impacts. Millions of automobiles pouring their exhausts into the air, thousands of housewives flushing phosphate detergents down the drain, and hundreds of plants dumping their chemical wastes into rivers and lakes — all exemplify decision makers failing to take the polluting effects of their actions into account because each actor is a tiny part of a huge collectivity, and his own actions affect others without flowing through markets. Economists have concentrated most of their theorizing and analysis in the past upon actions that do pass through markets; they have not focused much attention on the specific externalities that cause environmental deterioration. In contrast, ecology as a science encompasses *all* interrelations among the key actors (organic and inorganic) in any living system. Therefore, it has been ecologists — not economists — who have alerted us to the serious failure of modern economies to take sufficient account of direct environmental effects of the actions taken by market-oriented decision makers.

Economic Aspects of Some Antipollution Tactics. Although we admire the contribution of ecologists to our awareness of environmental deterioration, we must nevertheless apply careful economic analysis to their suggestions for counteracting pollution. Unfortunately, some ecological alarmists ignore crucial economic factors just as totally as most economists long ignored environmental externalities.

For example, consider the suggestion that we economically regress modern society to a far less specialized organization of production and consumption. In this theory, reverting to a simpler age would reduce the complexities and technical sophistication of human interactions and therefore produce fewer or less harmful spillover effects. This implies a return to a far less productive economy (measuring

production in terms of outputs which most of the world still values).
It would be one in which poverty was the lot of the majority, not of
only 12 percent of the population as in the United States today. I
strongly doubt that the vast majority of the people asked to make this
economically regressive move would be willing to do so, unless environmental pollution became far more obviously dangerous than it is
now. In fact, most citizens would have to be choking from air pollution on the way to the polling booth before they would vote for such
a change!

Another similar argument is that the underdeveloped parts of the
world should not be allowed to industrialize as Western societies have
because their doing so would dangerously raise world pollution levels.
Those who advocate this view from the comfort of their personal pros-
perity do not have much chance of persuading the world's undernour-
ished majority to adopt it. That majority desperately wants to achieve
even slight progress toward what they view as our incredibly affluent
standard of living — pollution to the contrary notwithstanding.

This conflict of viewpoints illustrates a key fact about all suggested
policies for controlling or even influencing the total ecological system of the earth. Each such ecological scheme embodies usually un-
stated implications concerning the distribution of income and power
that would result. Slowing down economic growth is all very well for
those at the top of the income pyramid, but how about those multi-
tudes at the bottom? Would they be better off remaining poor in a relatively unpolluted world, or getting wealthier in a more highly
contaminated one? Unless the degrees of pollution required to up-
grade their lot economically are very likely to be quickly fatal to them
and to everyone else, it is improbable that they will voluntarily give
up seeking economic advancement, even if it creates more pollution.

In my opinion, we should certainly not abandon technological
advances of the traditional type. Rather we should use some of the
fruits of those advances to improve greatly the technology of pollution control. We should also begin devising more effective ways of
getting the creators of pollution (including the millions of consumers who benefit from creating various forms of it) to take adverse
nonmarket spillovers into account in making their decisions. This
might indeed mean a lower gross national product as measured by
present techniques, since they do not include measures of environmental quality. But it would mean a higher gross national product as
measured by indicators which also took account of the quality of our
environment.

Reducing Prospective Environmental Spillovers. Three important observations can be made about the possibility of counteracting pollution by getting market-oriented decision makers to take more spillover
effects into account in advance. First, I believe that in most cases
the best way to do this is by converting present nonmarket effects

into market-oriented ones. This is superior to either banning most pollution-causing activities outright or trying to control them through direct public regulation of production. Such conversions could occur by taxing productive actions which cause pollution at the lowest of two rates. One rate would provide enough revenue for public bodies to offset fully the pollution created. For example, the City of New York ought to tax the publishers of *The New York Times* about six cents per copy of the Sunday *Times* sold in New York City, because that is just about what it costs to collect and dispose of the debris created by that massive tome. The second rate would impose such a high cost on each pollution producer that it would be cheaper for him to install antipollution equipment to offset its effect or to shift to some nonpolluting production process. Thus, it might be desirable to place such a high tax on nonreturnable or nonreturned soft-drink and beer containers that the distributors would shift to returnable containers and create their own incentive system to persuade the public to return them.

This approach of *taxing pollution* rather than *banning polluting activities outright* has the advantage of allowing some pollution to occur when the added positive benefits created in generating it exceed its social cost. It is naive to believe that it would be possible or even desirable to eliminate all environmental pollution. As pointed out earlier, pollution is often the obverse side of actions which provide tremendous benefits to society. Therefore, the socially optimal amount of pollution is surely not its complete absence. Rather, it undoubtedly involves acceptance of that degree of pollution with which society receives more benefits net of pollution costs than it would if the activity were banned altogether, or if steps were taken to suppress completely that degree of pollution. True, some types of pollution are so hazardous that even a small degree should be prevented through total prohibition of the activities which create them. But they are probably a minority of polluting activities.

The second observation is that no conceivable set of taxes, regulations, prohibitions, or other devices can possibly be successful in getting every human actor whose behavior creates adverse spillover effects to take those effects fully into account before he acts. The world is just too large, complex, interdependent, and dynamic. Hence the myriad actors in it cannot possibly foresee and take into account in advance all the ways in which their actions are likely to impact others. Even if these actors had perfect vision concerning all the effects of their actions, it would take eons for them to negotiate advanced settlements with all those impacted to be sure that few came out net losers. Therefore, even if it would be theoretically desirable to eliminate all polluting actions by coordinating decentralized decision makers, it will never be practically possible.

In view of this impossibility, some ecologists have proposed adoption of a single worldwide plan to control all pollution-causing activities. After all, we are all together here on "Spaceship Earth." Every really successful spaceship up to now has been operated in accordance with a minutely detailed comprehensive plan covering all aspects of its behavior. If we can solve the immensely complex problems of reaching the moon and returning safely, why could we not devise an immense computer center planning all the world's production and consumption so as to keep pollution within tolerable limits?

My third observation about taking pollution spillovers into account in advance is that development of an effective single earthwide environmental *control* center is now and will for some time remain neither possible nor desirable. It is impossible because no set of the largest computers yet conceived of can keep track of, or plan in advance, the immense number of human interactions involved in the behavior of more than three billion people. Moreover, within the foreseeable future, we will simply remain too ignorant about many of the basic causal relationships concerning environmental quality to devise any effective plan to control it. Furthermore, such an environmental control center would be undesirable for two reasons. First, its creators would have to design a single worldwide master development plan. To do so, they would have to invent solutions for immense conflicts of interest among huge groups of people across the world. In our present open and uncertain world, these conflicts can remain unresolved and problematic for decades. Thus, many parties concerned may mistakenly draw consolation from hoped-for future outcomes that are really inconsistent with each other. Attempting to resolve these conflicts explicitly and openly would create a level of tension and conflict which the world can ill afford. Second, even if such a plan could be created, enforcing it would require concentration of immense dictatorial powers in the hands of those few people operating this earth environmental control center. Many people would prefer having the earth's population slowly strangle on its own wastes to submitting themselves to such an ecological dictatorship. This does *not* mean that a single ecological condition *measuring*-and-*reporting* center for the whole earth is undesirable. On the contrary, I think it an excellent idea. But turning such a center into one that *controls* the earth's ecology should be regarded as a mythical horror story rather than a high-priority objective.

The Inherent Conservatism of Ecology. In my opinion, there is a basic conflict between the essential nature of ecology as a science and the key social and economic problems of the modern world. As an admittedly nonexpert outsider, I regard ecology as a basically conservative science. Its principal objective seems to be studying how *existing* life systems work so that they can be successfully maintained. Ecological balance appears to be a condition in which all the existing species in a given system are interacting in such a way that all are surviving, but none are either disappearing or gaining greater dominance over the others. This seems like a definition of the status quo in nature.

Yet nature and natural life systems really do not seem to have any specific goals or objectives other than those which human beings read into them. Nature itself (to personify it for a moment) does not appear to be interested in the survival of any particular species, since thousands of species have disappeared in the history of the earth. In fact, the word *system* as used in ecology has a radically different meaning from the same word as used in modern systems analysis and other technological orientations. The first step in analyzing any human systems is to *define their objectives,* which are imparted to them by their human creators. But what objectives do ecological systems have? If we assume that God created the world and has a definite plan to evolve it toward some specific outcome, then ecological systems do indeed have objectives. But even then we rarely know what they are. And many ecologists do not make this assumption, but instead look at ecological systems apart from such supernatural long-run planning. In that case, ecological systems contain only individual species struggling for survival, none of which have any conscious concern with the overall status or development of the system as a whole. Hence such systems have no real objectives as systems at all, other than what ecologists themselves assign to them. True, each such system moves toward some type of steady-state equilibrium within the general environmental conditions which prevail at a given moment. But any basic change in those conditions, such as a shift in climate, can wipe out or totally alter the whole system and its equilibrium position.

In contrast, *the fundamental problem of the modern world is discovering how to accommodate to and benefit from rapid technical change without destroying either the institutional or the natural bases for human freedom and development.* Thus, our basic challenge is not maintaining equilibrium within given conditions, but changing those conditions so as to improve the possibilities and choices of the billions of people who are now alive or will be in the future. This objective is fundamentally anticonservative. It aims at dynamic adaptation to changes in part generated through conscious planning within the system, rather than relatively static adaptation to existing circumstances determined almost entirely by forces external to the system. Furthermore, human social systems have parts (governments) specifically assigned responsibility for thinking about and acting to promote the welfare of the systems as a whole. True, the entire world has no single overarching government; hence it strongly resembles a set of different species struggling for survival with no agency responsible for the system as a whole. Nevertheless, I still believe the most profound objectives of human social and political systems are essentially different from those of nonhuman natural systems. Therefore, *it seems likely to me that the essentially conservative and nonobjective-oriented nature of ecology as a science or mode of thinking makes it ill suited to serve as the basis for developing the central public policies of the modern world.*

In contrast, theories of economic, social, and political development are essentially rooted in the concept of *expanding individual and social choices* through *transforming* nature and society. I believe our long-run welfare lies in accepting this perspective rather than that of ecology, which seeks to *preserve existing choices by adapting to nature* as it now exists. Certainly the science of ecology has a tremendous contribution to make in helping to guide human development so that we do not destroy ourselves in the process of seeking self-improvement. But its fundamental viewpoint should not replace the more dynamic and purposive prospective of development-oriented sciences and theories at the core of our social thought and policy orientation.

Nor can ecology generate some super overview that will eliminate our need to confront hard resource-allocation choices concerning improving the environment. These are the same kinds of choices we must face regarding all issues involving scarce resources. Such choices are almost never all-or-nothing, do-or-die matters. Rather they involve compromises and tradeoffs between alternatives — the basic stuff of economics and politics in all social systems. So improving the quality of our environment is, in the last analysis, still a matter of political economy, as I hope this analysis has demonstrated.

SUPPLEMENTARY READINGS

1. Kenneth E. Boulding, "The Economics of the Coming Spaceship Earth," in *Environmental Quality in a Growing Economy,* Henry Jarrett, ed., Baltimore, Johns Hopkins Press, 1966.
2. Edwin G. Dolan, *Tanstaafl: The Economic Strategy for Environmental Crisis,* New York, Holt, Rinehart, and Winston, 1969, Chapter 4 ("The Political Economy of Ecological Action"), pp. 40–54.
3. K. William Kapp, *The Social Costs of Private Enterprise,* Cambridge, Mass., Harvard University Press, 1950.
4. Allen V. Kneese, "Environmental Pollution: Economics and Policy," *American Economic Review,* 61, May, 1971, pp. 153–166.
5. National Urban Coalition, *Counter Budget: A Blueprint for Changing National Priorities,* New York, Praeger, 1971.
6. Gaylord Nelson, "This Generation's Strategy to Save the Environment," in *Agenda for Survival: The Environmental Crisis — 2,* Harold W. Helfrich, Jr., ed., New Haven, Yale University Press, 1971, pp. 185–195.
7. Mancur Olsen, *The Logic of Collective Action,* Cambridge, Mass., Harvard University Press, 1965.
8. Joseph L. Sax, *Defending the Environment,* New York, Knopf, 1970.
9. Charles L. Schultze, *The Politics and Economics of Public Spending,* Washington, D.C., The Brookings Institution, 1968, Chapter 4 ("The Role of Analysis in Political Decisions").

10. Charles L. Schultze, et al., *Setting National Priorities: The 1972 Budget,* Washington, D.C., The Brookings Institution, 1971, Chapter 12 ("Environmental Quality").
11. Stewart L. Udall, "Total Environment: A New Political Reality," in *Agenda for Survival: The Environmental Crisis — 2,* Harold W. Helfrich, Jr., ed., New Haven, Yale University Press, 1971, pp. 1–13.

4 The Political Economy of Water Quality Management

ALLEN V. KNEESE

WHAT HAVE WE LEARNED
FROM ECONOMIC RESEARCH?

In their theorizing about resources allocation, economists have long used the idea of external costs and have pointed out their implications for the efficient use of resources. External costs are costs imposed directly — not through the medium of a market — on other fiscally independent parties by a private or public production or consumption activity. This theoretical interest has grown considerably in the past two decades, and many notable contributions to the theory of external effects in market-type economies have been made. But it is only since 1960, and primarily since 1965, that economists have been willing to bite the bullet and try to apply their ideas empirically to the pollution problem which has long served them as an illustration of the external costs phenomenon. In this essay I stress in a first section what I regard as the main policy conclusions of this research, and in a second the political and economic problems in implementing them. No attempt is made to review the theoretical literature on

Reprinted from Downs, Kneese, Ogden, and Perloff, *The Political Economy of Environmental Control*, Berkeley, 1972, by permission of the publisher, Institute of Business and Economic Research, University of California, Berkeley. Acknowledgement is also due the Herman Royer Program in Political Economy, University of California, Berkeley, which sponsored the public lecture on which this essay is based, and to Dr. Kneese.

externalities or the many contributions to methodology which have been made by economists.[1]

To set the stage for a discussion of public policy, it is desirable to start with a broad perspective on the nature of the water-quality management problem. Then, in the remainder of this section, what I see as the main findings of empirical research on the economics of water-quality management are reviewed. The second section contrasts these findings with our present policy approach at the national level. Accumulating evidence shows the latter to be working very badly. It seems not unfair to say that a careful study of the political economy of this approach could have forecast its poor performance, and I try to adduce some evidence to that effect in the second section of this paper. But now for a look at the broader context in which water-quality management should be viewed.

The Broad Context. First, it should be understood that the problem of water-quality management is part of the class of problems associated with the efficient use of common-property natural resources. These are resources which for a variety of reasons are not in private ownership but rather in some vague sense collectively held though not really under the managerial control of anyone. Among the most important of these for our purposes are water bodies, the air mantle, and various other ecological systems. The United States has been highly fortunate to have had throughout most of its history a great abundance of clean air and water. These resources often came very close to being apt examples of the economists' concept of free goods. There was no great need to subject them to any coherent conservation or management since they were available in such abundance that few users would have been willing to pay anything to augment them. There are, of course, exceptions to this broad statement. In the West, because water has long been scarce and is clearly a major factor of production in one of the largest industries — irrigated agriculture — arrangements have been made to bring it under some form of more or less effective management. But even there the matter of water quality has taken a back seat, except sometimes when it directly affected this industry, until quite recent times.[2]

But in the postwar era, almost everyone has become at least vaguely aware and many have become acutely aware that the natural

[1] This has been ably done by others. See, for example, E. J. Mishan, "Reflections on Recent Developments in the Concept of External Effects," *Canadian Journal of Economics and Political Science*, February 1965; and E. J. Mishan, "The Postwar Literature on Externalities: An Interpretive Essay," *Journal of Economic Literature*, March 1971.

[2] See the sections on water pollution in Joe S. Bain, Richard E. Caves, and Julius Margolis, *Northern California's Water Industry* (Baltimore: The Johns Hopkins Press, 1966).

assets of air and water are no longer abundant, and that in fact their use for waste disposal is conflicting seriously with other services naturally yielded by these assets — such as life support, aesthetics, and recreational opportunities. The phenomenon which we have observed coming about in recent times is really quite beyond the scale of the economist's traditional example of a pollution-type externality. This typically involved two parties — sparks from a locomotive igniting a farmer's field, for instance — and was regarded as a somewhat random, if not freakish, event quite unrelated to the general processes of production and consumption. Rather we have seen the deterioration of natural assets on a truly massive scale from numerous sources of pollution which adversely affect the population at large. The quality of entire air mantles and watersheds has deteriorated markedly, and one can no longer view the imposition of damages as somewhat odd aberrations which might be effectively dealt with by ad hoc measures. Insight concerning the nature and scale of modern environmental pollution was rather slow to develop in the economics professions, but it is now becoming widely recognized that the reasons for degeneration of these natural assets can be greatly illuminated by the application of two concepts — that of common-property resources and that of the conservation of mass.

Basic Concepts. It is one of the most elementary concepts of physics that matter is created or destroyed only in the most minute amounts. Thus, it is clear that the production and consumption activities of society do not destroy the material substances which flow from our mines, farms, and forests through the economic system and finally to consumers, but that in fact their total mass must eventually somehow be returned to nature from whence it came.

Our historic, legal, economic, and governmental institutions were comparatively well designed to facilitate the process of extracting natural resources and guiding them rather efficiently to various uses in the economy. Furthermore, what environmental disruptions occurred in this process were generally accorded a low priority of attention relative to the goal of producing more goods. Thus, in general, our dependence on private property rights and the profit motive has served us well in developing our natural resources and converting them to useful goods. But, what happens to the material substances after they go through this process of extraction, production, and consumption and yield their utility to human beings? Clearly, the residual materials have to return in some form to one of our natural environments. It was fortunate for the smooth operation of our market-based economic system that the residuals-receiving capacity of our land, air, and water environments was for a long time sufficiently large relative to the demand put on them that, except for some local situations, no seriously adverse results followed from the free and unhindered use of these common-property natural assets for the disposal of residual materials.

Now the natural reservoirs of assimilative capacity are rapidly filling up, and waste disposers consistently impose important external costs by their activities. This is happening because for all practical purposes our air and water resources even today remain unpriced, although they have become scarce and valuable — the more so because a high-quality environment has been moving up rapidly in many people's preference scale. Moreover, unless large-scale material-saving technologies are employed, or extensive recycling is undertaken, or substantial changes in the structure of final demand occur in the future, we can expect these pressures on the environment to mount at least *pari passu* with our increases in production and consumption. Furthermore, it is a characteristic of such resources as air and water that their value as assets for other activities, such as life support and aesthetics, diminishes at a more rapid rate than that at which residuals are increasingly discharged to them over time. One main reason is that the probability of high concentration of residuals in the environment mounts faster than the *average* rate of discharge.[3] Another is that, after some point, damage begins to mount nonlinearly with additional degradations of the resource — indeed, sometimes disastrous discontinuities occur, as when a watercourse becomes anaerobic and its ecology changes spectacularly. It then becomes essentially useless for all purposes except waste disposal. When such an event occurs in an affluent society, we witness a profound failure in the incentive system generated by the market.

Clearly, the massive return of residuals to our common-property environmental resources confronts us with a deep and severe problem. This is primarily because the private-property and exchange institutions which we use for determining the value of resources and providing incentives for their efficient allocation cannot function for them. We are thus faced with a large-scale — indeed pervasive — and unfamiliar problem of collective action and collective management.

Another implication of mass conservation is pertinent in establishing the broad context within which water-quality management should be considered. A moment's thought will reveal that the treatment of waste materials, as such, does not reduce the mass of material which must be returned to the environment. Indeed, since treatment processes themselves require inputs, the total amount of mass to be disposed of is increased when treatment is applied. An intelligent treatment application transforms the residual mass to less damag-

[3] Robert U. Ayres and Richard P. McKenna, *Alternatives to the Internal Combustion Engine: Impact on Environment Quality* (Baltimore: The Johns Hopkins Press, 1972).

ing forms so that it can be disposed of with diminished harm. For example, a sewage treatment plant will remove some of the solids from the waste-water stream. The utility of this is that the more compact solids can often be disposed of in a manner less damaging than if they were discharged to a watercourse. However, if these solids are then incinerated, as is often done, they could contribute to an air pollution problem which might be even worse than the water pollution problem. If we pursue the control of discharges to watercourses in isolation from the management of the quality of our other common-property assets, we invite problems of this type. At the moment, economists are actively proceeding on development of residuals management models which systematically embody all the major residuals resulting from production and consumption activities.[4] Until this approach is applied in practice, it is highly important that a management agency with responsibility for one or the other of these media not neglect potential spillover effects on the others.

Another aspect of the broader context in which water quality management should be pursued follows from the inherent inseparability of water quality and water quantity management. Given some rate of discharge of effluents to a watercourse, the quality of that water body is highly dependent upon its rate of flow. Thus, depletion of water in, say, agricultural uses will not only reduce the amount of water available for further consumption downstream but will as well affect the quality of the water supply there. Analogously, water-quality improvement can be achieved by increasing the low flow of watercourses through releases from reservior storage or even, in some special cases, by pumping of groundwater for low stream-flow augmentation. Moreover, the storage of water may itself alter its quality. Thus, water released from near the bottom of deep reservoirs tends to be low in dissolved oxygen, whereas water stored temporarily in shallow reservoirs may carry more dissolved oxygen downstream than it otherwise would. High levels of dissolved oxygen are central to the support of higher forms of life in water bodies.

One must conclude, therefore, that water-quality management is really an integral part of total water resources management, including consideration not only of waste-water discharges but of the whole pattern of use and regulation of the watercourses. As in regard to the interdependency of different forms of residuals and of environmental media, in further discussion I isolate water-quality management

---

[4] See Clifford S. Russell and Walter O. Spofford, Jr., "A Quantitative Framework for Residuals Management Decisions," in Allen V. Kneese and Blair T. Bower, eds., *Environmental Quality Analysis: Research Studies in the Social Sciences* (Baltimore: The Johns Hopkins Press, 1971). See also, Allen V. Kneese, Robert U. Ayres, and Ralph D. d'Arge, *Economics and the Environment: A Materials Balance Approach* (Washington, D.C.: Resources for the Future, Inc., 1970).

somewhat artificially from this broader context. This is because I wish to maintain some degree of focus and simplicity in the discussion. But in actual water-quality management in a river basin, estuary, lake, or bay, these interrelationships would be neglected only at the hazard of severe miscarriages in the management of common property resources.

TEN YEARS OF ECONOMIC RESEARCH ON WATER QUALITY MANAGEMENT

Let me then turn to an examination of the main findings of some ten years of accumulating applied work on the economics of water-quality management. A significant share of this work was done at, or sponsored by, my institution, Resources for the Future. But large amounts of pertinent parallel work were also done by economists, engineers, and hydrologists in universities and government agencies. To understand the importance of this work, one must recognize that with one major exception — in the Ruhr area of West Germany — the sanitary engineering professions (until recently the only professions giving any significant amount of attention to pollution problems) and public policy in the United States have both seen the problem of managing water quality almost entirely in terms of the treatment of municipal and industrial waste waters. There was in the water pollution literature scarcely any examination of the many other technological alternatives applicable to the management of water quality; there was little or no concern for evaluating the damaging impact of waste-water discharges on the water resource and strictly zero attention to the economic incentives bearing on the generation and discharge of residual materials.[5]

One of the earliest efforts to define a research approach based on economic principles emphasized quite a different and at the time highly unorthodox view of the water-quality management problem. In a small book, *Water Pollution: Economic Aspects and Research Needs,* published in 1962,[6] I proposed a paradigm for work in this area. This was the concept of a hypothetical "basin-wide firm." It viewed the river basin or other watercourse as a multiproduct asset, the quality of which could be influenced by the wide array of technological and other management options. Specifically, it was hypothesized that in addition to treatment of waste water — *the* focal point

[5] Perhaps the engineer's vision was narrowed because he was seldom called on to do anything more than design a particular treatment plant. There is evidence that when, as in the Ruhr, he was privileged to view the problem in a broader context, his view of the range of options expanded. See, also, Edward Cleary's discussion of the Ohio River Survey in *The ORSANCO Story* (Baltimore: The Johns Hopkins Press, 1967).

[6] Allen V. Kneese, *Water Pollution: Economic Aspects and Research Needs* (Resources for the Future, Inc., 1962).

of the sanitary engineering literature — an optimum management system might include such other alternatives as stream-flow regulation, a variety of in-stream water quality improvement measures, the diversion of waste waters from sensitive areas, the use of waste waters for irrigation, short-term high-level treatment measures, and a revision of the incentive system bearing on the generation and disposal of waste waters. None of the technological options just mentioned was, strictly speaking, new. Most of them had found isolated application. But they were not regarded as possibilities to be considered systematically and routinely along with waste treatment in water-quality management.

Based on the framework described (which would come naturally enough to an economist schooled in such concepts as externalities and the production function), Resources for the Future launched a series of case studies to test the applicability of this approach to water-quality management in real situations. About the same time, parallel undertakings were started by other institutions. The results of much of this work are now available and, in my opinion, they provide compelling evidence that regional water-quality management, able to take advantage of an optimized set of technological options for managing water quality and of the power of economic incentives, could achieve enormous efficiency gains over the conventional approach based primarily on the imposition of more or less uniform treatment requirements at all existing outfalls. This would be true even if the latter approach were very effective, which it clearly has not been.

The Evidence. Some of the major evidence supporting the above assertion has been reviewed recently in a book by Blair Bower and myself, called *Managing Water Quality.*[7] But further evidence continues to accumulate. Studies of the Potomac River Basin, the Delaware Estuary area, the San Francisco Bay, the Raritan Bay, the Miami River Basin in Ohio, and the Wisconsin River Basin, among others, can leave little doubt about the general validity of the conclusion stated in the previous paragraph. Alternatives ranging from the direct mechanical reaeration of river basins to the pumping of groundwater for low-flow augmentation were components of cost-minimizing schemes for achieving water-quality standards in the watercourse in every case. Reduction in costs from conventional approaches for achieving the same standard was usually found to be large — often differing by a factor of two or more.

More fundamental, perhaps, than the matter of exploring and implementing a wide range of technical options is the question of eco-

[7] Allen V. Kneese and Blair T. Bower, *Managing Water Quality: Economics, Technology, Institutions* (Baltimore: The Johns Hopkins Press, 1968).

nomic incentives. Economists have long advocated, in abstract terms, the so-called Pigovian solution — a tax on the externality-causing activity reflecting the external costs imposed. However, this approach has remained quite foreign to the sanitary engineering profession, and to those most responsible for public policy in this area, until quite recently — and it has usually been greeted with much skepticism when it has become known to them. Even those, including some economists, who feel the approach had much theoretical merit, have sometimes been very dubious of its applicability in practice. Some others have felt that if applied it might fail to result in an effective incentive to reduce residuals generation and discharge. Questions of this type have, for example, been raised repeatedly in Congressional hearings on water pollution policy.

Again, economic research has tended to support the practical value and effectiveness of an effluent charges or taxes approach, although in research applications the focus came to shift — quite appropriately I think — from the economist's traditional two-party case to the more realistic one of multiple users of a common-property asset.

The most pertinent case study in this connection is of the Delaware Estuary area. It was found that, assuming that either an effluent standards direct-order approach or an effluent charges approach could be effectively implemented, the latter would have substantial advantages. It turned out, for example, that a water-quality standard in the estuary — established through benefit-cost analysis and a related process of political choice making — could be met at something like half the real cost if a uniform effluent charge were levied on all waste dischargers rather than if they were all required to achieve uniform levels of treatment. There are complicating factors which I have explored elsewhere,[8] but the general reason for this would be immediately clear to an economist. The effluent charge will tend to elicit residuals-control activities at various points of discharge until the marginal cost of achieving further reductions at any given point is about equal to that at other points. In so doing, it will tend to concentrate residuals control at those points where costs of accomplishing it are least. With the uniform treatment requirement, gross differences in marginal cost occur so that cost reductions for a given total level of discharge could be achieved by rearranging quantities discharged at different locations.

Important efficiency results which could be achieved by economic incentive techniques are also amply illustrated by studies of individual industries and their residuals generation and disposal activities. It has been shown that through internal redesign of processes resulting in greater production of the primary product or the recovery of

[8] Allen V. Kneese, "Environmental Pollution: Economics and Policy," *American Economic Review,* May 1971.

salable by-products or a change in the quality of inputs, generation of industrial waste waters can be reduced drastically. If the industrial firm is given real incentive to do so, such as in effluent charge, it can often reduce residuals much more cheaply by controlling their generation than by building a treatment plant to attempt to reduce them after they are already generated. The efficacy of this approach is also supported by the response of industrial firms when sewer surcharges have been implemented by municipalities. These are charges, geared to the amount and strength of waste waters, which are levied for the service of treating industrial wastes in municipal plants. Where such charge systems have been introduced, even though the level of charges is much lower than a true effluent charge would be, the reduction in wastes discharged to the sewer system have usually been rapid and dramatic.[9] As I point out in the next section, current policy approaches essentially ignore all possibilities for industrial waste reduction except treatment after the residuals are generated.

Finally, the effectiveness and efficiency of a regional water-quality management approach is supported by study of the activities of the water management authorities in the Ruhr area of West Germany, where the approach has been based on the application of a broad range of technological opitions systematically combined according to economic criteria and in response to economic incentives. These agencies have, over a period of some seventy years, very successfully developed full-scale regional management programs for the river basins in what is rather generally known as the Ruhr region. Economists were not involved in the enterprise, but because of the broad management mandate established for these agencies and the principles of water-quality management laid down for them in their basic charter, they have evolved an approach and a set of facilities and policies which in general resemble those that a basin-wide firm might adopt.[10]

Conclusion. I must admit to possible bias because of my deep and long involvement in many of the economic research programs on water-quality management. Nevertheless, I feel that a compelling case has been made for an approach based on regional river-basin management authorities and the far-reaching use of economic incentive devices to control the generation of residuals. Our national policy toward water quality — as expressed in a long series of national legislation over the past twenty years — is, however, quite different from, if not totally contrary to, the approach which economic research would suggest is appropriate. The case for reorienting our present

[9] See Kneese and Bower, *Managing Water Quality,* for a discussion of these cases as well as a review of some of the results of studies of particular industries.
[10] *Ibid.*

national approach in the direction indicated by the economic research programs of the past decade is considerably strengthened
when one looks at how our national water-pollution control program
has actually operated in practice. It seems fair to say that it has been
costly, scattershot in its effects, very limited in its achievements,
and has not laid the basis for any long-term management approach
to the important common-property assets represented in our watercourses. In the next section I undertake to examine our present
strategy and to propose an alternative which I think is much more
in keeping with the results of economic research and promises to be
highly effective in dealing with a major continuing problem of
residuals management.

THE PRESENT NATIONAL WATER-POLLUTION
CONTROL PROGRAM AND AN ALTERNATIVE

I now turn to the present strategy for water-pollution control in the
United States as embodied in policies of the federal government and
propose an alternative, the rationale for which was developed above.
A complete treatment of the current approach would, of course, have
to include a discussion of state programs. These programs usually
have about the same elements as the national programs, and therefore have similar problems as well as some others, but they vary
widely in details and in effectiveness. Nominally, the major powers
to control water pollution belong to the states, but in practice these
have usually been quite limited in effect. In some states a condition
has been achieved where most municipal waste waters get at least
some treatment. Effectiveness against industrial waste discharge has
in general been very modest. Large industrial waste dischargers are
usually politically powerful in the states, and aggressive action has
often been inhibited by fears of losing present and potential industry
or political support. Ordinarily, success has been somewhat better in
influencing the design of new industrial plants. Discussion of the
national program gives a reasonable idea of the problems that afflict
the state program, only usually in even higher degree.

The Present National Program. To start with, I would like to charac-
terize briefly what I take to be the present strategy of the federal
government for achieving water pollution control in the United States.
One has to be a bit cautious on this point because the present approach seems not to have evolved out of a coherent strategic concept,
but rather to have grown by bits and pieces to a point where one can
identify at least an implicit strategy. It is based on two main elements.

The first is financial support for waste treatment plant construction. This support started with the Federal Water Pollution Control

Act of 1965 and has continued under higher levels of authorization since then. The 1966 act authorized $3.4 billion for municipal sewage plant construction grants over the period 1968 to 1971, but expenditures have run well below this rate. Under the act it is possible for municipalities to obtain up to 55 percent of the costs of waste treatment plant construction from federal grants. Industries can benefit from this provision to the extent that they are connected to municipal sewer systems. Furthermore, in the Tax Reform Act of 1970, Congress permitted rapid write-off for industrial waste treatment plants. So the first element in our present strategy is subsidies for municipal and industrial waste treatment.

The second main element is enforcement actions directed toward individual waste dischargers. This power was introduced in a weak form against interstate polluters in the early post-World War II period and has been strengthened since then to include, in principle, virtually all sources of pollution, whether interstate or intrastate. Another act of importance which was intended, at least in part, to strengthen federal enforcement capability is the Water Pollution Control Act of 1965. This required that all states set water-quality standards on their interstate and boundary waters. These standards were to be completed and reviewed by the Secretary of the Interior by mid-1967. The standards are to be accompanied by a proposed program for achieving them which could be used as a benchmark against which to judge the need for federal enforcement actions. Failure to comply with the program could be considered prima facie evidence of a violation. At this time only twenty-nine states have fully approved standards and implementation plans. Furthermore, as we will see later, it appears doubtful that this act will really support the enforcement effort. Actually, although the federal government in principle possesses strong powers to bring enforcement proceedings against polluters, these powers have been used only to a very limited extent.

Disenchantment with the Present Strategy. There is a growing disenchantment with our national pollution control programs. For a long time, discussion of them revolved around such matters as underfinancing and the lack of sufficient personnel for enforcement activities. No doubt these are significant explanations for the slowness or absence of progress in our national effort. But it is also becoming clear that there are much more fundamental deficiencies in the strategy that we have chosen to adopt. It is our main objective here to illuminate the character of these deficiencies and to relate them to performance under the program. Doing this is significantly aided by the availability of three recent reports. Two of these were made by government agencies, the third by a private group. The former are a General Accounting Office study entitled *Examination into the Effectiveness of the Construction Program for Abating, Controlling, and*

Preventing Water Pollution[11] (referred to as "the GAO Report") and a report by the Environmental Protection Agency, *Cost of Clean Water*[12] (referred to as "Clean Water"). The third is by Ralph Nader's Task Force on Water Pollution and is called *Water Wasteland*[13] (referred to as "the Nader Report"). Following analysis of the present strategy, an alternative approach to our water-quality problems is outlined — one which I feel holds the promise of cutting through most of the difficulties inherent in our existing approach and putting us on the road to continuing, coherent, and efficient management of our water quality.

Federal Subsidies for Waste Treatment Plant Construction. As already pointed out, the present federal strategy is based on two main elements. First is the provision of subsidies for municipal and to some extent for industrial waste treatment plant construction, the latter via rapid tax write-offs. The second is enforcement actions against individual sources of waste-water discharge.

The first is often called an incentive program, although in my opinion that is a misapplication of the term. If the dictionary definition is accepted that an incentive is that which incites to action, certainly the term is not apt. In the absence of other inducement, the mere provision of a subsidy will not cause a municipality or an industry to reduce its waste discharge whatsoever. Even though, say, half the cost of the treatment plant is paid for externally, it is still much cheaper to discharge the waste water than to build the treatment plant. Consequently, this program must be linked in some fashion to the enforcement program if present strategy is to have any effectiveness and coherence at all. This integration has not happened and consequently the provision of federal funding has been based on considerations other than the most effective ways of reducing pollution of our waterways. The available grant funds have been allocated to municipalities that for some reason or other were ready and willing to act, and then on the basis of a more or less chronological priority system. In many cases these have been small towns that are more subject to political pressure than the larger sources of waste discharge. The GAO Report provides a penetrating analysis of the results of this program. I shall have more to say about it later.[14]

[11] The Comptroller General of the United States, Washington, D.C., November 3, 1969.

[12] Environmental Protection Agency, Water Quality Office, Washington, D.C., March 1971.

[13] Center for the Study of Responsive Law, Washington, D.C., 1971.

[14] In an appendix to the GAO Report, a study by the consulting firm of Camp, Dresser & McKee is reported. They apply systems analysis techniques to the Merrimack River Basin to determine what cost savings might accrue from a coherent regional cost-minimizing program of constructing treatment plants as contrasted with the rather arbitrary arrangement that now exists. They find the cost savings to be significant.

Because the allocation of federal funds under the grant program has been essentially arbitrary from an economic efficiency point of view, various cost increasing results have followed. As among states, the present program allocates funds based on a combination of state per capita income and population. This has resulted in funds being quite abundant in some states and very stringent in others, relative to requirements. Where the funds have been available in large supply, this has reinforced the local officials' tendency to grossly overdesign public works to avoid having to go to the electorate very often for authorization of bond issues. This, coupled with possible uncertainty on the part of local officials about the permanence of the subsidy program, has resulted in a situation where fully one-quarter of metropolitan area waste treatment capacity is less than half utilized and nearly 20 percent is overloaded.[15] This once again illustrates the difficulty of devising subsidy schemes for particular actions which do not generate substantial biases toward inefficiency.

Another excellent illustration is provided by a limitation written into the tax write-off provisions for industry. The tax write-off does not apply to a treatment process which results in salable, recovered materials. The intent of writing in this provision is obvious, but the resulting bias against recycling is highly unfortunate in our present circumstances.

An additional shortcoming of the program subsidies is their emphasis upon the construction of waste treatment plants and virtual absence of attention to operation of the plants once built. This means that a plant could well be put on line and then operated far below its capability. Under the present program there is hardly any incentive to operate existing plants effectively. Similarly, plants can be overloaded and provide greatly diminished treatment without any public body taking adequate notice or having effective recourse. The governing philosophy appears to have been that once a treatment plant is built, a problem is solved. This is by no means the case.

But the most fundamental objection to the subsidy arrangements in our present strategy is that they do nothing to remedy the perverse incentives with respect to the use of the common-property assets. They do nothing to bring the social costs of production into closer conformance with the private costs of production. They do nothing to mitigate the excessive generation of wastes — especially industrial wastes — in the first place. They generally neglect all methods of water quality management other than conventional treatment.[16]

In brief, the intricate problem of linking subsidies to enforcement has not been solved at all; the subsidy arrangement has been linked to the use of a particular technology for improving water quality when others are available and often more efficient; attention has been focused on the construction of treatment facilities and not their opera-

[15] Environmental Protection Agency, *Clean Water*, Vol. II, p. 72.
[16] Cf. Chapter 2, pp. 47–49.

tion; and nothing has been done to change the economic incentive to overuse and misuse the common-property assets.

The Enforcement Program. The second element in our national strategy, the enforcement program, has displayed equally grave shortcomings. The Federal Water Pollution Control Act of 1956 launched the present approach and established what remains as its kingpin, the so-called enforcement conference. An enforcement conference may be called by the administrator of the Environmental Protection Agency (EPA)[17] when water pollution crosses state lines or by the administrator if requested by a state governor when a pollution problem is intrastate.

In addition, there is the "Shellfish Clause" which allows the administrator to call an enforcement conference without regard to whether the pollution is interstate or confined within one state. All he must do is find that the interstate sale of shellfish suffers economic injury as a result of the pollution.

The administrator is legally required to call an enforcement conference if one of two circumstances prevails. The first is if a governor or state agency requests a conference on an intrastate problem. The second is if investigations show to his satisfaction that an interstate pollution problem exists or shellfishing is being injured. In the latter cases, there is no legal obligation to make such studies or to heed their results. His action, if any, is purely discretionary.

The Nader Report describes the conferences and possible follow-up aptly:

> These are purely informal convocations, market places of pollution control ideas from which the conferees are supposed to issue advisory recommendations to the Administrator of EPA. When "official" clean-up recommendations may or may not be adopted by the Administrator and thereby become official suggestions of the conferees, they are purely exhortatory and have no force of law. After a minimum period of six months has elapsed, the Administrator again at his complete discretion may go to the next stage of the Conference procedure by convening a hearing board. Deliberations of the hearing board are formal but nevertheless result in yet another set of "recommendations." Another period of six months must elapse before the Administrator may — once again, this is discretionary — invoke the third and final stage of the conference procedure. He may ask the U.S. Attorney General (who presumably could exercise his own discretion and his views) to initiate injunctive proceedings in Federal Court to abate the pollution.[18]

The Federal Water Quality Act of 1965 endeavored to shortcut some of this lengthy and cumbersome process by requiring the states to set

[17] The statutory authority for enforcement has always belonged to the man with overall administrative responsibility for the Federal Pollution Program, i.e., the Surgeon General of the United States Public Health Service until 1961, the Secretary of HEW until 1966, and the Secretary of the Interior until the December 1970 reorganization which created EPA.

[18] Center for the Study of Responsive Law, *Water Wasteland*, VI-5.

federally approved water quality standards on their interstate waters. They are also required to submit an implementation plan for achieving these standards. The stream standards logically imply some pattern of systematic control of effluent, presumably through effluent standards if the regulatory approach is used. State implementation plans have in fact proved much vaguer than this and really do not provide a firm basis for bringing action against individual points of waste discharge. The Nader Report concludes that because the lines between stream standards and effluent requirements are so weak, the requirements placed upon individual waste dischargers are almost certainly unenforceable at law.[19]

Experience Under the Present Strategy. Let me turn then to a discussion of experience under this strategy. A coherent discussion of accomplishments and failures is greatly hampered by the lack of systematic data. Accordingly, the presentation is unavoidably somewhat anecdotal.

One way to look at the question of effectiveness is to inquire how frequently and in what manner enforcement provisions have been used. Since 1956 the federal government has initiated official discussions on fifty-one different pollution problems. None of these conferences is listed as ever having been officially "closed." Many have been reconvened several times over the years to look at new information, or to see if any progress has been made. For example, the Conference on the Potomac has recently been reconvened for the fifth time. In only four instances has the government stopped the conversation and proceeded to the hearing board stage. In only one case has the process run its full course to a legal proceedings — against St. Joseph, Missouri. The suit against St. Joseph was brought in 1960, and full compliance has not been achieved there yet.

This is not to say that the enforcement conference has not produced some results. Forcing the waste dischargers and state agencies to make public statements and giving cleaner water advocates a forum has often produced a degree of action on the part of waste dischargers involved in the conference. But the whole process, from the selection of problem situations and sources of waste water to be discussed through the stage of achieving some sort of conference consensus, is highly subject to political manipulations and delaying tactics on the part of waste dischargers.[20] Moreover, the process tends

[19] Center for the Study of Responsive Law, *Water Wasteland*, XIV-19. Support for this point of view is provided by a memorandum prepared for the United States Chamber of Commerce by the law firm of Covington and Burling, "Water Quality Standards under the Federal Water Pollution Control Act," April 4, 1968.

[20] Chapter VIII of *Water Wasteland*, entitled "With a Little Help from Their Friends," provides case studies of this process. Another illuminating case study is found in Alexander Polikoff, "The Interlake Affair," *The Washington Monthly*, March 1971.

to lose credibility when the enforcement procedures are practically invoked.

There is a long history of expressing good intentions on the part of waste dischargers and then subsequent foot dragging delays, sometimes for many years. Delays are beneficial from the waste dischargers' narrow point of view, because there is no penalty whatsoever for not staying on schedule or for delay in establishing a schedule. The prospect of procedures moving to an actual court order is virtually nil, and in most instances the maximum that could happen is that the dischargers would find the conference reconvened and would once more be exposed to a somewhat public scrutiny.

The enforcement officials face another obstacle: they are almost wholly dependent on the residuals dischargers themselves for information concerning what is being debouched to the watercourses and what the options and costs are for reducing it. Not only does this mean that they frequently need to depend on highly selected, if not totally inaccurate, information, but that to get any at all they must often cultivate a friendly relationship with the waste dischargers whom they are allegedly regulating. At the conference stage it is not possible to force the waste dischargers to divulge any information.

With regard to the "Shellfish Clause," which apparently gives the administrator so much discretion, experience has not been any more inspiring. According to the Nader Report,[21] the clause could have been invoked in at least 427 areas but, in fact, has been used only five times since its enactment in 1965.

Even if the procedural difficulties in the present enforcement strategy were remedied — and the Nixon Administration has imposed a bill that would do some of this — to make the regulatory strategy work in a systematic manner would require a veritable army of bureaucrats and lawyers. It has been estimated that to pursue enforcement activities vigorously in only four Missouri Basin states would require between 200 and 300 regulatory personnel, whereas at the present time twelve are assigned to this region. In other words, a twenty-five-fold staff expansion would be needed. If the conclusion is correct that the water-quality standards and compliance schedules required under the 1965 act would not, in fact, simplify the enforcement process, then present strategy requires dealing individually through the whole procedural process with each separate source of pollution in the United States. It means dealing with them in a process involving collecting information under difficult circumstances and essentially bargaining about every individual case. Some perspective on this appalling task may be obtained by noting that there are at least 40,000 dischargers of substantial amounts of industrial waste waters directly to water courses in the United States. The difficulty of making this system an integral part of a coherent strategy for con-

[21] Center for the Study of Responsive Law, *Water Wasteland*, VI-16.

tinuing management of one of our major common-property assets boggles the mind.

What Has Been Accomplished. Perhaps a more telling way to look at the question of the efficacy of the present strategy is to see what has been accomplished in the control of residuals and in improving the quality of our watercourses. Unfortunately, this is very difficult because hardly any systematic information exists. It may come as a shock to the uninitiated that for the most part we do not even know what effluents industry is discharging to watercourses. We will no doubt know more about this in a few years, but at present we must depend on ridiculously gross estimates.[22] It was estimated that in 1966 waste loads generated (measured in BOD — biochemical oxygen demand — a measure of the burden put on dissolved oxygen in watercourses) were 22 billion pounds by industry and 7 billion pounds from the sewered population of the United States (about one-third of the U.S. population is not served by sewers). How much is discharged to waterways by industries and municipalities after treatment is not known with any accuracy, but probably the proportion is even higher for industry. About one-fifth of the BOD load which industry generates is discharged to municipal sewers and roughly 45 percent of the BOD going into municipal sewers comes from industry. The subsidized construction of municipal waste treatment plants, if it has any effect at all, can therefore have only a small influence on the discharge of industrial waste.

According to the Council on Environmental Quality,[23] since 1957 government subsidies have been provided for 10,000 waste treatment plants at a total cost of about $6.5 billion, of which around $1.5 billion came from the federal government. Over this period the number of people served by some kind of treatment has increased by 51 million. But this gain has mostly been cancelled by a population growth of about 36 million persons. Moreover, there is grave doubt in many people's minds whether the federal subsidy program accelerated the construction of waste treatment plants at all. In fact, many observers believe that it has slowed down the process. Thus, municipalities wishing to improve water in their own areas or anticipating external pressure have tended to link their plans to the availability of federal funds. It is quite possible, and perhaps even probable, that there would be greater degree of treatment of municipal wastes today had we not had the federal subsidy program at all.

[22] Under the 1899 Refuse Act, discharge permits are now being issued to industries discharging directly to watercourses, and the applications contain information about their discharge. Not included are industries discharging to municipal sewers. EPA is also increasing its surveillance of industrial waste discharges.

[23] *Environmental Quality: The First Annual Report of the Council on Environmental Quality* (Washington, D.C.: United States Government Printing Office, 1970), p. 46.

Moreover, the figures above relate only to the construction of treatment plants. A recent government report[24] confirms what many observers of the water quality management scene have believed for a long time. Over half of the sample of plants that were studied provided substandard service, either because they were poorly operated or did not have sufficient capacity to treat the waste load delivered to them. Again this situation is largely a result of the present strategy's single-minded devotion to the construction of waste treatment plants. Once again the Nixon Administration has proposed certain reforms which might make the program work somewhat better.[25] None of the proposals would, however, deal with what I regard as the basic question of how the warped incentive structure, which is inducing the problem in the first place, can be changed once more to align the private interests in profits and economic growth with the broader social interest. This observation is especially pertinent in the case of the generation and discharge of industrial waste water.

Little or no systematic information is available on what has happened to industrial waste discharges over the years — even if one focuses exclusively on a useful but limited measure like biochemical oxygen demand. However, a series of case studies contained in the GAO Report suggests that whatever modest gains may have been achieved in municipal waste treatment have, in many river basins, been substantially outweighed by increases in industrial waste discharges. The GAO Report does not name the basins studied, but the most dramatic case was one in which, between 1957 (when the federal programs began in earnest) and 1968, eighteen grants totaling about $7.7 million were made in the basin for the construction of municipal waste treatment plants. A reduction of 147,000 population-equivalent BOD was accomplished by plants built in the basin. During the same period, industry *increased* its discharges by at least 2.4 million population equivalents. Moreover, despite the federal subsidy and enforcement programs, the raw sewage of about 525,000 persons was still being discharged into the river.

Of course, this is a rather spectacular instance, and across the country residuals discharges have not grown so dramatically. A rather heroic effort (in view of the fact that at this moment we don't have the slightest idea of what most industries are putting into our watercourses) was made by the authors of Clean Water to estimate the

[24] *Need for Improved Operations and Maintenance of Municipal Waste Treatment Plants*, General Accounting Office, Washington, D.C., 1970.

[25] To boost the program, the President has proposed that a billion dollars a year be provided in federal subsidies over the next four years. This is a large increase from what has been extended in recent years. It is also proposed to provide a financing authority to aid localities in financing treatment plants. Greater attention to monitoring performance is also foreseen. Whether these proposals will become actualities is still very much an open question. Moreover, they can be viewed as simply shoring up a grossly defective program.

change in two types of residuals discharge since 1957. They are BOD and plant nutrients (phosphorus). Estimates of the former are heavily built on coefficients from the 1966 calculations mentioned earlier. The estimates suggest that discharge of BOD has increased a little less than 10 percent, whereas plant nutrients have about doubled. According to these estimates also, BOD has started to decline in the last several years, whereas the discharge of plant nutrients has continued to increase strongly.[26] The authors admit that their estimates are extremely crude, especially for industry. Little is known about the generation of industrial residuals and *less* is known about the amount of treatment performed after generation. Even given the rough assumption about facilities in place, one may be dubious about the estimate of discharge, because it is based on the assumption that facilities are operated effectively. This seems highly doubtful in view of what is known about the effectiveness of municipal treatment plant operations — and industries are operating under a similar set of incentives. A striking feature of the Clean Water estimates is the spectacular growth of industrial BOD *generation*. It about doubled between 1957 and 1968, a period during which industrial production as a whole grew around 60 percent. If at all correct, this is a striking illustration of the failure of our present policies to discourage generation of residuals.

It was not possible, on the basis of available data, even to estimate crudely the tendencies in the generation and discharge of many other very important industrial residuals including suspended matter, acids, and toxic materials.[27]

The GAO Report concludes, and it is not difficult to agree, that underfinancing of federal programs, scattershot assistance unrelated to systematic plans for improving water quality, and most of all the overwhelming growth of industrial waste generation have largely mitgated the effectiveness of the federal programs.

Lack of Attention to Institution Building. In discussing the limitations of the present approach I have not yet mentioned what I regard as one of the most fundamental failures of all in our policy strategy — the lack of attention to institution building. In the first section of this paper I indicated that economic engineering has made a compelling case for the systematic management of entire river basins using a wide

[26] See Environmental Protection Agency, *Clean Water*, Table II, p. 29.

[27] Especially in view of the crudeness of the estimates of how much is being discharged to watercourses, it would be desirable to have a direct assessment of what has happened to their quality. No such assessment is available. *Clean Water* gave a rather impressionistic assessment of their present situation. It was found that almost a third of the United States stream miles are polluted in the sense of being persistently below the standards set for them. For obvious reasons, *miles of stream* are not a good measure of how often or how long people are exposed to poor quality water or of the effects on ecosystems — as on anadromous fish, for example.

array of technologies in addition to the reduction of discharges at individual outfalls. Furthermore, there are major "nonpoint" sources of residuals, such as runoff from agricultural land. For these, measures to improve the assimilative capacity of streams may be the only practical way to achieve better water quality. The present strategy embodies virtually no support for the development of this vital part of any systematic and efficient management program. Title 3c of the Federal Water Quality Act does provide for planning grants to states and regional agencies to develop coherent approaches to the problem. It is the only support for regional planning and institution building available from the federal government, and in recent years expenditures under this program have been running around $2 million a year. A degree of perspective on this figure can be achieved if one notes that this amount of money would not buy one respectable interstate highway interchange. In the longer perspective, and especially if one notices the interrelationships among water quantity and water-quality management and the need to develop programs for management of the nonpoint source residuals like agricultural runoff, the failure to build institutions which can undertake efficient management on a regional river-basin basis is perhaps the most profound deficiency of the entire approach.

An Alternative Strategy. An alternative strategy for dealing with our national water pollution problems grows rather naturally out of the economic research which has been done, the main results of which were reviewed briefly above. This strategy is based on two main elements.

The first rests on the concept that the waste discharger should, as far as possible, bear the costs that his waste disposal activities impose on the common property assets of society. The second is based on the recognition that in many of our highly developed basins, where pollution problems are concentrated, great gains in effectiveness and efficiency can be obtained by introducing a systematic and well-integrated water-quality management program on a regional basis. These are propositions which, as we have seen, are heavily underpinned by research results.

The first element would be implemented by the imposition of effluent charges, the amount of the charges to reflect the quality of the discharge. Our present subsidy arrangements are quite different in their impacts from the proposed effluent charges system. First, the system of effluent charges is based on the concept that payment for the use of valuable resources is necessary for efficiency, whether they happen to be privately or collectively owned. These payments will affect industrial producers' decisions to generate and discharge residuals. The type and quality of inputs, the kind of production processes used, and the type of final product produced will all be influenced. The charges not otherwise absorbed will also be reflected in the price of intermediate and final goods, so that a broader incentive will be provided to consumers to shift to goods with a lesser environmental cost. The present system of subsidies has the unfortunate effect of subsidizing most those goods the production of which, directly or indirectly, makes the heaviest use of common-property assets. Thus it aggravates rather than mitigates the most fundamental cause of the problem.

Second, to the extent that the subsidy-enforcement system is effective in reducing discharge, it tends to bias the choice of techniques in an inefficient direction, since as a practical matter only treatment plants qualify for subsidies. This provides an incentive to construct treatment plants with federal subsidy, even though — as in many, if not most, instances — internal controls would be cheaper. Effluent charges are technologically neutral and tend to induce the discharger to select the least-cost means for reducing residuals generation and discharge.[28]

Finally, the effluent charges system yields revenue rather than further straining an already seriously overextended tax system. This revenue can be put to useful public purposes including improvements in the quality of our environment. From a fiscal policy point of view, the best imaginable tax base is an activity that generates external costs. Taxes on such activities not only yield revenue but, if properly designed, improve the allocation of resources by moving private costs closer to social costs. This is important because most conventional taxes tend to distort efficient resources use in one way or another.

So far this discussion of charges has emphasized industry, but municipalities too are paying only part of the social costs associated with the waste waters they generate. And what they pay is rather capriciously distributed depending on how much treatment they have implemented and whether they have qualified for federal subsidies. The effluent charges system would give these municipalities an incentive to proceed expeditiously with the effective treatment of waste. Moreover, the effluent charges system focuses on what is put into the stream and thereby offers an incentive for effective operations of existing facilities. Finally, about half the residuals treated in municipal plants come from industrial sources. Thus, a charge on municipal discharges, passed back to these industrial sources, is necessary if the latter are to have the proper incentive to curb residuals generation.

Thus we see that, in principle, an effluent charges approach could remedy many of the difficulties and inefficiency-inducing features associated with our present subsidy-enforcement strategy. But despite what appear to be compelling reasons for favoring the effluent charges system as one of the cornerstones of effective and efficient national and regional water-quality management, it may be difficult for particular states and regions to pioneer such a substantial departure

[28] Cf. Chapter 2, pp. 40–47.

from previous practice. Although initiatives have been taken in several states and regions recently, the federal government's greater insulation from powerful local interests provides an opportunity for leadership.

In addition to the strategic advantages the federal government may have in this connection, there is much to be said for levying a national minimum charge which would establish the principle universally and at least partially blunt industry's threats to move to more permissive regions. Moreover, the charge could provide an immediate incentive to reduce discharges to the nation's watercourses. This charge could be considered a base which could, at their discretion, be exceeded by a state or regional agency having responsibility for water-quality management. Revenues obtained by the federal government could supplement funds from general tax sources and be made available for purposes of financing the federal program with the excess turned over to other governments of general jurisdiction. An illustrative calculation of the possible amount of revenue generated may be useful. If the charge for BOD were set at 10 cents per pound, the revenue would be about $1.5 to $2 billion per year. Ten cents per pound would produce a very strong incentive effect, because it is well above the costs of higher level treatment, except at the smallest outfalls, and much above the cost of process changes in many industries. On the assumption that charges for other substances would yield a similar amount, total revenues would be $3 to $4 billion. But the amount would fall rapidly — after several years probably to less than $1 billion.

The revenues could be used, and I think there is much to be said for this, to help establish regional water-quality management agencies, which are the other element in the proposed strategy. The rationale for this element was rather fully discussed earlier. One way for the federal government to encourage regional agencies would be to establish incentives and guidelines for the organization and operation of regional management agencies, either under state law or through interstate arrangements. An agency with adequate authority to plan and implement a regional water-quality management system would be eligible for a grant of funds to support a portion of its budget to help staff the agency and to make the first data collections, analyses, and formulation of specific measures for water-quality management. Some of the money would also be made available for retraining some of the present surplus of scientists and engineers to do this work.

If the federal government is satisfied that the regional agency's proposed program and the plan for its implementation satisfy criteria for effective and efficient operation, the agency might be eligible for a grant to assist it with actual construction and operating expenses. Such a system might approppriately be limited to the early implementation stage — say, five years. During this period, longer-term arrangements for financing the agency would have to be worked out. Clearly, the proposed effluent charges system could play a major role in this. Presumably, administration of the effluent charges system would be turned over to the regional agencies with the federal level of charges continuing to be regarded as a baseline. In this manner, regional scale measures for the management of the common-property asset would be financed while at the same time providing incentives to waste dischargers to cut back on their emissions. Special provisions might be included in the federal law affecting marginal industrial plants which might go under in situations where there was a broader social interest in protecting them. A possible pattern here would be the trade adjustment provisions of our international trade law. In these special assistance efforts, strong attention should be given to helping the reemployment of labor. This might take the form of assistance for retraining and subsidized movement. Assistance to the industrial plants themselves is less desirable, because plants which would have to shut down under the program outlined here are probably in deep trouble for other reasons anyway.

It should be noted that where serious efforts to implement regional water-quality management have been undertaken (as in the Delaware and the Miami basins, for example), one of the most serious problems has been to set up adequate financing arrangements. Existing regional agencies which would probably meet the criteria — like the Delaware River Basin Commission — would be immensely boosted by the regional institution-building strategy based on effluent charges if it were put into effect. It would make regional water-quality management virtually an immediate reality in these important areas.

What Are the Prospects for a New Strategy? Despite what seem to me extremely persuasive arguments in favor of the charges and regional institution-building approach, there has been much resistance to its adoption. Most of the resistance seems to center around the matter of charges on effluents.

One difficulty is the sheer momentum of an approach to a problem once it has been in operation for a period of time. Political points have been made on the basis of the subsidies and enforcement strategy. A substantial bureaucracy has been built up to implement the strategy, and its expertise and loyalties lie with it. Lawyers have written the basic statutes virtually without advice from economists, and they continue to have a vested interest in the legalistic approach they have nurtured. Moreover, the idea of using regulatory agencies to control major problems associated with our industrial and technological society is deeply embedded in our system of government despite the fact that its history is by no stretch of the imagination a tale of unmitigated successes. Indeed, the statement that the regulators are captured by the interests they are supposed to regulate has almost become a cliche. But so entrenched is this particular approach to public policy that many people can hardly imagine that things could be done any other way.

Another central source of opposition to the effluent-charges route is found in the industrial community. All sorts of reasons are given by industrial spokesmen for opposing it. Some argue that the charge is punitive and will tend to elicit an uncooperative attitude from industry. The argument that the charge is punitive is totally false; quite in contrast to the normal enforcement proceeding, no fault is implied. The charge is simply a payment made for the use of a resource, quite similar to payments which would be made for any other resource. The burden-of-proof problem is accordingly much simpler under charges than under the traditional approach because no problem of fault liability arises.[29] Showing that a measured amount of residual requires a certain dollar amount of payment involves none of the complexities of showing specific injury, technical and economic feasibility, and the like, which seems to have been the Achilles heel of the enforcement approach. The effluent charge is *not* punitive; it is aimed at producing a more efficient use of the nation's resources including its common-property resources.

Another argument made by industry is that it is unfair to ask them to continue to pay the charge for residual waste discharges if they have met some kind of a predetermined standard or are evidencing good faith in trying to deal with the problem. Once more the view fails to recognize that what is at issue is a question of the efficient use of natural resources and that efficiency requires that its users pay for their use whether that use is large or small. Also, political and possibly legal resistance to the charge as unequal in application should be reduced if it applies uniformly to all waste discharges. The charge can remain in effect for emissions levels below the point at which courts might legitimately object to the use of regulatory standards under the police power.[30] The conceptual, legal, and administrative advantages of having the charge apply to all levels of waste discharge are compelling.

Industry also often argues that it will have a "cash flow" problem, because it will be necessary to expend funds for payment of charges which could otherwise go into abatement activity. Aside from the deep question as to whether the funds would go into abatement activity (there seems to be no good reason to expect them to), this argument is blunted if a procedure is used which begins with a low level of charges and gradually increases in some firmly preordained manner. Referring again to BOD, one might start with a two-year grace period

[29] This point is explored in an excellent report by Adrian J. B. Wood, J. Serge Taylor, Frederick R. Anderson, and Laurence Moss of the National Academy of Engineering staff, "Strategies for Pollution Abatement Comparisons of Direct Regulation, Economic Incentives, and Control by Litigation" (unpublished).

[30] *Ibid.*

and then raise the charge in yearly increments, reaching 10 cents per pound (if that is the chosen level) in another five years.

Some members of the industrial community have argued that the charge is unfair because it will increase the price of certain goods where large residuals loads make control costly and that this is unfair to the consumer. Once more the larger question of efficiency is ignored. Clearly, a basic reason for many of our environmental problems is that goods whose social costs go unpaid are artificially cheap and consequently consumed in excessive amounts. The systematic passing forward of social costs is indeed a necessary element of efficient resources use. One of the hardest educational tasks facing those interested in effective management of our common-property resources is to break the frame of mind, built up during our history, that the use of these resources should be free.

In my personal opinion the most important source of opposition from industry is the recognition that the charge, in contrast to the enforcement procedures which have been set up in the United States, is much more nearly unavoidable and unevadable and will have a broad immediate effect on all waste dischargers. It is, I think, the effectiveness of the charge in a program for water-quality management that distresses industry most. The basic charge, once established, will be impersonal and relatively immune from economic or political interference or personal prestige.[31]

It has sometimes been argued that the effluent charge and effluent tax would encounter insurmountable legal or constitutional objections. This issue has been examined and seems to be totally false.[32] The Supreme Court has ruled that ". . . it's beyond serious question that a tax does not cease to be valid merely because it regulates, discourages, or even definitely deters the activity taxed. . . .The principle applies even though the revenue is obviously negligible . . . , or the revenue purpose of the tax may be secondary. . . . Nor does the tax statute necessarily fall because it touches on activities which Congress might not otherwise regulate."[33] Firms might wish to subject emissions taxes to court tests, but the incentive to do so is less than in the case of standards. Standards are postponed by litigation, whereas a tax is always paid while court action is taking place. This means that the effectiveness of a regulating tax cannot be delayed by court action and that the costs of losing a case are composed of both legal fees and tax payments. In the case of litigation over standards,

---

[31] As Robert K. Davis has pointed out, the "impersonal nature of a tax deserves some emphasis." He quotes a statement of an enforcement official excusing slow action, as reported in *Audubon,* March 1970, "we're dealing with top officials in industry, and you just don't go around treating these people like that." Elvis J. Stahr, Robert K. Davis, and Roland C. Clement, "Anti-Pollution Policies, Their Nature, and Their Impact on Corporate Profits" (unpublished manuscript).

[32] Wood *et al.,* "Strategies for Pollution Abatement."

[33] *United States* v. *Sanchez,* 340 U.S. 4244, 1950.

a firm could pay legal fees up to the costs of compliance during the time consumed by the litigation and still be no worse off — even if it expected to lose the case. The present strategy does seem to provide an effective incentive for employing lawyers.

Conservationists: Opposition and Support. Another source of resistance to a charges or taxation approach has been found in recent years among some members of the "conservation" movement. I interpret their resistance as reflecting their desire for total prohibition of the use of environment for the disposal of residual materials. If such total prohibition is unobtainable, at least they want the positiveness of direct control. I think it has now become clear to many conservationists that total prohibition of all discharges is virtually impossible in a society remotely resembling the one we have. If one reflects on the implications of conservation of mass, it soon becomes clear that literally to stop discharge of residuals materials to the environment, a degree of recycling would be needed beyond that ever achieved in a spacecraft. Moreover, I feel that the conservationists have come to appreciate, as have many others, that the apparent positiveness of direct controls is a mirage and that, in fact, a well worked out system of economic incentives will almost without doubt be more positive and more broadly effective than the present regulatory approach could hope to be. The argument of some proponents of the regulation approach — that theirs is the positive and direct program, while the effluent charges approach is uncertain — is almost exactly backwards. Accordingly, there has recently been a noticeable change of attitude among the conservation groups. The Sierra Club and the Audubon Society as well as the National Wildlife Federation leadership have gone on record in favor of the charges or taxation route. This is one of the most encouraging elements in the present situation.

Effluent Charges Supporters. There are other reasons to be somewhat hopeful that the incentives institution-building approach, which makes so much more sense from a political economy point of view, is getting some serious consideration in policy-making quarters and seems to be developing a certain degree of momentum. There is as yet no ground for strong optimism, but there are some encouraging developments. In its *Counterbudget* the National Urban Coalition has come out foursquare for the effluent charges regional management approach.[34] The prestigious Brookings Institution has taken a similar strong stand.[35] Senator Proxmire has introduced a bill containing many of the features of the approach advocated here and so has Con-

---

[34] The National Urban Coalition, *Counterbudget: A Blueprint for Changing National Priorities, 1971–1976* (New York: Praeger, 1971).
[35] See Charles L. Schultze, Edward R. Fried, Alice M. Rivlin, and Nancy Teeters, *Setting National Priorities: The 1972 Budget* (Washington, D.C.: The Brookings Institution, 1971).

gressman Aspinall in the House. Representative Reuss raised the possibility of hinging a charges system to the permit requirements of the 1899 Refuse Act, which act will now apparently be implemented in some manner. Other members of the Congress have expressed an interest in pursuing an effluents charges technique. The State of Vermont has passed a Water Pollution Control Bill containing some major features of an effluents charges approach. There is activity in a number of other states directed toward getting effluent charges bills introduced. On the international scale, effluent charges are embodied in water-quality legislation in Canada, France, and Czechoslovakia, and expressions of interest in the approach have come from other countries, most notably the Federal Republic of Germany. The process of information and education on this matter has been going forward for several years, and most persons in positions of power in government, industry, and other salient groups at interest are becomingly relatively well acquainted with this alternative strategy.

In laying emphasis on effluent charges, I do not mean thereby to imply that administrative rulings and legal remedies have no role to play in water-quality management. Indeed, the discharge of many substances (primarily heavy metals and persistent organics) should probably be prohibited entirely, and Professor Sax has argued cogently that the courts could be made to play a more constructive role in environmental management.[36] But I am persuaded that economic incentives and regional management must move to center stage if we are to come to grips with the water-quality management problem effectively and efficiently.

It seems to me we have before us an important test of whether the political process in this country can learn from policy research on pressing issues of the day, can learn from accumulating experience with a defective program, can overcome the pressure of special interests, and if it can then put us on the road to effective management of a continuing and worsening problem affecting our valuable common-property assets.

I would like to conclude with a couplet by that famous economist-bard, Kenneth Boulding:

> What this country lacks is
> a system of effluent taxes.

SUPPLEMENTARY READINGS

1. Joe S. Bain, Richard E. Caves, and Julius Margolis, *Northern California's Water Industry,* Baltimore, Johns Hopkins Press, 1966, pp. 113–116, 521–524, 590, 668–669.
2. Center for the Study of Responsive Law, *Water Wasteland* (A Ralph Nader Task Force Report), Washington, D.C., 1971.

[36] Joseph L. Sax, *Defending the Environment* (New York: Alfred A. Knopf, Inc., 1970).

3. Comptroller General of the United States, *Examination into the Effectiveness of the Construction Program for Abating, Controlling, and Preventing Water Pollution*, Washington, D.C., 1969.
4. Council on Environmental Quality, *Environmental Quality: First Annual Report*, Washington, D.C., 1970.
5. R. K. Davis, *The Range of Choice in Water Management*, Baltimore, Johns Hopkins Press, 1968.
6. Environmental Protection Agency, Water Quality Office, *Cost of Clean Water*, Washington, D.C., 1971.
7. General Accounting Office, *Need for Improved Operation of Municipal Water Treatment Plants*, Washington, D.C., 1970.
8. Allen V. Kneese and Blair T. Bower, *Managing Water Quality: Economics, Technology, Institutions*, Baltimore, Johns Hopkins Press, 1968.
9. Marc J. Roberts, "River Basin Authorities: A National Solution to Water Pollution," *Harvard Law Review*, 83, May, 1970, pp. 1527–1556.

5 The Technology, Economics, and Industrial Strategy of Automotive Air Pollution Control

Since World War II, air pollution in metropolitan areas of the United States by automotive vehicles has become increasingly apparent as a physiological irritant to human lungs and eyes and a general health hazard, an enemy of many types of vegetation, a major aesthetic nuisance, and a meteorological phenomenon persistent enough to alter micro-climates significantly.

This development has engendered political action to impose regulations of progressive severity on the permissible emissions of uncombusted gasoline and of certain combustion products from motor vehicles. The first action was taken in California in 1962, largely because its South Coastal Basin had a combination of topography, climate, and a very large number of vehicle miles traveled per capita that combined to produce first among metropolitan areas an extensive and intensive atmospheric "smog." Subsequently, California has imposed progressively more severe and comprehensive regulations, and the federal government entered the picture in 1967 with the Federal Air Quality Act.

The status of the automotive air pollution problem and of existing and proposed automotive emissions regulations in the latter part of 1970 may be summarized briefly as follows:

By Joe S. Bain, reprinted from *Western Economic Journal*, VIII: December 1970, pp. 329–356, with permission of the Western Economic Association.

Grateful acknowledgment is made to the Institute of Business and Economic Research, University of California, Berkeley, for financial support of part of the research underlying and the preparation of this paper.

1. Automotive emissions of both uncombusted hydrocarbons (hereafter, HC's) and carbon monoxide (hereafter, CO) per mile of driving have been drastically reduced since precontrol years. The biggest contributor to the reduction has been the introduction in the earlier 1960's of positive crankcase ventilation systems to carry noxious gases from the crankcase to the combustion cylinders. Other contributors have included adjustments of combustion cylinder design, of air-fuel ratios in the mix fed to cylinders, of spark timing, and of choke, generally adopted in 1968 models by American automotive producers. On most models, air injection into the exhaust line was earlier relied upon.

2. The intensity of photochemical smog in metropolitan areas has declined appreciably since 1966,[1] but smog still constitutes a persistent problem in such test cities as Chicago, Cincinnati, Denver, Philadelphia, St. Louis, Washington, D.C., and San Francisco. Though somewhat ameliorated, smog remains very much more persistent and intense in the South Coastal Basin of California than elsewhere. CO pollution remains serious in metropolitan areas generally.

3. The automotive air pollution problem in metropolitan areas threatens to become more severe over the next decade and beyond because of an increased automotive population, unless something much more drastic and costly than previously is done to alter or augment the design of automotive engine systems, and possibly the composition of commercial gasolines.

California has imposed automotive emission regulations which, beginning with 1970 model-year vehicles, become progressively more severe through the 1974 model-year cars, and is considering proposed regulations for 1975 which are much more severe. The federal Congress has in effect regulations generally comparable to California's for 1971 vehicles and is seriously considering regulations for 1973 through 1975 which would be somewhat more severe than the California ones.[2]

4. To comply with these standards as they become effective the American automotive industry has formulated and with the 1971 model year has begun implementing redesign plans geared to the introduction in 1975 model-year vehicles of exhaust-gas reactor systems, with the petroleum industry generally cooperating to supply

[1] W. G. Agnew, "Science and Technology in Automotive Air Pollution Research," paper presented at Symposium on Science and Technology of Aerosol Pollution in Modern Society, Royal Society of London (mimeo), February 1968, Tables 1 and 5.

[2] United States Department of Commerce, Technical Advisory Board Panel on Automotive Fuels and Air Pollution, "The Implications of Lead Removal from Automotive Fuel," an interim report, June 1970 (mimeo), Table 1; and California Air Resources Board, *Air Pollution Control in California,* Annual Report (Sacramento, January 1970), pp. 11–24.

modified gasolines as required by these exhaust treatment devices. To bolster specific announced auto-industry and cooperating petroleum-industry plans, California in late 1970 passed legislation which (a) forbids the sale in California of autos requiring gasoline with greater than 91 octane rating to run properly, beginning with 1972 models, and (b) imposes an added annual registration tax on all autos with compression ratios above 8.5:1, not meeting emission standards, beginning with 1975 models. The meaning and advisability of this legislation should emerge below.

I will turn to these plans momentarily, but first should enter a caveat concerning the importance of automotive air pollution in total air pollution.

A CAVEAT

Although we have been emphasizing automotive air pollution, in substantially all metropolitan areas total air pollution is generated in proportions ranging from appreciable to major by nonautomotive sources. Other major sources include petroleum or coal burning plants used to generate electricity, plants emitting organic solvent vapors, metallurgical and chemical plants, petroleum refineries, and burning of solid wastes. Indeed a recent study by the California Air Resources Board found that in the state's South Coastal Basin, where automobile use is more extensive and intensive than anywhere else in the world, motor vehicles in 1968 accounted for 88 percent of the tonnage of the major air-pollutant emissions — including HC's, nitrogen oxides (hereafter, NO_x), CO, sulfur dioxide, and particulates — and 64 percent of such emissions other than CO. But in the San Francisco Bay Area basin, where automotive use per capita is probably above the national metropolitan average, motor vehicles accounted for only 67 percent of total pollutant emissions, and 45 percent of those other than CO.[3] In industrialized metropolitan areas in the midwestern and northeastern parts of the United States, the proportionate contribution of automotive vehicles to air pollution is undoubtedly smaller, whereas steam plants for electric power generation become more important sources of air pollution, and selectively metallurgical, chemical, and organic solvent-using plants. Mineral and chemical plants are important sources of sulfur dioxide and particulate emissions, as are electricity-generating steam plants, which are also important sources of NO_x emissions. Thus the proportionate importance of automotive emissions as a source of air pollution varies among areas — although it always remains important — as does the composition of the total pollutants in the air. Generally, cleaning up all air pollu-

---

[3] *Ibid.*, California Air Resources Board, pp. 33–34.

tion requires about equal attention to nonautomotive and automotive sources of air pollution.

Nonetheless, automotive emissions have attracted a disproportionately large amount of attention because they are the major source of the pollutants that are converted into photochemical smog (uncombusted unsaturated HC's and NO_x). This smog, in addition to forming a pervasive artificial fog or cloud, causes eye irritation, impairs lung function, damages or destroys vegetation, and discolors the atmosphere. In addition, autos are the predominant source of health-impairing CO and emit polynuclear HC's that have proven carcinogenic tendencies. By contrast, most other major sources emit pollutants whose major persistent effects are usually dirt, odor, and visibility reduction, excepting perilously high sulfur dioxide emissions. Otherwise, automotive emissions at present levels in general are the most dangerous and annoying air pollutants.

OPTIONS OPEN TO THE AUTOMOTIVE AND PETROLEUM INDUSTRIES

In the move to comply with much more severe regulations of automotive emissions by 1975, a number of options are open to the automotive industry and reciprocally to the pertoleum refining industry.

The options currently emphasized by Detroit are: (1) foremost, the ultimate choice, to be implemented in 1975, between two general types of exhaust-gas reactors, both still in the later stages of development; (2) an interim choice (for the 1971 through 1974 model-year vehicles) as to whether or not, when, and to what extent to reduce the compression ratios in their engines to accommodate gasolines that have lower octane (anti-knock) ratings because they do not contain tetraethyl lead, and because lead removal will not be fully compensated for by altering the mix of different types of HC molecules in gasoline. This choice is related to three facts. First, appreciable amounts of tetraethyl lead in automotive exhausts are demonstrably poisonous to and would render commercially nonfeasible one of the two major types of exhaust-gas reactors — catalytic reactors. Second, the petroleum refining industry would need several years to equip itself to produce enough high-octane HC's to compensate at all fully for the general removal of lead from all gasolines. Third, such a full compensation would greatly increase the photochemical reactivity of exhaust emissions.

A second option emphasized by the automotive industry has become forced choice — in California beginning with 1970 model-year vehicles and federally beginning with 1971 models. This is the installation of devices to reduce greatly the evaporation of gasoline in the vehicle prior to its reaching the combustion cylinders. These devices, which include altered filler caps on the gasoline tank and tightened controls at the fuel pump and the carburetor, are being generally included on 1971 model-year vehicles.

An option that has been hardly mentioned by American automotive makers is whether or not to reduce the size of their engines, as generally measured by the interior volume of their combined cylinders — their "displacement." Years of driving experience, partly documented, suggest that in autos of the same year much greater displacements are significantly linked with much larger fuel use per mile. This seems due partly to design choices that use added power to improve performance at the expense of fuel economy, and partly to the driving habits of users of very powerful cars. Exhaust emissions would also rise in pace with fuel use if compensatory emission controls more effective than used on smaller engines were not used on big-displacement engines. Such controls being equal, larger displacements should lead to larger emissions. Current American engines, especially V-8's, are held to provide a large unusable power surplus, so that abundant performance and lower emissions per mile can be had from notably smaller high-compression engines.

The options open to the petroleum refining industry are mainly in the area of redesigning a part of their gasolines in various ways, mainly to supply redesigned new-model cars beginning with the 1971 models — a need that will increase progressively over time beyond 1975. In choosing among options, refiners have commercial incentives, as well as incentives to cooperate in the effort to reduce automotive air pollution, to dance more or less to a tune played by Detroit, which determines engine designs that constrain the properties of the gasolines they should best use from the standpoint of efficiency and of limitation of air polluting emissions. The choice among options is likely to differ somewhat between an interim period from late 1970 to 1980 or later, when there will be a maximal emphasis on producing gasolines that will practically minimize highly pollutant emissions from vehicles not equipped with exhaust-gas reactor systems, and the period beginning some years subsequent to 1975, when the bulk of vehicles on the road will presumably be equipped with exhaust-gas reactors and the pollutant emission potentialities of gasolines will become much less important.

For the designated interim period, the petroleum industry's immediate option is whether or not to comply with Detroit's request (as presented most strongly by General Motors) that they produce a lead-free or low-lead gasoline of reduced octane rating to provide the desired fuel for the lower-compression engines offered in 1971 auto models and presumably to be offered at least through the 1974 models. The petroleum industry appears to be in the process of complying with this request. As time progresses toward 1975, it has the further option of deciding whether or not and to what extent to augment refining facilities for producing greatly increased amounts of high octane HC's to replace lead in all gasolines in the long run. In making this decision, it needs to gamble on whether or not the exhaust-gas reactor ultimately adopted by Detroit will be incompatible with leaded gasoline. Its decision on this matter will be simplified if American auto makers announce soon what type of exhaust-gas reactor they will adopt in 1975. If it knows that an exhaust-gas reactor incompatible with leaded gasoline will be introduced in 1975, it further needs to gamble on whether or not American auto makers, given the reactor to control exhaust emissions, will proceed thereafter to return to high-compression engines, which would require production of substantially larger amounts of high octane gasoline components and more refinery equipment to produce them. Meanwhile, the petroleum refining industry has the subsidiary option of reducing or eliminating from gasoline a group of hydrocarbons with high photochemical reactivity comprising the more volatile olefins — an option that it may or may not systematically exercise.

PURPOSE AND SCOPE OF THIS PAPER

In moving rapidly toward a drastic reduction in automotive air pollution, an extremely difficult set of problems involving numerous variables and susceptible of a variety of solutions must be solved. The economist, therefore, becomes naturally interested in what the range of optimal and near-optimal solutions is, with respect both to sequential solutions in the interim period before the introduction of exhaust-gas reactors and to the ultimate solution involving the choice of a type of reactor and a gasoline to go with it. These problems are going to be solved primarily by a few large auto producers, petroleum refiners cooperating, in a context wherein Detroit is evidently going to try to meet progressively severe legislative standards for automotive emissions but is going to do it in a way of its own choosing, unless the present rules of the game are changed. The economist is thus likewise interested in evaluating the industrial strategies that are taking shape for responding to governmental regulations of automotive emissions.

We are undertaking here a preliminary examination of the optimality problems mentioned and a preliminary evaluation of evolving industrial strategies and their alternatives, within the confines of the assumption that in the medium term automotive vehicles will be powered by gasoline-burning internal combustion engines.

Any productive discussion of this sort, however, needs to be prefaced by a brief review of selected crucial aspects of (1) petroleum refining technology, (2) automotive engine technology as related to gasoline combustion and to combustion products, (3) the ingredients and mechanisms of smog formation from automotive emissions, and (4) the technology of exhaust-gas reactors and associated equipment. We shall deal with them shortly, but first review the present solutions that have been proposed and are being implemented by the automobile industry.

SOLUTIONS PROPOSED BY THE AUTOMOBILE INDUSTRY

By 1968 or 1969, with rapidly developing California and federal legislative action to regulate automotive air pollution, American auto makers were in a position that favored their developing a concerted general strategy for coping positively with regulatory constraints they faced or were about to face — a strategy that would put them in the driver's seat in selecting specific reactions to regulatory pressures, while still leaving room for about as much nonprice rivalry as they desired. The high concentration of the industry together with the existence of a common "opponent" made the adoption of such a positive strategy feasible.

Previously, the auto industry had not been especially given to the common adoption of positive strategies, but had favored negative ones of foot-dragging resistance to the regulation of its products, as in its response to demands for making autos safer. Its shift toward a positive strategy for coping with automotive air pollution was thus somewhat surprising. Perhaps lessons learned in the battle over auto safety convinced the industry that it was advantageous to take the lead in deciding what should be done to meet a large problem of public concern, trying not to leave the mode of solution up to governmental authority. At any rate, the industry did come forth with a positive strategy, to which we now turn.

The Current Strategy. The going strategy of American auto makers, announced early in 1970, is a general one basically propounded by General Motors, and adhered to with individual variations by the other three major American producers.

The initially announced intentions of General Motors were (a) to modify *all* its 1971 model-year engines (and presumably those for 1972 through at least 1974) so that they would operate on a "regular grade" 91-octane unleaded gasoline, with about 8.5:1 compression ratios and no increase in engine displacements, and (b) to introduce exhaust-gas reactor systems, either catalytic or thermal, probably incorporating improvements not yet discovered, in its 1975 model-year vehicles.[4]

One modification in this program was tentatively introduced in March of 1970, when General Motors said it was ready to modify its position temporarily to allow low-lead gasoline (containing 0.5 cc. of lead per gallon from 1972 through 1974), but still with a 91-octane

[4] California Air Resources Board, Hearings on Fuel Composition and Emissions Control, Sacramento, March 4–5, 1970, 2 Vols. (mimeo). (Page references are omitted because copies are not generally available to the public.) Testimony of Mr. Cole, President of General Motors.

rating.[5] This change in gasoline specifications was justified as permitting a lesser addition of photoreactive hydrocarbons to the gasoline in order to reach 91 octane, since the 0.5 cc. of lead should add about 2.5 octane numbers. This modification had the effect of liberalizing the instruction given to or order placed with the petroleum industry, at no known cost to General Motors other than exposing the arbitrary character of its initial insistence on lead-free gasoline four years prior to the introduction of exhaust-gas reactors.

In its revised plan for gasolines, General Motors proposes for 1972 through 1974 just two grades of gasoline: 91-octane low-lead regular and 97-octane normal-lead premium, followed by a gradual phasing out of the lead almost entirely.[6]

In March of 1970, Ford announced that 90 percent of its 1971 engines would be designed to operate on 91-octane unleaded fuel (100 percent of its 1972 engines) and implied aiming at introduction of exhaust-gas reactor systems with the 1975 model year.[7] Chrysler announced that, starting with the 1971 model year, 93 percent of Chrysler engines would operate on regular-grade fuel, leaded or unleaded, with about 8.5:1 compression ratios, but would need 94-octane gasoline if operated without spark-retard. It implied comparable timing of the introduction of exhaust-gas reactor systems.[8] American Motors said that with 91- or 92-octane fuel available, it would stay with its previous 8.5:1 compression ratio on six-cylinder engines, but maintain a 9:1 ratio on its V-8 engine[9] (the latter probably implying reliance on a leaded premium fuel).

As to what the auto firms actually did with 1971 models, General Motors introduced its 1971 basic Chevrolet 6 and V-8 engines with 8:1 ratios (down from 8.5:1 and 9:1 respectively from 1970), as did American Motors with its 6-cylinder engine. As did Chrysler in its basic engines, General Motors did reduce the compression ratios of the engines in its medium-price class and Cadillac models only to 8.5:1 (from 10:1), perhaps on the theory that in those models surplus power was sufficient to absorb spark-retard or to avoid noticeable knock with gasolines of insufficient octane. Ford dropped V-8 compression ratios only to 9:1 in 1971 models.

The responsive strategy of major petroleum refiners supplying the Pacific Coast (probably representative of major refiners nationally) was generally cooperative, but with variations. Announced as planning to produce a 91-octane unleaded gasoline beginning in the Fall of 1970, *in addition to* the two previous leaded regular and premium grade gasolines (octane ratings about 94 and 100), were Standard

[5] *Ibid.*
[6] *Ibid.*
[7] *Ibid.*, Testimony of Mr. Misch, Vice President, Ford Motor Co.
[8] *Ibid.*, Testimony of Mr. Bornhauser, Vice President, Chrysler Corp.
[9] *Ibid.*, Testimony of Mr. Adamson, Vice President, American Motors Corp.

of California, Shell, Atlantic-Richfield, and Texaco — the two previous leaded grades being retained to fulfill the needs of the multitude of pre-1971 relatively high-compression vehicles now on the road. Humble and Gulf now offer three grades, one low-lead. Planning to produce only two grades of fuel, a 91-octane low-lead gasoline and a 97-octane leaded premium gasoline, were Union and Phillips.[10] The petroleum refining industry generally appears sensibly to be leaving its options open with respect to the design of gasolines for 1975 and beyond, waiting to find out what type of exhaust-gas reactor the auto makers will choose, and what they will do about compression ratios once exhaust-gas reactors are in use.[11]

It is clear that the automotive industry has a two-part short-term strategy, one part applying to the interim period from the introduction of 1971 model-year vehicles to the introduction of exhaust-gas reactors with 1975 model-year autos, and the other applying to the choice between types of exhaust-gas reactors to be introduced in 1975. Before appraising this strategy, let us turn to some of the technological information needed to formulate such an appraisal.

PETROLEUM REFINING TECHNOLOGY

Since petroleum refining technology as a whole is complex, we shall concentrate on a few aspects of the technology of producing gasoline, referring also to significant chemical properties of the main components of gasoline and to some cost factors.

Gasoline is initially extracted from crude petroleums, which are mixtures of HC molecules of widely varying specific gravities and volatilities, by a process of fractional distillation. The molecules distilled for gasoline have boiling points ranging from 10° F. to above 350°. The crude petroleums, and thus the gasoline fractions distilled from them, are preponderantly either paraffins (saturated open-chain HC's) or naphthenes (saturated cyclic hydrocarbons). A minor proportion of these natural HC's have moderately to very high octane or antiknock ratings, but the bulk of them do not and require blending with high-octane HC's and/or the addition of tetraethyl lead to produce gasolines suitable for use in modern high-compression engines.

[10] *Ibid.*, Testimony of Mr. Walker, Vice President, Shell Oil Co., Mr. Chambers, Vice President, Atlantic-Richfield Corp., Mr. Hartley, President, Union Oil Co., Mr. Meisel, Manager of Research, Mobil Oil Co., and Mr. McReynolds, Phillips Petroleum Co. Also, observation of press-announced and physically implemented policies of various petroleum firms selling gasoline in the far western states.

[11] As petroleum refiners' policies actually evolved, the major firms have generally come to offer either just two grades of gasoline — a low-lead (0.5 cc. per gallon) grade with about 93.5-octane rating, and a leaded premium grade with a 97-octane rating or greater — or three grades, including the two just mentioned plus a 91-octane unleaded gasoline.

Generally, they have a low photochemical reactivity, or smog-forming propensity.

Because gasoline is potentially by far the most valuable product of crude oils, American refiners for several decades have significantly increased their gasoline outputs by thermal and catalytic cracking of petroleum distillates heavier than used in gasoline — processes that crack heavier petroleum molecules into smaller and more volatile ones within the gasoline range. Such cracking produces more volatile paraffins and naphthenes, but also reforms the molecular structures of a part of the cracked molecules to produce HC's with higher octane ratings. Important among these reformed molecules are olefins, which are unsaturated chain-form hydrocarbons; olefins have relatively high octane ratings, but they are the most photoreactive chemically of the principal HC's in gasoline. As one of several common products of cracking processes, they are relatively inexpensive as compared to other high octane manufactured HC's.

Octane ratings of distilled and cracked gasolines were initially (and still are) raised by mixing them with small quantities of tetraethyl lead, in amounts ranging roughly from 1.5 to 4 cc.'s per gallon. This mixing on the average raises the octane rating of gasolines from 6 to 8 octane numbers, as measured on the scale of 94- and 100-octane ratings in current regular-grade and premium-grade leaded gasolines. It does so inexpensively, at a cost in the neighborhood of a cent per gallon.

The World War II demand for very high octane aviation gasolines, followed by the development of automotive engines with much higher compression ratios, created a need for producing in volume gasolines with much higher octane ratings than previously. This was accomplished mainly by reforming the molecular structures of basic paraffin and naphthene gasolines to produce a group of HC's known as aromatics, which are unsaturated cyclic molecules. They are produced principally by catalytic reforming, with a feed stock made up mainly of naphthene and paraffin gasolines.

Aromatics have the primary advantage of possessing very high octane ratings — ranging for nearly all particular subvarieties from 100 to 120, with most above 110, thus furnishing the blending stocks needed to produce high octane gasolines in volume. They have two main disadvantages. Their cost is high, because of the high value of the feed stocks used to produce them, 20 percent loss in gasoline volume in processing, and added processing costs. It has been estimated that the cost of raising the octane rating of leaded premium gasoline from 99 to 104 would be about four cents per gallon.[12] And

[12] F. W. Kavanagh, J. R. MacGregor, R. L. Pohl, and M. B. Lawler, "The Economics of High Octane Gasolines," paper presented at West Coast Meeting, Society of Automotive Engineers, Los Angeles, August 1958 (mimeo), pp. 8–10.

aromatics are quite photoreactive chemically, so that as emitted unburnt from auto exhausts they have important smog-forming pro-
pensities.

A typical 100-octane leaded premium gasoline today might contain
about 30 percent aromatics, 15 percent olefins, and 55 percent paraffins plus naphthenes. Maintaining octane rating while removing lead
requires raising the content of aromatics significantly, and thus the
cost of gasoline. The comparative intractability of the smog problem
in the last two decades is not unconnected with the emergence of
aromatics as important components of commercial automotive
gasolines.

In the preceding synoptic discussion, a number of other less important refinery processes that increase gasoline output and/or raise
octane ratings have been neglected. Let us turn now to automotive
engine technology as related to gasoline combustion and its products.

AUTOMOTIVE ENGINE TECHNOLOGY
AND GASOLINE COMBUSTION

Because modern automotive engines and their technology are very
complex and involve many variables, space does not permit any comprehensive discussion of them. We shall limit our discussion to the
major aspects of engine design that are related to the generation and
control of automotive exhaust emissions, neglecting evaporative emissions because by now they are pretty well taken care of. It is convenient to deal in turn with (1) the composition of exhaust emissions
and their sources; (2) the effects of tetraethyl lead in gasoline on
exhaust emissions and on automotive components; and (3) the effects of principal alterations in the design and adjustments of automotive engines on exhaust emissions and on the operating efficiency
of these engines.

Composition of Exhaust Emissions and Their Sources. In present-day
automotive engines, exhaust emissions are made up first of products
of combustion of gasoline and second of uncombusted HC's. With the
major combustion products being carbon dioxide and water, the remaining important ones are CO, NO_x, sulfur dioxide, and lead or lead
salt particulates. All these four remaining ones are atmospheric pollutants, with CO being the most serious from a public health standpoint. NO_x is both a component and an important building block of
photochemical smog.

Uncombusted HC emissions include the original gasoline fed into
the engine combustion chambers and HC molecules "produced" in the
combustion process by alterations in the composition of the molecules
in the original gasoline. The emissions of uncombusted original gasoline of course include paraffins, aromatics, and olefins, of which the
latter two are highly photoreactive chemically. The "produced" emis-

sions of unburnt hydrocarbons importantly include olefins (the properties of which were previously discussed), which constitute a large percentage of total olefin exhaust emissions. They also include aldehydes, which are oxygen-containing HC's and are characterized as "instant smog" in that they produce eye irritation and odor without reacting with anything else. Further, they include in small quantities polynuclear aromatic HC's, some of which are proven carcinogens.

In late model autos, fortunately, total uncombusted HC's emitted from exhausts are estimated to comprise from ½ to 1 percent of the total gasoline fed into engines.[13] Unfortunately, this is much too much in metropolitan areas.

Effects of Tetraethyl Lead. The effects of using tetraethyl lead in gasoline on exhaust emissions require careful treatment. To decompose the automotive air pollution problem in an analytically useful way, it is desirable to isolate the effects of lead per se, *ceteris paribus* with respect to several other variables. Unfortunately, a number of analyses have approached the "lead effect" on emissions by comparing the emissions from a relatively high-compression engine burning leaded gasoline of relatively high octane rating with those from a lower-compression engine burning unleaded gasoline, frequently without a specification as to whether or to what extent compensatory adjustments in the air-fuel ratio in the combustion mix, spark timing, etc., were supposed to have been made in shifting to no lead and a lower compression ratio. Here we shall first try to isolate the lead effect.

Some recent research by scientists of the Bureau of Mines provides most of the ingredients for such an isolation.[14] They tested for the comparative volume and degree of photoreactivity of emissions of leaded and unleaded gasolines of equal octane ratings, burned in identical engines, with octane ratings in the unleaded gasolines being maintained by increasing the proportion of aromatic HC's in them. Burning both types of fuel in nearly new engines with some accumulated lead deposits, they found that lead may either decrease or increase gross HC exhaust emissions per mile of driving from slightly to appreciably. Using lead instead of aromatics to maintain octane rating decreased the volume (weight) of HC emissions by about 6½ percent for premium-grade fuel; for regular-grade fuel it either increased or decreased these emissions by about 1 percent, depending on whether the unleaded regular-grade gasoline was low or high in olefin content. NO_X emissions were not appreciably affected.

13 Confidential industry source.
14 B. Dimitriades, B. H. Eccleston, and R. W. Hurn, "An Evaluation of the Fuel Factor Through Direct Measurement of Photochemical Reactivity of Emissions," *Journal of the Air Pollution Control Association*, March 1970, 20, 158–59.

Other tests, however, have revealed that with the persistent use of leaded gasoline, the accumulation of lead deposits in engines increases the volume of HC exhaust emissions by about 7 percent as compared to clean engine operation, but does not appreciably affect NO_X emissions.[15] The long-term effect of lead in gasoline on the volume of HC exhaust emissions per mile is estimated to increase it about 7 percent with either grade of gasoline.

But in unleaded gasoline of equal octane, the content of aromatic HC's is significantly greater, and so is the aromatics content of exhaust emissions. Thus, using lead instead of increased aromatics decreases the specific photochemical reactivity (smog-forming propensity) of exhaust emissions. Substituting aromatic HC's for lead to maintain octane rating in the Bureau of Mines experiment increased the photochemical reactivity of HC exhaust emissions (as measured on a chosen scale) by about 28 percent for premium fuel, and by either 38 or 21 percent for regular-grade fuels, respectively of low- and high-olefin content. Leaded as compared to unleaded fuel, however, perplexingly had on the average only slight effects on the eye-irritant content of exhausts.

Combining the effects of lead on the volume and photoreactivity of HC exhaust emissions, the effect of using lead instead of increased aromatics to maintain 1970 octane ratings should be to decrease the aggregate photochemical air pollutant potential of exhaust HC's per mile from 15 to 20 percent.

Octane rating being held constant, lead probably affects gasoline economy adversely in terms of miles per gallon (in proportions similar to those of the increase of volume of emissions), but this diseconomy would be offset by the fact that substituting aromatics for lead would probably increase the cost of gasoline by at least 3 or 4 cents per gallon. It is not clear whether shifting from leaded to unleaded gasoline in engines that have previously accumulated lead deposits would in the long run reduce their volume of exhaust emissions. It would not do so on impact, but might with the accumulation of a number of thousands of miles of driving on unleaded gasoline.

As to the effect of lead on exhaust emissions other than those of HC's and NO_X, its use results in emitting lead salt particulates, which at present levels do not have demonstrated clinical effects on human health, but are suspected by some investigators of having cumulative subclinical effects. If lead affects aldehyde emissions, as it probably does, it retards them. As compared to unleaded gasoline of equal octane rating, leaded gasoline appreciably reduces the emission of polynuclear HC's. It has no appreciable effect on CO emissions.

The major nonemission effect of lead — and the only one which might counterbalance its numerous cost-saving and antipollution

---

[15] U.S. Department of Commerce, Technical Advisory Board Panel on Automotive Fuels and Air Pollution, *op. cit.*, p. 14.

virtues — is that it is sufficiently deleterious or poisonous to catalytic exhaust-gas reactors to be substantially incompatible with their use. But this is apparently not true of at least some types of thermal exhaust-gas reactors. On the positive side for lead are the facts that complete lead removal from gasoline would result in valve-seat recession on many present automobiles, due to loss of lead lubrication, and that the substitution of some types of aromatics for lead until gasoline is made up of well over 50 percent aromatics may damage engine operation, though some say lead effects are worse. Auto firms now committed to a design program linked to unleaded gasoline also charge lead with corroding exhaust systems, decreasing spark-plug life, clogging exhaust recirculation devices if they are introduced, and shortening the life of crank-case oil. The magnitude or cost of these claimed effects has not been established.

In conclusion, given the prohibitive cost and pollution increasing effects of replacing lead with aromatics sufficiently to maintain present octane ratings in gasoline, lead removal tends to put us in the bind of accepting, prior to the fairly widespread use of exhaust-gas reactors, significantly lower octane gasoline, lower compression ratios in engines and their adverse effects on engine efficiency, performance, and gasoline economy, and either unchanged or somewhat increased automotive air pollution — *almost* entirely in aid of making catalytic exhaust reactors workable, and this in a context where thermal exhaust reactors, which are relatively insensitive to lead, may turn out to be equally feasible technically and economically.

Engine Changes: Compression Ratios. Let us turn now to principal pollution-connected changes in the design and adjustments of automotive engines, considering first engine compression ratios, the reduction of which is inextricably linked with plans to accommodate engines to lower octane, unleaded gasoline.

First, it is well established that increases in compression ratios of engines (gasoline octanes being adapted) result in increases in their power and efficiency, continuously over a wide range of ratios up to 14:1, but at a decreasing rate as the compression ratio increases.[16] In the currently relevant range of compression ratios, from 8:1 to 12:1 this increase is still distinctly significant. If the benefits of increasing compression ratios are taken largely in the form of gasoline economy (performance being held constant by simultaneously lowering rear-axle gear reduction ratios), controlled experiments have shown that increasing compression ratios from 8.5:1 to 10.1:1 will increase miles per gallon about 6 percent in average overall driving.[17] If the advantages of higher compression ratios are taken entirely in increased power, a movement from 8.5:1 to 10:1 should increase

[16] Kavanagh *et al.*, "High Octane Gasolines," pp. 5–7, 14–16.
[17] *Ibid.*, Charts 9–12.

brake horsepower by about 7 percent and improve acceleration performance.[18] Historical data for a cross section of basic engines in nine American auto models from 1955 to 1970 confirm this tendency.[19] With typical compression ratio increases over that 16 years of from 1 to 2 points (e.g., approximately from 8:1 to 9:1 or to 10:1), brake horsepower per cubic inch of engine displacement increased modally by 13 to 15 percent for one-point increases in compression ratios and by 22 to 25 percent for two-point increases, although associated engine design changes undoubtedly accounted for a significant part of these increases.

The effect of changing compression ratios on exhaust emissions is complicated by the fact that although lower compression ratios result in burning more gasoline per mile, they also reduce the volume of exhaust emissions per gallon of gasoline used. Thus, although reducing compression ratios from 10:1 to 8.5:1 should increase gasoline consumption per mile by about 6 percent (or from 5 to 10 percent, according to other estimates), it should decrease HC exhaust emissions *per gallon* by about 10 percent.[20] The net effect on HC emissions per mile might range from negligible to a reduction in their volume per mile of about 5 percent. A comparable reduction of NO_x emissions might result.[21]

Engine and Fuel Changes: Low Compression Plus Low Octane Gasoline. Let us now consider the combined effects on exhaust emissions of reducing engine compression ratios and using low octane, unleaded gasoline. The initially announced General Motors combination for 1971 involved compression ratios of about 8.5:1 and the use of unleaded gasoline of 91-octane rating. Putting aside for a moment the question of whether engines with 8.5:1 compression ratios will run effectively on 91-octane gasoline, the effect of this change should be to reduce the volume of HC exhaust emissions per mile approximately by from 7 to 12 percent for "regular" grade gasoline. At the same time, compensation for the removal of lead from regular grade fuel by increasing aromatics sufficiently to attain an unleaded 91-octane rating should raise the aggregate photochemical air pollutant potential of HC exhausts per mile from models that used regular fuel in 1970 by 10 percent or more. Moving from leaded premium fuel to 91-octane unleaded should reduce the potential moderately. Any reduction in NO_x emissions would contribute toward reduction of increases in the smog-forming potential of total emissions. No important reduction in CO emissions should be obtained[22] and emissions

---

[18] *Ibid.*, Charts 20, 24.
[19] Calculated from *Automotive News Almanac* (annual), 1955–70.
[20] Confidential industry source.
[21] *Ibid.*
[22] This assumes no change in fuel mixture or spark timing.

of lead-salt particulates would be eliminated. For the interim period involving the 1971 through 1974 model years prior to the scheduled introduction of exhaust-gas reactors, this appears to be a more costly package than the 1970 one, because of reduced gasoline economy and somewhat increased cost of gasoline, with net disbenefits if anything from the air pollution standpoint.

In this connection there is more than the shadow of a doubt as to whether automotive engines with 8.5:1 compression ratios will operate satisfactorily and without knocking, using 91-octane gasoline, unless the engines are detuned by retarding the spark timing. Controlled research results indicate that efficiently tuned engines with the 8.5 ratio require 94-octane gasoline for 95 percent satisfaction in performance.[23] Chrysler has stated that its 1971 models (with compression ratios of about 8.5:1) will require 94-octane gasoline for effective operation,[24] and the history of increasing compression ratios and gasoline octanes over the last 16 years reveals that when principal automotive models designed to run on regular-grade fuel had compression ratios of about 8.5:1, the regular-grade gasolines being supplied had octane ratings from 92.5 to 94. Moreover, there have been numerous instances in the last decade in which various models were advertised as designed to run on regular-grade gasoline (of 93 or 94 octane), but were not. Typically they were delivered to buyers with the engines sufficiently detuned by spark retard to avoid knocking with regular-grade gasoline, but the engines could achieve their inbuilt performance potential and efficiency only after retuning by advancing spark timing and shifting to premium-grade gasoline.

Retarding spark timing from the designed optimum as a compensatory device to adapt an engine to gasoline of insufficient octane rating (and the limit on this compensation is to adjust for about a 2.5-octane deficiency on a 100-octane scale) not only reduces performance but lessens fuel economy by 5 to 10 percent.[25] Should 91-octane gasoline prove insufficient for 8.5:1 compression ratios, compensatory spark retarding would increase operating costs and virtually aggravate the air pollution problem by increasing HC exhaust emissions. However, spark retard per se should not increase and might slightly decrease nitric oxide emissions. Alternately, a shift to 94-octane unleaded gasoline would, as indicated above, more appreciably increase the aggregate photoreactive potential of HC exhaust emissions.

The Air-Fuel Ratio in the Combustion Mixture. Another adjustment in engines that is important from an air pollution standpoint is the

[23] Kavanagh *et al.*, "High Octane Gasolines," Chapter 5.
[24] California Air Resources Board, Hearings on Fuel Composition and Emissions Control, Testimony of Mr. Bornhauser, Vice President, Chrysler Corp.
[25] W. G. Agnew, "Automotive Air Pollution Research," p. 16; and confidential industry sources.

determination of the ratio of air to fuel in the mix fed into combustion cylinders. If exhaust emissions were not a problem, the auto maker could choose between a ratio designed for maximum power (typically a relatively rich mix of about 12:1 air to fuel) and one designed for the maximum fuel economy consistent with smooth, reliable engine operation (typically a relatively lean mix of about 15:1) — or he might make a "stoichiometric" compromise between these limits, which one research endeavor has set at about 14.5:1. Unfortunately, for the automotive designer and all of us, moving toward leaner or richer air-fuel ratios has opposite effects on the emissions of different principal pollutant exhaust emissions. Briefly, a relatively rich mix such as 12:1 produces relatively high emissions of uncombusted HC's and CO but relatively low emissions of NO_x, with poor fuel economy. Leaning the mix from there up to 15:1 increases NO_x emissions by about 300 percent but reduces HC emissions by about 70 percent and carbon monoxide emissions by about 95 percent. Greater leaning of the fuel mix brings NO_x emissions down steeply and further reduces other emissions, but the very lean mixes required are incompatible with smooth and reliable engine operation.[26]

There is thus a quandary. It is desirable to keep HC and CO emissions low, which suggests a lean mix, but relatively low NO_x emissions are needed (suggesting a rich mix), particularly because NO_x in the air is critical in the process of forming the oxidants that participate in the formation of photochemical smog. In recent years, auto makers have turned toward leaner fuel mixes of the range of 14:1 to 15:1, reducing HC and CO emissions but more or less maximizing NO_x emissions. With the introduction of exhaust reactors which substantially eliminate HC and CO emissions, an indicated course appears to move toward richer fuel mixes to reduce NO_x emissions, at the expense of fuel economy. But a NO_x problem would still remain, unless a commercially satisfactory exhaust reactor that eliminates NO_x can be perfected. An auxiliary device to reduce NO_x formation by recirculating some reactor-treated exhaust gas to the combustion cylinders is well along in development, but this would result in an undetermined loss in fuel economy. All prospective systems for greatly reducing NO_x as well as HC and CO emissions threaten to be expensive because of decreased fuel economy as well as the cost of hardware.

Engine Size or Displacement. A final engine-design variable deserving mention is the displacement of the engine, or total interior volume of its combustion chambers. As noted frequently, American auto manufacturers since 1955 have on the average increased the displacements of basic engines by about 30 percent. Increasing engine displace-

---

[26] *Ibid.*, pp. 15–16; and confidential industry sources.

ments is generally the cheapest way, in terms of manufacturing costs, of increasing power. The potential of increased power has generally been exploited through linked design choices, involving rear-axle reduction ratios and carburetion, that increase performance, also increase gasoline use, and exhaust emissions unless specially controlled.[27]

In this connection, it is notable that performance can be maintained with decreased engine displacements by introducing more complex (and more expensive) transmissions, with an increased number of forward-speed gear ratios, as amply demonstrated in various European designs. We thus discover an alternate or supplementary route to decreased exhaust emissions. Also, several "semicompact" European models in 1970 and immediately previous years, with engine displacements of about 120 cubic inches (as compared, for example, to 250 cubic inches for the Chevrolet 6) and compression ratios generally in the 8.5:1 to 9.0:1 range, were obtaining ratios of brake horsepower to cubic inches of displacement as high as 0.98:1, 0.94:1 and 0.87:1 (for the Swedish Volvo and the West German BMW and Mercedes), as compared to a modal ratio slightly above 0.7:1 for basic engines in a representative cross section of American autos. This suggests that engine design alternatives are available which should both increase fuel economy and generate exhaust emissions significantly smaller than those attainable with present American designs, making feasible the reduction of engine displacements without a significant loss of performance. The European models are more expensive than full-size American "low-price" and "medium-price" models at the production volumes attained in making them. We have no data on how expensive vehicles embodying their different design features would be at Detroit production volumes.

INGREDIENTS AND MECHANISMS
OF SMOG FORMATION

Consideration of exhaust reactor devices should be prefaced by a synoptic discussion of the mechanisms and ingredients of smog formation. Neglecting such smog as is directly emitted from automotive

---

[27] As engine displacement is increased, the number of cylinders remaining constant, the total surface area of the combustion chambers increases less than proportionately with displacement (in accordance with the operation of familiar physical laws); as displacement decreases, this surface area decreases less than proportionately with displacement. Therefore, "wall-quenching" becomes proportionately less important with larger displacements; exhaust emissions of unburnt hydrocarbons should therefore increase less than proportionately with fuel consumption as displacements increase, and vice versa for decreases in displacement. In the net, however, increased displacements virtually tend to increase exhaust emissions per mile.

exhausts, atmospheric smog formation results from a complicated process of photochemical reactions, involving conversion of nitric oxide (NO) into nitrogen dioxide (NO_2) by combination with atmospheric oxygen (O_2) and the complex effects of the solar irradiation of NO_2 and unsaturated HC vapors or aerosols.

After formation NO_2 is broken down by sunlight into NO and atomic oxygen (O), wherafter oxidant gasses — primarily ozone (O_3) — are formed by reactions of O and O_2. The formation of oxidants is critical in smog formation, and that of NO_2 is critical in the formation of oxidants.

Unsaturated HC vapors or aerosols also react with O atoms under irradiation in a way that seriously builds up NO_2 and oxidant (O_3) levels. This and other mechanisms involving reactions between oxygen and NO_2 and the oxidation of unsaturated HC's combine to produce the principal end products of photochemical smog. These include aldehydes, peroxy acyl nitrates and nitrites (PAN), ozone, nitrogen dioxide, and large quantities of photochemical aerosols that contain or tend to form aldehydes, PAN, etc. To these smog products may be added carbon monoxide, particulate matter, and nonphotochemical aerosols. Weather conditions especially conducive to the formation of photochemical smog include direct sunlight, relatively still air (poor natural ventilation), and the persistence of temperature inversions.

For purposes of our further discussion, it is important to note that emissions of both NO and unsaturated HC's are critical in smog formation.

CATALYTIC AND THERMAL EXHAUST REACTORS

The primary purpose of exhaust-gas reactors and associated equipment is to eliminate or very greatly reduce emissions of uncombusted HC's, CO, and NO_x from automotive exhausts. At this writing, several types of systems are in relatively advanced stages of development, but none is known to be perfected sufficiently to justify widespread installation on new automotive vehicles; an expert panel[28] this year estimated that it would take three or four years for major design improvements to find their way into full automotive production.

In this context, there are two major types of systems based on two distinctly different types of exhaust-gas reactors (each with two or more subvarieties), with distinctly different attributes from the standpoint of fuel requirements, between which auto makers must choose in the near term. The risks of making an ultimately inferior choice seem quite significant if the expert panel referred to is correct in telling us in one breath that, because exhaust emissions technology is

[28] United States Department of Commerce, Technical Advisory Panel, "Implications of Lead Removal," p. 23.

evolving rapidly, governmental regulations should account for and encourage innovation, and in the next breath that it is imperative that the automotive industry should make the major choice by early in 1971.[29]

The two major types of exhaust emissions control systems are based respectively on a thermal exhaust-gas reactor (exhaust afterburner) and a catalytic reactor. To make a choice between them, or to decide which offers the economically more attractive alternative, one needs to compare their efficacy in reducing noxious exhaust emissions, the service lives of their major components, their initial and maintenance costs, their costs in extra or more expensive fuel consumed, the effects on automotive performances associated with their adoption, and so forth. Unfortunately for us at this time, we are unable to make any close comparisons of the alternative systems in the form they will have assumed in 1973 or 1974, and in addition the developers of the system, auto producers and others, have been remarkably stingy in releasing specific cost and related information concerning their devices in their present stage of development,[30] although various broad qualitative claims have been made.

About all we can do at this juncture is to review available information on the characteristics, strengths, and weaknesses of the systems and their subvarieties in their present stages of development, and possibly arrive at some tentative qualitative judgments. We should be dealing here not with a cost-minimization problem, but rather with one of finding an optimal relationship of costs to benefits, in a context where benefits and disbenefits are more numerous than the single benefit of erasing specified automotive exhaust missions.

Thermal Exhaust Reactor Systems. A thermal exhaust-gas reactor (EGR) is a high-temperature chamber, attached to the engine next to its exhaust ports, in which hot exhaust gases made up of HC's and CO complete their oxidation — in simple terms, an enlarged and specially lined and insulated exhaust manifold receiving sufficient air to accomplish the effects described.[31] The apparently feasible subvarieties include (1) a "rich" exhaust-gas reactor (REGR) requiring a moderately rich fuel mixture in the combustion cylinders and an engine-driven pump to inject air, and operating at internal temperatures of about 1700° F.; and (2) a "lean" reactor (LEGR) that operates with a very lean engine fuel mixture (i.e., one with excess air), thus deals with a lower output of unburned HC's, requires no air pump, and operates at lower internal temperatures.[32]

[29] *Ibid.*, pp. 6, 23.
[30] *Business Week*, "On the Inside Track in the Muffler Race," May 2, 1970, p. 112.
[31] Agnew, "Automotive Air Pollution Research," pp. 14, 18.
[32] United States Department of Commerce, Technical Advisory Panel, "Implications of Lead Removal," pp. 18–19.

According to their strong proponents, both thermal reactors are entirely compatible with the use of typical leaded gasoline and should have service lives equal to the life of an automobile.[33] The expert panel referred to concurs on lead compatibility in the case of the LEGR, but not in that of the REGR. This compatibility with typical leaded gasoline, for one or both types of thermal reactors, constitutes a large plus in their favor, since their use need not involve the losses in auto performance and fuel economy associated with lowered engine compression ratios (or, alternatively, with the substantially increased cost of high octane unleaded gasoline).

According to the panel, the REGR operated with a semirich fuel mixture would reduce fuel economy by 5 to 15 percent below that of an engine with no reactor; its major proponent characterizes the fuel-economy reduction as "small." All parties seem agreed that little or no fuel-economy penalty is incurred with the LEGR. In its present state it has the virtual disadvantage of requiring close control of the air-fuel mix fed to the engine, and of its distribution among cylinders, thus posing some added production problems. Both types of thermal reactor are difficult to install on the fat V-8 engine, because of frame interference, but easy to install on an in-line engine.[34] This may constitute an important disadvantage to American auto makers, with their heavy past investments in perfecting V-8 engines, but not necessarily a significant disadvantage to the public, if we consider undoubted European success in developing high performance and economical in-line engines with four or six cylinders.

Neither type of thermal reactor considered here will reduce NO_x emissions sufficiently to meet forthcoming air pollution control standards, and both will require either an exhaust-recirculation device that feeds a small fraction of reactor-treated exhaust back into the engine combustion chambers (thus lowering combustion temperatures and keeping NO_x formation within tolerable limits) or an alternative supplementary device that might be developed. Information on the efficacy of such a recirculation device seems scarce, and we have not seen a believable estimate, made by a disinterested party, of the fuel-economy loss associated with exhaust recirculation. It may be appreciable.

To bring a thermal reactor system using leaded gasoline up to full parity in emissions control with a very effective catalytic reactor system using unleaded gasoline, the thermal system needs additionally a supplementary lead particulate trap placed on the exhaust line beyond the reactor. As understood, it would involve a trap chamber and a cyclonic precipitator. There are working prototypes of par-

[33] California Air Resources Board, Hearings on Fuel Composition and Emissions Control, Testimony of Mr. Dawson, Vice President, duPont Co.; and of Mr. Blanchard, Executive Vice President, Ethyl Corp.

[34] United States Department of Commerce, Technical Advisory Panel, "Implications of Lead Removal," pp. 19–20.

ticulate traps that remove 65 percent of lead particulates from the exhaust, and those who are developing them expect to achieve 90 percent removal.

Estimates of the cost of thermal reactor systems are scanty and also vary widely. One organization engaged in developing this system has estimated the fabricated cost of one good thermal reactor at $22, and the cost of a lead particulate trap at about the same amount.[35] We have not seen estimates of the cost of an exhaust-gas recirculator, but it should be relatively low. The panel referred to, after stating that the LEGR would be less expensive than a REGR, estimated the cost of thermal exhaust reactors as between $150 and $300 apiece, including some oven temperature control, but evidently not including the cost of a particulate trap. These estimates of reactor cost are astoundingly different, and from extraneous information the smaller estimate seems unrealistically low, and the larger estimate probably high.

In sum, with respect to thermal exhaust reactor systems, the LEGR version appears to have substantial net advantages in terms of initial cost, fuel economy, and lesser high temperature problems as mounted in the engine compartment.

Catalytic Exhaust Reactor Systems. A catalytic exhaust-gas reactor is a mufflerlike chamber, placed close to the exhaust manifold, through which hot exhaust gases are passed. The reactor contains one or more beds of catalytic material which induce reactions in the exhaust gases that convert unburnt HC's and CO into carbon dioxide and water, and in some versions also induce reduction of NO_x. These reactors are mechanically simple but use very expensive catalytic materials, the durability of which is a problem. They are generally incompatible with typical leaded gasolines, which rapidly deteriorate the catalysts, and must be run with fuel that is either lead-free or contains only miniscule amounts of lead.[36] In evaluating their costs, it must be remembered that to any fuel-economy losses associated with their use must be added a further economy loss of about 6 percent if they are coupled with low-compression engines.

The simplest variety of catalytic reactor being seriously considered uses a single bed of oxidizing catalyst that induces oxidation of HC's and CO but does not control NO_x emissions. Thus it must be coupled (like thermal reactors) with exhaust-gas recirculation systems to reduce NO_x formation. The reactor is run with a relatively rich air-fuel mixture, which imposes a fuel-economy penalty of about 5 percent. This penalty, added to that of a low-compression engine, results in a gross penalty of about 10 percent in increased fuel use, as compared

[35] California Air Resources Board, Hearings on Fuel Composition and Emissions Control, Testimony of Mr. Diggs of duPont Co.

[36] United States Department of Commerce, Technical Advisory Board Panel, "Implications of Lead Removal," pp. 20–21.

to none for a thermal LEGR (estimated ultimate added cost to motorists, $30 apiece or an aggregate of $3 billion annually). The fuel cost penalty could not be reduced by shifting to expensive nonleaded high octane gasoline compatible with high-compression engines. A trap for lead particulates would not be needed, so the cost of that would be avoided, and this is generally true for lead-sensitive catalytic reactors. The panel referred to reported that considerable testing will be required before this simple catalytic reactor is a proven device. A major present problem, not encountered with thermal reactors, is attrition of the catalyst in rough driving.[37]

A second variety under consideration is a dual-bed catalytic device, incorporating an oxidizing bed of catalyst to induce oxidation of HC's and CO, and a reducing bed to dispose of NO_X. Its effective operation again requires a fuel-rich mix, and its total fuel-economy penalty is about the same 10 percent attributed to the simple oxidizing device. Total catalyst costs are undoubtedly higher, but the costs of exhaust-gas recirculation to reduce NO_X formation are avoided. It is reported that the dual-bed device is subject to an emissions penalty during the warmup of the oxidizing bed, the seriousness of which is not appraised.[38] Attrition of the catalysts with rough driving is presumably also a problem with this version of a catalytic reactor.

A third variety considered is a single-bed device that removes HC's, CO, and NO_X. Though virtually attractive, its operation requires very highly precise control of fuel-air mixtures used in combustion, sufficiently precise that an improvement in present carburetion techniques, or possibly a shift to fuel injection with a feedback control, would be required. The panel referred to above concluded that associated technical risks and coordinating problems make development of this device by 1975 less than promising.[39]

We have discovered no cost data on these catalytic exhaust reactors to compare with varying cost estimates for thermal reactors, other than a business-periodical estimate that one would cost $100 to $150.[40] A total catalytic system would require at least one less supplementary device than a thermal system using leaded gasoline — namely a lead particulate trap — and possibly two less, in varieties that do not require exhaust-gas recirculation. Nonetheless, the high cost of catalytic materials is such that one would not expect a huge original-cost advantage for any catalytic system, and such advantage as it might have would probably be offset by fuel-economy penalties associated with the more promising catalytic systems.

Tentative Evaluation of Thermal versus Catalytic Devices. It is evidently too early to decide at all firmly which type of exhaust reactor

---

[37] *Ibid.,* p. 21.
[38] *Ibid.,* p. 22.
[39] *Ibid.,* p. 21.
[40] *Business Week,* "The Muffler Race."

system will or would turn out to be superior in terms of relationships of costs to benefits, but we can observe the straws in the wind. The critical comparison at this time would seem to be between a thermal system based on the LEGR reactor, on the one hand, and a catalytic system based either on a single-bed oxidizing catalyst or on a dual-bed of oxidizing and NO_x reducing catalyst.

The two systems apparently promise to be about comparably effective in eliminating HC's, CO, NO_x and lead particulate exhaust emissions, though the dual-bed catalytic system has the bonus advantage of circumventing the technical and cost uncertainties associated with exhaust-gas recirculation, and probably of accomplishing a higher percentage reduction in NO_x emissions.

The LEGR-based thermal system has the distinct advantage, because of its compatibility with customary leaded gasoline, of permitting the continued use of high-compression engines with their superior performance and efficiency, without the large cost penalty associated with producing high octane unleaded gasoline. This advantage looms larger if one feels that there is a substantial risk that after emission-control systems are introduced, American auto makers will replay their past rivalry to produce high-performance engines by increasing compression ratios up to 1970 levels.

Initial plus gasoline costs of using the two systems, assuming the catalytic system would continue to be linked with low-compression engines and low octane fuel, promise to be roughly comparable. If the catalytic system were used with high-compression engines and high octane unleaded fuels, it would probably have a distinct cost disadvantage as compared to the LEGR-based thermal system.

An important unknown in the problem, as noted, involves the efficacy of, and possible cost and other penalties associated with, exhaust recirculation devices, which are linked to thermal systems but not to the dual-bed catalytic system. If such a possible cost penalty turned out to be sizable (e.g., imposing a fuel-economy penalty of 10 percent or more), the comparative position of the dual-bed catalytic system would improve. If the penalty were negligible or small, the LEGR-based thermal system seems probably superior in terms of the relation of costs to benefits.

Putting this issue aside, a further consideration involves the comparative service life, durability, and maintenance costs of the thermal and catalytic systems. Although the thermal system includes more components than the dual-bed catalytic system (an added exhaust recirculator and a lead particulate trap), it is composed throughout of strong metals or other materials and would probably be fairly rugged under actual service conditions and would require relatively low maintenance costs. A catalytic system, by contrast, is very probably more fragile intrinsically, as is suggested by expert opinions that its catalysts are subject to attrition by rough driving. This would suggest a higher cost of maintenance or replacement of components.

Subject to a reservation concerning possible costs and other disadvantages of exhaust-gas recirculators, we find the LEGR thermal system to be preferable at this time, and this leads us strongly to support a policy of pushing its development hard and not precluding its introduction by making a premature decision in favor of a catalytic system.

EVALUATION OF THE PRODUCT STRATEGIES
OF THE AUTO INDUSTRY

On the background developed above, let us turn to an end appraisal of the previously outlined Detroit strategies for product changes.

The Interim Strategy. The interim strategy of lowering engine compression ratios and pushing the use of low octane unleaded gasoline from 1971 to 1974 should contribute toward meeting progressively severe gross but unselective HC emission standards, and may help in meeting slightly more severe NO_x emission standards. But it does not promise to reduce appreciably the aggregate smog-forming potential of exhaust emissions per vehicle mile, and in addition is distinctly costly in gasoline consumption and reduced vehicle performance. Even allowing for appreciably reduced lead particulate emissions, this interim strategy is evidently not worth its cost in terms of reducing air pollution before 1975 — and especially not because of uncertainties concerning the adequacy of 91-octane gasoline to fulfill the needs of 8.5 : 1 compression ratios.[41] The strategy looks slightly better from an emissions standpoint if low-lead gasoline is used instead of no-lead, but this raises the question of why the lead content of gasoline should be curtailed drastically or at all during the interim period.

One argument advanced for the apparently premature introduction of engines that run on unleaded gasoline is that it will provide a needed incentive for petroleum refiners gradually to augment their capacity to produce aromatics to replace lead in gasoline as an octane booster. But the incentive provided is actually small, and the petroleum refiners very probably do not need this sort of incentive anyway. If asked only progressively to substitute 91-octane unleaded gasoline for leaded regular and premium grade gasoline, large refiners can generally comply with at most only a very modest gradual increase in present capacities to produce aromatics. A big increase

---

[41] This problem potentially remains except for Chevrolet engines in 1971 models in which General Motors has actually dropped the compression ratio to 8 : 1, and American Motors sixes. Such a reduction of compression ratios does not greatly alter the judgment offered above, when the counterbalancing of slightly increased gasoline use against slightly lowered exhaust emissions per gallon of gasoline is considered.

would be required only if after 1974 they were asked to produce *high octane* unleaded gasoline for high-compression engines. If that is a presumption, the automotive firms haven't mentioned it. Should the automotive producers project a distinctly increasing need for aromatics production beginning in 1975 (linked to an anticipated restoration of high compression ratios), what petroleum refiners require is something like a three-year advance promise from the automotive industry that this need will arise. Such a promise should represent as negotiable a currency as recent promises to reduce compression ratios and shift to low octane, low- or no-lead, and comparatively low-aromatics gasoline.

Another reason advanced for an otherwise premature shift to low-compression engines is the standard Detroit argument that auto producers require a 30-month lead time from decision to implementation in introducing design changes. This is hardly applicable to engines with approximately 8.5:1 compression ratios, of which American firms produced a few tens of millions in the model years from 1958 through 1962, having adequate opportunity to develop and perfect them. The one technique they might have to learn is how to make an 8.5:1 engine run efficiently on 91-octane gasoline.

On balance, we conclude that the interim strategy now being pursued by the automotive industry is uneconomic in that it involves substantial added costs — generally not borne by the automotive firms — while yielding at best rather slight benefits, and that it is being implemented quite prematurely, even if the ultimate choice is made in favor of a catalytic exhaust-gas reactor that is incompatible with leaded gasoline. There is a distinct suspicion in some quarters that the automotive producers have already made a provisional decision in favor of catalytic reactors. In this connection, it is pertinent to paraphrase the statement of one petroleum firm executive to the effect that the lack of experience with catalytic exhaust reactors and need for their fuller development before introduction makes a massive move by petroleum refiners (as encouraged by automotive producers) to produce unleaded gasolines premature.[42] To this we might add that the announced interim strategy of the automotive industry bears markings of a grandstand play, directed in considerable part toward deterring governmental agencies and legislatures from exploring and perhaps requiring quite different redesign strategies that are not of the automotive firms' choosing.

Alternatives to the Interim Strategy. We have already suggested that a more efficient interim strategy might be to retain previous high-

---

[42] California Air Resources Board, Hearings on Fuel Composition and Emissions Control, Testimony of Mr. Burnap, Executive Vice President, Continental Oil Co.

compression ratios for most of the 1971 through 1974 period, using leaded gasoline, and to notify the petroleum refining industry by sometime in 1971 what type of exhaust-gas reactor system had been chosen for introduction in 1975 models and whether or not compression ratios would be low in those and later models. This strategy would be less costly, overall, would not result in an appreciably greater aggregate smog-forming potential in 1971 through 1974 models, and should not be significantly hampered by lead-time problems.

A more attractive alternative interim strategy would be to do about the same thing, but also to reduce engine displacements appreciably. Given the substantial power surplus built into typical 1970 engines, which is overdue for elimination, a reduction in typical V-8 engine displacements of from 15 to 20 percent, and in six-cylinder engines of 10 percent or more, compression ratios being moderate and design choices adapted, would lead to a loss of performance that would hardly be missed by most drivers, would reduce fuel costs, and could be made to rate somewhat better from an air pollution standpoint than the present interim strategy. Moreover, such a strategy might create needed incentives for American automotive producers to develop engines that yield more horsepower per cubic inch of displacement. Lead-time problems would not be serious, because of prolonged industry experience with smaller-displacement engines. But this strategy probably appears to be an appreciably less profitable one to American automotive producers.

The Choice of an Exhaust-Gas Reactor System. The second strategic choice to be made by automotive producers is that between catalytic and thermal exhaust-gas reactor systems. The comparative merits of these systems in their present stage of development and the uncertainty as to which will turn out to be preferable have been discussed above.

Because of this uncertainty, it is very unfortunate that in making this choice automotive producers evidently do need something like their standard 30-month lead time between decision and implementation, largely because of complementary engine-design changes which will be associated with the adoption of either type of reactor system. In the improvement of the alternative systems, lead time is not so fixed; developers of either device need as much time as they can be allowed to improve and perfect their devices. However, an early choice of type is needed in order to allow for building of capacity to produce the selected type of reactor system. In this connection it is interesting that the development of exhaust-gas reactors, both catalytic and thermal, has been left by American auto makers in important part to other, nonautomotive firms. At least eleven different firms are considered "in the running" as potential suppliers of catalytic systems,[43] and duPont Company and Ethyl Corporation (both suppliers of tetraethyl lead) are leading in the development of thermal systems and in their vigorous promotion.[44]

The decision that American automotive producers will make is currently open to conjecture, although certain considerations suggest that they are more likely than not to select a catalytic reactor system. First, their very early implementation of plans to supply engines that run on unleaded gasoline and to encourage petroleum refiners to increase their capacity to supply it might be read not simply as a move to leave their options open (for only six or nine months) in choosing between reactors — the official explanation — but as an indicator that they have already tentatively decided in favor of a lead-incompatible catalytic reactor.

Second, the production difficulties likely to be encountered in fitting thermal-reactor exhaust manifolds into an engine compartment already crowded by a V-8 engine is likely to be a deterrent to the adoption of a thermal exhaust-gas reactor system. And the profits of automotive producers would probably be hurt if they overcame this problem by investing heavily in the further perfection of in-line four- or six-cylinder engines which would easily accommodate thermal-reactor manifolds, even though the buying public would not suffer much if any net loss.

Third, any adverse effect on the profits of automotive producers is likely to be less if they introduce a reactor with lower initial cost and higher costs of maintenance and of fuel, than if they introduce a reactor with a higher initial cost which is fully offset by better fuel economy and lower maintenance costs — this on the theory that automotive buyers are likely to be more sensitive to immediately visible increases in the purchase prices of new vehicles than to poorly apprehended increases in the costs of vehicle operation.

In general, supposing that the two types of reactor systems would be about equally effective, we may have a situation in which the choice that is most profitable or least unprofitable to automotive producers is different from the choice that would be most economical to the public. But if the decision is left up to the automotive producers, the most profitable choice from their standpoint is likely to be made.

CONCLUSION

It is an adage that the principal disadvantage of monopoly (and thus of joint monopoly exercised by a very few oligopolists) is that monopoly unduly concentrates a large amount of discretionary power

[43] *Business Week,* "The Muffler Race," p. 112.

[44] California Air Resources Board, Hearings on Fuel Composition and Emissions Control, Testimony by officers and personnel of duPont Co. and Ethyl Corp.

over prices, product designs, and other things in the hands of very few people. To which it may be added that this discretionary power is likely to be exercised in a manner consistent with maximal profits for those holding it.

We encounter this disadvantage in the case of the American automotive industry, unless countermeasures are taken to remedy it. It is dangerous to leave the choice of the type of redesign of automobiles to accomplish given goals of reducing air pollution almost entirely to the discretion of three large firms, one of which is comparatively dominant, when their pursuit of profits is likely to lead to decisions that are suboptimal from the standpoint of the public. Governmental authority, administrative and legislative, probably should play a more active role in determining the choice to be made, by assuming unto itself a significant share of the discretionary power now held by the private industry.[45] Doing this effectively in the case at hand would require developing really sophisticated expertise in the area of automotive engineering within the personnel of governmental agencies, and a heavier reliance of legislative bodies on the recommendations of genuinely independent experts in the area. But the episode we have been discussing suggests strongly that, from a social standpoint, this sort of development should more than repay its costs.

AUTHOR'S NOTE, 1971

After this manuscript was sent to press late in 1970, the following developments of relevance to the preceding text ensued. First, General Motors announced its decision to use an exhaust-gas control system based on some oxidizing catalytic reactor and an exhaust-gas recirculation device for limiting NO_x emissions — to be installed on some 1973 models and all 1975 models. The system is incompatible with leaded gasoline.

Second, on December 18, 1970, Congress passed a Clean Air Act (Public Law 91-604) which requires a reduction of permissible emissions per mile from automobiles to 90 percent below the emission levels permitted by federal law in 1971, this 90 percent reduction to be accomplished for HC and CO emissions by 1975, and for NO_x emissions by 1976. These represent extremely stringent emissions standards.

SUPPLEMENTARY READINGS

1. California Air Resources Board, *Air Pollution Control in California* (Annual Report), Sacramento, Calif., 1970.
2. Robert S. Decker, "The Dynamics of Unconventional Motor Vehicles and the Reduction of Air Pollution," *Western Economic Journal*, 8, December, 1970, pp. 357–363.

[45] Cf. Chapter 2, p. 51.

3. B. Dimitriades, B. H. Eccleston, and R. W. Hurn, "An Evaluation of the Fuel Factor Through Direct Measurement of Photochemical Reactivity of Emissions," *Journal of the Air Pollution Control Association,* 20, March, 1970, pp. 158–159.
4. John Espositor et al., *Vanishing Air,* New York, Grossman Publishers, 1970, Chapter 2 ("The Auto Industry").
5. Institute of Public Administration, *Governmental Approaches to Air Pollution Control,* Washington, D.C., 1971.
6. A. Jamison, *The Steam Powered Automobile,* Bloomington, Ind., Indiana University Press, 1970.
7. Allen V. Kneese, "Air Pollution Control — General Background and Some Economic Aspects," in *The Economics of Air Pollution,* Harold Wolozen, ed., New York, W. W. Norton, 1966, pp. 23–39.
8. Lester B. Lave and Eugene D. Seskin, "Air Pollution and Human Health," *Science,* 169, August, 1970, pp. 723–733.
9. Edwin S. Mills, "Economic Incentives in Air Pollution Control," in *The Economics of Air Pollution,* Harold Wolozen, ed., New York, W. W. Norton, 1966, pp. 40–50.
10. Ronald G. Ridker, *Economic Costs of Air Pollution,* New York, Praeger, 1967.
11. U.S. Department of Commerce, Technical Advisory Board Panel on Automotive Fuels and Air Pollution, *The Implication of Lead Removal from Automotive Fuels* (an interim report), Washington, D.C., 1970 (mimeo).

6 Environmental Issues and Policies Concerning Rural Recreational Resources

INTRODUCTION

A very significant aspect of the total environments of a majority of Americans is provided by rural natural resources that supply or support recreational benefits. These are the recreational resources that are distinctly out of town, and that are typically used recreationally on annual or other vacations of a week or more and on weekend trips. We will confine our attention here to rural recreational resources — in fact, only to a major part of them — neglecting equally significant outdoor recreational resources within or closely proximate to cities and metropolitan areas.

Our citizens' use of rural recreational resources has increased progressively and severalfold over recent time. This is attributable in some part to population growth, but more to markedly increasing affluence for most of the population, the very rapid spread in the ownership of automobiles, and the concurrent rapid augmentation and improvement of rural highways and roads. Even from 1955 to 1970, records kept for principal rural recreational sites suggest that recreational visits per year to rural areas more than doubled.

This rapid expansion in public vacationing has created a demand for the use for recreation of much more of our rural natural resources than heretofore. And it has tended generally to produce crowding or congestion at attractive and readily accessible rural recreation sites, as the provision of ready access to added sites has lagged badly behind the growing demand. This is one of the problems that will concern us here, but there have concurrently been other developments that have had at least equal impact on the quality of our rural recreational environment.

Because this is an essay and not a monograph or tome, we will not endeavor to deal with the "congestion problem," or with the other developments just mentioned, with reference to all types of rural natural resources that support recreation (we will omit mention of deserts and seashores), or with reference to recreational environment that is predominantly created by large capital investments — such as skiing facilities and golf courses. Rather we will center attention on the two seemingly most important broad categories of recreational resource: (a) inland water resources and (b) forests or forest land.

Concerning water and forest resources suitable for rural recreation, we will be concerned with three sorts of development (or nondevelopment) which have had clear impacts on our rural recreational environments:

1. A rapid progressive "development" of our rivers for commercial uses through the building of dams and associated reservoirs that are used (for a variety of purposes) drastically to modify natural time patterns of streamflows, as well as to divert streamflows for uses away from streams. This development is progressively and on a broad scale substituting large numbers of not particularly attractive still-water reservoirs for naturally flowing streams as recreational resources.

2. The progressive destruction of forest habitat and watersheds — mainly but not entirely on privately owned forest lands — through destructive logging practices that disregard their adverse external effects on the forest environment. These effects include prominently promotion of erosion, lessening of the capacity of forest land to support reproduction of trees, severe degradation of myriad small streams, and increases in the intensity of floods and flood damage within and outside forest areas.

3. The failure of federal, state, and other governmental agencies (and private owners of forest land) to provide relatively easy access to the greatly increased amount of forest land that by now would have high recreational values if made easily accessible — coupled with badly lagging programs to set aside greatly increased amounts of forest land as recreational preserves not available for logging or other commercial uses.

(The first and third of these developments involve mainly the allocation of natural resources among uses, which has been subjected to abstract analysis on pp. 22–28 of Chapter 1. The second involves external environmental costs of private production, analyzed on an abstract level on pp. 11–20 of the first chapter.)

We will discuss these problems below in the order just enumerated, considering in each case both the scope and nature of the difficulty,

and remedial public policies that seem appropriate. Before beginning this discussion, however, a word of caution is in order. Because
of the great diversity of preferences among groups and individuals
concerning the sort of rural recreation they want (if any) and a similar diversity of value judgments concerning the significance of the
problems enumerated, it is quite impossible to discover a strong consensus attitude toward any of these problems. Among those favoring
water-oriented recreation, a large group prefers still-water recreation
(including water skiing, boat fishing, power-boat cruising, etc.),
whereas a group either larger or smaller prefers recreation based on
free-running streams. Of those who visit forests, some prefer to camp
in congested crowds, others want various measures of privacy and
solitude, and still others seek true "wilderness" areas. And the degree
of concern with the destruction of forest habitat by bad logging practices varies greatly among individuals and groups. As proposed remedial policy measures aimed at the problems are considered, some
considerable effort must be made to be objective about such varieties
of attitudes and to weigh policy alternatives accordingly.

A final prefatory remark is necessary. Although we have a very
affluent society generally, families with incomes in the lowest 15 or
20 percent within the population generally lack very much or any
access to rural recreational resources; for them the "great outdoors,"
and the quality of its recreational resources are not especially meaningful. There is thus likely to be a noticeable income-distribution bias
in evaluations of rural recreation environment and of policies affecting it in most of the writing on these matters (including this essay).
Deep concern with the problems discussed here rests on some system
of priorities concerning what environmental problems deserve major
attention.

ENVIRONMENTAL CONSEQUENCES OF LARGE-SCALE
RIVER DEVELOPMENTS

The natural flows of fresh-water streams, in addition to providing
valuable recreational habitat, may be exploited for a number of non-
recreational commercial uses. These include the supply of water for
agricultural irrigation and for domestic, commercial, and industrial
purposes. They include also the generation of hydroelectric power,
whenever the gradients of streams are steep enough that the force of
falling water is sufficient efficiently to drive power-generating turbines, and, selectively, the provision of navigable watercourses valuable in commerce. And because, if uncontrolled, streamflows also
may destroy property and even lives by periodic floods, controlling
floods with dams and reservoirs is a significant commercial development of rivers.

The systematic fluctuation of streamflows within years (and also
between years), moreover, has the effect of diminishing their values

in productive uses, because the time patterns of streamflow water supplies differ significantly from the time patterns of demands for their use, with a resultant lessening of their commercial values. Thus, for example, streamflows are typically at their largest during winters and periods of spring snowmelts, and in surplus supply relative to demands for their use; in summer and early fall periods they are, respectively, smaller and smallest, and in short supply relative to demands for their use.

The major economic purpose of constructing dams on streams is to impound or store streamflows in reservoirs in periods of economically surplus natural flow, and then later to release the stored water in periods of economically deficient natural flow — thus improving the coordination of the time pattern of below-dam released flows with the time patterns of demands for streamflows. At the same time that dams perform this basic function, they may perform a number of related ones. One is the raising of the level of water impounded in reservoirs well above stream-bed levels to concentrate at one point a long and steep "drop" of water through pipes or other conduits into electricity-generating turbines, with increased velocity and turbine-driving power (returning the diverted water to the stream either just below the dam or some distance downstream). In addition, dams are frequently used as diversion points from which water is artificially conveyed in aqueducts to offstream locations for "consumptive" use in irrigation or for domestic, commercial, and industrial purposes — correspondingly reducing the annual flow of the stream. Finally, they are used to regulate the below-dam flow of the stream — with successive accumulation and release of river flow — to reduce the probability of floods and in some cases to sustain navigability of streams.

In any event, reservoirs behind onstream dams are generally built to be "filled up" (retarding streamflow) and "drained down" (augmenting streamflow) in a regular periodicity. They are thus typically artificial lakes of markedly fluctuating levels, located best to produce commercial as distinct from recreational value.

The Explosive Recent Increase in River Development. We have had considerable dam-reservoir development of our rivers with us for a very long time, but for most of that time this development did not faintly approach imposing severe regulation and alteration of the character of the bulk of our myriad streams. Since the mid-1930's, however, and particularly since the end of World War II, we have witnessed a literally explosive increase in river development, which is well along the way to altering irreversibly the primary characteristics of our inland water resources. By far the largest and most important new developments — and the largest addition to onstream reservoir capacity — has been made by the federal government under Congressional authorization and financing.

Its principal instruments in this development have been the

Bureau of Reclamation of the Interior Department (limited by law to river developments in the seventeen westernmost states — ex Alaska and Hawaii[1]), and the Corps of Engineers of the United States Army, which may operate anywhere in the United States. Both agencies are charged with the primary responsibility of planning and building multipurpose and single-purpose river development projects. Both are powerful bureaucracies which promote river projects, and both enjoy strong Congressional support, stemming from the desires of Congressmen to secure federally financed public works for their states. As Congressional and bureaucratic policies have developed since the 1930's, the Bureau and the Corps have become predominantly concerned with huge projects oriented to the comprehensive development of the waters of entire major river basins, with tendencies toward leaving few if any significant streams in a river basin undeveloped.

Some notion of the magnitude of this still-galloping program of river development is supplied by statistics describing the extent of dam-reservoir developments constructed or operated (or both) by the Bureau and the Corps by about 1970. In that year, the Bureau of Reclamation had constructed or was operating, or both, 239 reservoirs with the staggering aggregate storage capacity of 165,767,000 acre feet of water. A substantial majority of this capacity had been constructed since World War II, and nearly all of it since the mid-1930's. A very large fraction of Bureau resorvoir capacity was concentrated in the California Central Valley, the Columbia River Basin, the Colorado River Basin, and the Missouri River Basin, with a scattering of the remainder among several smaller river basin projects.[2]

The Corps of Engineers, as of June 30, 1968, controlled 121 multipurpose (with power generation or irrigation or municipal water supply functions in addition to flood control) reservoirs, with an aggregate storage capacity of 155,968,000 acre feet of water (almost as much as the Bureau of Reclamation total). Nearly half of this capacity was in the Missouri River Basin (which originates east of the Continental Divide in Montana and Wyoming) and comprised essentially a large part of the Bureau's Missouri River Basin Project. Corps dams and reservoirs also provided minor but significant complements to the Bureau's facilities in its Columbia River Basin Project and its California Central Valley Project. Otherwise, the Corps had distinctly major dam-reservoir development in the Texas-Oklahoma-Arkansas-Kansas river complex, in the central border (Mason-Dixon line) states, and in the southeastern United States, as well as lesser developments elsewhere. Over 90 percent of the total reservoir ca-

[1] The eastern fringe of these seventeen states comprise North Dakota, South Dakota, Nebraska, Kansas, Oklahoma, and Texas.

[2] Bureau of Reclamation, *Statistical Compilation of Storage Dams and Reservoirs on Bureau of Reclamation Projects, June 30, 1970* (Washington, D.C.: 1970).

pacity referred to had been completed since the end of World War II.[3] This listing for the Corps omitted its very numerous single-purpose flood control reservoirs (generally of small to moderate size) which are scattered across the country, in a number estimated by extrapolation of data from 1960 as at least 300.

With Bureau plus multipurpose Corps reservoir capacity totalling about 322 million acre feet, nearly all completed since the mid-1930's and most of it since 1950, it would appear that in the last thirty-five years, primarily in the last twenty-five, the Bureau and the Corps have constructed more reservoir capacity in the United States than existed in total in the mid-1930's, and have generally done so with much more massive dams and reservoirs possessing much more stream-altering potential than was familiar theretofor.

Of course, not all river development has been carried on by these two federal water agencies. Prior to the middle 1930's, a very large amount — a preponderant proportion — of dam-reservior development had been undertaken by privately owned public utilities for hydroelectric power production, by municipalities for securing urban water supply, by local public irrigation districts, and by state and local agencies for a variety of purposes. The geographical distribution across the country of these developments and their primary purposes, of course, depended on the water-consuming population, on the relative abundance or scarcity of rivers, on terrain (especially important for hydroelectric power generation), and on the presence or absence of considerable demands for irrigation water. The demand for some flood control has been perhaps most widespread, though with differences in intensity among regions. By the mid-1930's, nonfederal agencies were mainly responsible for a national reservoir storage capacity (excluding natural lakes) that has been variously estimated within a range of from 125 to 175 million acre feet[4] (which we may compare with over 300 million acre feet added by the Bureau and the Corps since that time).

The nonfederal agencies have, of course, been active too in developing dams and reservoirs since the mid-1930's. We lack comprehensive and organized national data on the exact amount of their contributions, but sampling of developments in several states suggest that the nonfederal addition to reservoir capacity over the last thirty-seven years has not exceeded 20 percent of the federal addition, and is probably closer to 15 percent.

Given this explosive recent increase in river development, a pertinent question is how far we have proceeded down the path of placing major dam-reservoir interferences on every river with a significant flow and how much we have left of free-flowing and substantially un-

[3] Untitled printed report of the Corps of Engineers (Washington, D.C.: 1968).
[4] Cf. Outdoor Recreation Resources Review Commission, *Water for Recreation — Values and Opportunities*, Washington, D.C., 1962, p. 4.

dammed "wild" rivers. The data available for determining this are in such unorganized and scattered form that half of a man-year of work would be required to answer even with rough estimates. Sample calculations for three states, however, suggest that we are well along in the process of universal damming, and that wild rivers are becoming increasingly a very scarce natural resource.

Every one of the even slightly significant rivers (about twenty in number) that flow from adjacent mountains into the great Central Valley of California (450 miles long and from thirty to sixty miles wide) is significantly developed with dams and reservoirs, with the reservoir storage capacity on individual rivers typically ranging from 20 to 80 percent of the annual flow of the river, and exceeding 100 percent on three rivers. No wild rivers flow into the Central Valley. The same is substantially true for all coastal rivers south of the San Francisco metropolitan area, and for all such rivers as there are in Southern California. There are two major, substantially wild rivers in northwestern California that flow into the Pacific — the Klamath and the Eel. The third major previously wild river of the area, the Trinity, has been severely tamed (with reservoirs having a capacity of over 60 percent of its large flow) since 1960, and both the federal agencies and the California Department of Water Resources have well-developed plans for similarly damming the Klamath and the Eel. In addition, there are about seven minor coastal streams between the San Francisco area and the northern border of California that are still substantially wild rivers.[5]

In the much less populous state of Washington, the great Columbia River proper is of course highly developed with a series of dams which support reservoirs with a total capacity of over 16 million acre feet of water (about 11 percent of the annual flow of the Columbia near its mouth). In that part of the Columbia River basin that lies in Washington, every one of its eleven principal tributaries has been dammed — six to a major extent and five to a very minor extent. Of the nine significant coastal rivers of Washington that flow directly to the Pacific, all are dammed — three to a major extent and the rest in a minor way.[6] A number of sizeable rivers in that state have thus as yet not moved very far out of the wild-river category — largely because the onstream Columbia developments have provided a superfluity of hydroelectric power and because irrigation demands are comparatively small.

The third state we examined was Pennsylvania, as perhaps typical of a populous and industrialized large state on the northeastern sea-

[5] See J. S. Bain, R. E. Caves, and J. Margolis, *Northern California's Water Industry* (Baltimore: Johns Hopkins Press, 1966), pp. 45–52.

[6] Data compiled from State of Washington Department of Conservation, Water Supply Bulletin No. 15 (Olympia, Washington: 1962); and from International Commission on Large Dams, *World Register of Dams* (New York: 1963), plus supplements for later years from the same source.

board. It is bisected by the extensive but relatively low Allegheny Mountains. Of the nineteen principal rivers in the state, ranging from quite small (55,000 acre feet of flow annually) to very large (14 million and 26 million acre feet flow per year respectively for the Allegheny and Susquehanna Rivers), all are dammed, but only eight of them have substantial reservoir capacity relative to flow. The remainder have relatively minor developments. The predominant function of Pennsylvania dams is flood control, with hydroelectric power generation being undertaken on six of the nineteen rivers.[7] The relatively low average level of river development undoubtedly reflects deficiencies of terrain from the standpoint of hydro-power generation, and a negligible demand for irrigation water. It is pertinent to note, however, that even streams at higher elevations in Pennsylvania are frequently plagued with pollution stemming from coal mining and industry, so that commercial activities other than river development have deprived them of wild river characteristics.

These findings, together with more casual surveys of the intensity of river development in other areas, support the qualitative generalizations that we have proceeded a long way down the road of damming nearly every river (and plan to proceed further) and that, although wild rivers remain here and there, they are a species of especially significant wilderness resource that is in danger of extinction unless preventative measures are taken.

Sufficient concern has been stirred in Congress that some protection of wild rivers (however minimal and inadequate) has been provided. The Wild and Scenic Rivers Act, passed in 1968, had the purpose of preserving *stretches* of wild and scenic rivers in their natural state. It named eight rivers or stretches thereof for preservation in their wild state, and designated twenty-seven more rivers to be studied in order to determine if they qualified for preservation. The act also authorized acquisition of a strip of land up to 300 yards wide on each side of a designated wild river, for bank preservation (a seemingly very inadequate protection). Apparently, we are still studying the tweny-seven rivers designated for study. The protective legislation to date smacks strongly of "tokenism" and is aimed at reserving a few wild rivers as natural curiosities, rather than at any broad protection of natural river resources for recreation.

Interferences of Reservoir Operations with the Quality of Recreational Habitat on Rivers. What effects do the construction of dams and operation of reservoirs have on the recreational environment provided by flowing streams? Any reservoir operation that is substantial relative to the flow of a river has a number of well-recognized deleterious

---

[7] Data compiled from United States Geological Survey, *Surface Water Supply of the U.S.* (Washington, D.C.: 1961); and from International Committee on Large Dams, *World Register*.

effects. One effect on rivers that support runs of anadromous game fish like steelhead trout and salmon (largely rivers draining into the Pacific north of San Francisco and rivers of northern New England) is the blockage of these runs by high dams, preventing the migrant fish from reaching much of their spawning grounds and ultimately destroying or greatly damaging a highly prized sports-fishery resource.

For rivers in general, the following environment-degrading effects may be noted:

1. Elimination or substantial diminution of floods greatly diminishes their periodic flushing of stream channels, this leading to siltation of deep pools and of spawning beds for fish, thus progressively destroying the pools, the beds, and the fish.

2. The siltation process described above induces the encroachment of weeds and brush onto the river banks, destroying the accessibility and beauty of the rivers, and also providing a further base for silt accumulation.

3. Regulation of below-dam river release flows for commercial purposes results in periodic severe reductions of such flows sufficient — because of water shortage and increased water temperatures — to induce a high mortality of game fish species. Also, sudden changes in release flows (which are common) tend to destroy game fisheries.

4. In the case of reservoirs operated for power generation, river flows are frequently diverted in large part out of natural stream channels, carried by conduit offstream to a turbine installation several miles below the reservoirs and thereafter returned to the natural stream channels. This results in flows in the by-passed stream channels being insufficient to sustain game fisheries.

5. Drowning out of river gorges and rapids with reservoirs, destroying further the natural amenities of wild rivers.

6. Elimination of opportunities for many of the recreational uses of free-flowing streams, including bank fishing, float-trip boating, and white-water canoeing.

7. Substitution of slack-water reservoirs for free-flowing streams — a matter which we will discuss separately below.

Not all of these external recreational costs of dams and reservoirs are significant for every reservoir or reservoir system on every river — as the varying purposes or functions of reservoirs lead to various patterns of effects — but these externalities are generally experienced with reservoirs and systems thereof.

The effects mentioned are intrinsic in the operation of most reservoirs for the usual variety of commercial purposes, although some effects can be (and occasionally are, grudgingly) ameliorated somewhat by stipulations concerning such matters as minimum release flows below dams. But they are disregarded generally as external costs by federal, state, and local water-development agencies. And in spite of much lip service paid to the importance of recreation, neither state departments of fish or game nor the United States Fish and Wildlife service have been successful in hearings before the boards that must authorize water projects (Bureau and Corps projects are either legally or in practice exempt from such review hearings) in securing more than minimal ameliorative alterations in project designs and operations. There is no significant case on record wherein the location, design, and size of a proposed water project was appreciably changed — or a project forbidden — because its external recreational disbenefits would affect a flowing stream.

It is not difficult to explain why these important environmental costs are so systematically disregarded by water-development agencies. The federal agencies (Bureau and Corps) and some state agencies are now ordinarily instructed to regard the enhancement of recreation as one of the multiple purposes of their water projects. But with irrigation, hydro-power generation, flood control, etc., being first in the list of purposes, recreation with great regularity comes distinctly last — a residual claimant. The same applies to private electric utility companies and to myriad local agencies, although state laws guiding regulatory boards usually mention the provision of recreation as one of the purposes that should be served by dams and reservoirs. Nothing has really been done as yet, however, to retard the substantial neglect of in-stream recreational disbenefits that regularly result from dam-reservoir water projects.

In dealing with recreational benefits, the federal agencies and several significant state agencies, as well as private companies and local agencies, have managed to disregard (and not count as water-project costs) the external environmental costs regularly inflicted on stream habitat by ingeniously changing the subject. This change involves forgetting about the recreational values of the streams and emphasizing and publicizing loudly and at length the positive recreational benefits provided by their still-water reservoirs — for boating, boat fishing, swimming, water skiing, and so forth. These benefits are counted whereas onstream disbenefits are never mentioned. Yet few have been assertive in pointing out that this "confidence game" is just that. Let us now consider how this tradeoff of still-water reservoirs for running streams affects the overall recreational environment.

The Comparative Recreational Benefits of Still-Water Reservoirs. The progressive accumulation of onstream reservoirs throughout the history of this country, capped by an explosive increase in the numbers and aggregate capacity of such reservoirs in the last thirty-five years, has left our population supplied with a plethora of artificial lakes. Statistics on their present number and distribution of sizes are relatively deficient in coverage. Complete statistics on federal reservoirs are ten years out of date; systematic statistics on nonfederal reservoirs are unavailable; and the last estimate of overall reservoir numbers and their aggregate size refers to 1954. Combining a variety of dated statistics with measures of new reservoir building in the last eighteen years, however, and employing some extrapolations of scraps of data on nonfederal reservoirs in some individual states, we have produced the following estimates, which may range from 20 perecent too low to 20 percent too high.

At the beginning of 1972, the approximate number of onstream reservoirs with individual storage capacities in excess of 5,000 acre feet of water was in the neighborhood of 1,200. The aggregate acreage of their water surfaces appeared to be roughly 15 million acres, or about 23,400 square miles; and their total shoreline, about 96,000 miles. Their aggregate water storage capacity was, very approximately, 500 million acre feet of water. These reservoirs ranged in size from quite small to gigantic; it is important to note that about half of their storage capacity, and a third or more of their surface acreage, was accounted for by about the thirty largest reservoirs.

A large proportion of these reservoirs are open to the public for recreational use, accessible by automobile, and have at least some shoreline development to accommodate visitors for camping, picnicking, swimming, boating, etc. And they are used for recreation. Again depending on the manipulation of incomplete data, we estimate that in 1970 all reservoirs in the United States accommodated in the neighborhood of 300 million visitor days oriented to recreation. What proportion of the national population accounted for this large number of visits is not discoverable; various circumstances suggest that significantly less than half of the population was at all involved. In any event, it is clear that the onstream reservoirs of the country provide, quantitatively, a very important recreational resource. It is unfortunate that no comparable data are available on the intensity of use of streams.

What is the general quality of the recreational environment provided by onstream reservoirs? The usual reservoir bears one primary resemblance to a natural lake. It is a body of flat, or still, water largely contained by natural land of higher elevation, differing in this respect from a lake in that it is in minor part contained by a dam. In a number of respects, the usual reservoir differs from and as recreational habitat is inferior to natural lakes.

First, its location is seldom chosen with the purpose of placing it in surroundings that are aesthetically pleasing in terms of terrain and vegetation. Engineering considerations as related to the commercial purposes of the reservoir dictate reservoir locations, and if one happens to end up in good or superior aesthetic surroundings, this is a happy — and atypical — coincidence. By contrast, geological processes — particularly of the last great glacial or ice age — seem generally to have operated to locate natural lakes in surroundings with topography and vegetative land cover that are aesthetically very pleasing and often more or less spectacular. Further, natural lakes most frequently occur at altitudes where forests thrive and where summer temperatures are pleasantly below that of adjacent lowlands. On the other hand, most reservoirs, other than those built primarily to support hydro-electric power generation (including importantly those with flood control as one of their major functions), tend to be located at relatively low altitudes not too far above the river valleys below them, in order to secure maximum impoundments of river flow. This favors reservoir locations at sites with relatively high summer temperatures and mediocre vegetative cover.

Second, reservoirs are, for the most part, lacking in the important recreational amenities of naturally formed shores and littoral zones. Unlike natural lakes, they have not been present for the thousands of years required for wave action to form more or less gradually shelving beaches, shores, and adjacent underwater littoral lands. Except as sand or gravel is occasionally imported to reservoirs to build artificial areas of beach, reservoirs tend to be ringed by abrupt cut banks or bulldozed and barren slopes of dirt, devoid of vegetation that might proceed pleasantly close to the water line. Their bank or shore areas in fact tend to be especially barren and unsightly because of typically substantial annual fluctuations of reservoirs levels (resulting from periodic accumulation and release of water). This fluctuation tends to result in wide and often steep stretches of barren mud or clay or natural soil aggregate being exposed in summer recreation seasons. Artificial assists to access to the reservoir surface usually mitigate the resulting impediment to reaching it, but the aesthetic results are distinctly unpleasant.

The fluctuation of reservoir surfaces in the course of a year tend to be very substantial — especially when irrigation-water supply and flood control are major reservoir purposes, and less so when hydro-power generation is the dominant purpose. In California, for example, the very large multipurpose Shasta Reservoir on the Sacramento River (with a storage capacity of 4½ million acre feet) from 1944 to 1959 had a median annual drop in level from June 15 to September 15 of 43 vertical feet. Two other large reservoirs in the state — Folsom and Pine Flat — with a million acre feet apiece of storage capacity — had median vertical drops in level during the three-month summer vacation season of 49 feet and 96 feet respectively in the latter half of the 1950's.[8] National average fluctuations in reservoir levels are undoubtedly smaller but still substantial, with corresponding deleterious effects on the recreational habitat provided by reservoirs.

Third, in all but very large and, especially, very deep reservoirs,

[8] Outdoor Recreation Resources Review Commission, *Water for Recreation*, pp. 21–32.

there is a tendency for water temperatures to exceed substantially those of the flowing streams they have replaced, and this has definite effects on the quality of the sports fisheries that reservoirs can support. Summer water temperatures become too high for the survival of the more highly prized fresh-water game fish, like trout, but are at levels quite acceptable to generally less prized game fish like bass, and to nongame pan fish. Experience with large and deep reservoirs, moreover, suggests that, although during their early years they are quite successfully stocked with trout and support good trout fishing — in part evidently because of food debris left in the reservoir bottom — as they mature past a couple of decades, they fail to develop the fresh-water food chains that ultimately support the predator trout, and their trout fisheries tend to decline rapidly.

In spite of the comparative deficiencies of reservoirs in providing water-oriented recreational environment, they can be used, of course, for about the full variety of recreational pursuits supported by natural lakes: pleasure boating, boat fishing, water skiing, swimming, camping near their shores, and so forth. And they are quite heavily used for all of these pursuits.

The question is whether or not individual reservoirs, or reservoirs as a group, have either deteriorated or improved our rural recreational environment by widely substituting still-water artificial lakes for flowing streams. No one to date has been able to answer this question by measurements of the comparative values of the two types of inland water resources to recreationists. And no very simple answer is ever likely to be forthcoming, because of the wide diversity of preferences of different groups of people seeking inland water-oriented recreation.

On the one hand, there is an evident multitude (never tabulated systematically) of individuals who definitely prefer recreation — fishing and other — on free-flowing streams or wild rivers, and who have been progressively deprived of the resources which would enable them to secure the sorts of recreational satisfactions they prefer. The scarcity of free-flowing streams, reasonably accessible to much of our population, moreover, probably has induced many people to shift to the distinctly second-best choice of using reservoirs for water-oriented recreation. To the extent that stream-fishing habitat has generally deteriorated, and also to the extent that shifts to second-best reservoirs have resulted, there has been a serious though unmeasured environmental cost of dam and reservoir development.

On the other hand, there is also an evident multitude of people whose preference is strongly in favor of still-water recreation of the variety mentioned, and who prefer even a reservoir with many aesthetic and physical deficiencies over a free-flowing stream as the site for their sorts of water-oriented recreational pursuits. In the way of man-made lakes, they will settle for what they can get in order to run power boats or ski on the water or fish from boats. For this group, the burgeoning supply of reservoirs has probably provided a very substantial, though again unmeasured, environmental benefit.

Can anything more be said of the overall effect (plus or minus) on environmental values of the widespread building of reservoirs? One thing, based on a generalization drawn from analytical economics, can be said. This proposition is that if two or more substantial fractions of a total group of consumers seeking a given general sort of good prefer distinctly different types of that good (connected costs to them being considered), total consumer welfare will be increased if the two or more types of the good are supplied at least roughly in the proportions that they are sought. A variety of product types adapted to the variety of consumer tastes for these product types will tend to maximize consumer satisfaction. Supplying one of the types as a proportion of the total output of the general good which is substantially in excess or short of the proportion of that good which is preferred by any "preference group" of consumers will diminish total consumer satisfaction, perhaps very seriously.

This rule is clearly applicable to the proportions in which inland water resources are supplied in the form of free-running or wild streams and in the form of still-water reservoirs respectively. The problem is whether they are being supplied more or less proportionately to consumer preferences for them, or quite disproportionately — in favor either of stream resources or reservoir resources. Lacking meaningful measures both of the volume of stream-oriented recreation activity and of the value of either stream-based or reservoir-based activity, we cannot supply a quantitative answer to this question. But the preponderance of qualitative evidence and of incomplete statistics on the recent reservoir boom suggest strongly that, relative to the respective demands for them, stream-based recreational habitat is in relatively short supply relative to preferences for it — and consequently reduced in value by congested use — and reservoir-based habitat is in relatively superfluous supply. The effects of the explosive development of onstream reservoirs since the mid-1930's have thus very probably been to reduce the value of rural water-based recreational environment substantially and to impose a large gross environmental loss in this area of recreation. Further progress along the line of river development will impose generally greater and increasing gross environmental losses.

Overall Economic Welfare Results of Dam and Reservoir Building to Date. Suppose that we accept either as a tentative conclusion, or as one entertained only for purposes of argument, the judgment that onstream reservoirs have already been sufficiently overbuilt that from a recreational standpoint a large gross environmental loss in the recreational sphere has been imposed by destroying more open-stream recreational benefits than it has created still-water recreational benefits. (This writer is more or less convinced of the accuracy of this conclusion, but certainly cannot prove or disprove it with the data and analytical technique now available.) Still, granted the supposition, there is an important remaining issue, to the following effect: Have the values of the time streams of commercial net benefits (stemming from hydropower, irrigation, flood control, municipal water supplies, and so forth) of important increments to our river developments of the last twenty-five or more years exceeded their capital costs sufficiently to outweigh the gross environmental losses imposed by these increments, so that they have resulted in net increases in aggregate economic welfare? Or, pushing the inquiry further, have their commercial net benefits exceeded their capital costs at all, or have they been as large as these costs, so that there was any commercial net benefit to offset the losses in the value of recreational environment?

Not enough independent and dispassionate studies of the ratio of commercial net benefits to capital costs of a small multitude of river development projects have been made to support a definitive answer to these questions, but these are important straws in the wind. All Bureau of Reclamation and Corps of Engineers river projects since World War II have been required by law to be justified by these agencies through analyses showing that their benefits should be expected to exceed their costs, and these justifications have been forthcoming for every river project proposed. But a considerable number of retrospective analyses of major and minor individual Bureau and Corps river projects — conducted dispassionately and clinically by experts in no way associated with these federal agencies — have shown that typically the actual commercial benefits of these projects are below their costs and thus have reduced aggregate economic welfare. This is the case even when, as is typically so, external environmental costs of these projects are not counted as part of their costs. The discrepancy between the predictions of the federal agencies that their projects always will have benefits exceeding costs, and the later findings of disinterested parties that the same projects almost always have costs in excess of benefits, seems attributable to some constitutional overoptimism of federal agencies whose business it is to build water projects and also to the use by the agencies of irrelevantly low discount rates in calculating the present values of far future net benefits.

An extended survey of published and unpublished independent studies of the benefit-cost ratings of federal water projects has convinced this writer of two things:

1. A large proportion of federal water projects built since World War II have had either zero or negative net commercial values as built on the scales that they were, and thus no redeeming economic features to offset the gross environmental losses that they tended to impose.

2. A part of these "losers" might have yielded enough net commercial value to offset their environmental costs if built on smaller scales, with fewer and smaller features, including fewer and smaller dams and reservoirs.

The tentative conclusion is that large gross environmental losses imposed by the bulk of federal water projects in the last twenty-five or more years have not been compensated for by commercial net benefits, and have resulted in net losses in overall economic welfare. We have constructed far too many and too large river-development projects from a net welfare as well as from an environmental standpoint — and are planning to do more of the same. This is an economic disaster with an adequate political explanation.

The Problem of Public Policy Remedies. Effective public regulation to arrest or retard the ongoing process of river developments, by withholding governmental permission to build water projects which will degrade our recreational environment without generating appreciable excesses of commercial benefits over costs, is difficult to fashion and politically very hard to secure. The political difficulty stems in largest part from the unwillingness of the federal Congress to subordinate to either executive or independent bureaus or commissions its substantially unfettered discretionary power to authorize as well as to finance river-development projects to be constructed by the Bureau of Reclamation and the Corps of Engineers.

Nevertheless, the time has long since come when organized conservationist groups should mount a large campaign to secure a major augmentation of recent environment-protective legislation along the following lines: That is, an independent federal commission should be created which would have first the duty of conducting its own investigations of all proposed Bureau and Corps projects (really auditing the project appraisals submitted by those agencies), with an eye both to determining the physical amount of environmental damage that any project would probably inflict and to finding if the project really would generate enough net commercial benefits (net of capital as well as other costs) to offset that damage. Second, it should have the power to declare ineligible for Congressional authorization any proposed Bureau or Corps project which would produce either no such net commercial benefits or net commercial benefits insufficient to offset the environmental damages it would inflict. These review and licensing powers could readily be extended to nonfederal water projects as well, in conformity with well-established legislative precedents, and probably should be so extended. Such a review of proposed projects should result in prohibiting the construction of part of them and in the building of others at smaller scales and with revised designs. The political hurdle to be crossed in inducing Congress to provide the necessary legislative authorization for the establishment of the sort of commission described may well be insurmountably high, but with the growing strength of the environmental protection movement that hurdle could conceivably be surmounted.

Meanwhile, the time is overdue for the executive branch of the federal government, with the concurrence of Congress, to implement rapidly the provisions of the Wild and Scenic Rivers Act of 1968 that provides for study of twenty-seven wild rivers (in addition to the nine such rivers already protected by the act), to the end of placing most or all of these added rivers in the category of recreational preserves not open to commercial development. (To date, no action has been taken with respect to any of the twenty-seven designated rivers.) The act, moreover, should be amended to include a considerable number of other substantially wild rivers as candidates for preservation, including the few remaining big ones, and those which are otherwise threatened with early development by the federal water agencies and some state agencies. In this area, action should replace legislative rhetoric on a broad scale.

If we are correct in concluding that at present we are already rather badly oversupplied with river development projects and their dams and reservoirs, can anything be done to remedy our past mistakes of project overbuilding, ultimately to restore some of recreational habitat previously provided by free-flowing streams? Here, we are squarely faced with a conundrum of the following sort: The great bulk of Bureau and Corps water projects yield time streams of net commercial benefits after construction with values which are not much greater than, or are less than, their capital costs — and were thus not ever economically justified when environmental losses are counted. But once these projects have been built, the capital investment in them thus "sunk" beyond recall and "hardened in concrete," from then on their time streams of net benefits (i.e., benefits minus only operating and maintenance expenses) are typically of very substantial value. And then far more is contributed to aggregate economic welfare by "operating a mistake" (the capital costs of which are lost anyway) than by abandoning or destroying it. Thus, restoring stream environments by dynamiting dams to improve stream environments would generally entail a loss in aggregate economic welfare — and most people who understand this would probably not recommend any widespread destruction of existing dams and reservoirs for the sake of improvement in our outdoor recreational environment. Moreover, the problem described is extremely persistent, since the major features of most water projects will ordinarily last for a century or more.

Some ameliorative measures affecting the operation of existing dams and reservoirs could be imposed, under additional legislation — e.g., in the direction of requiring the maintenance of larger and less fluctuating below-dam instream flows, at the sacrifice of some commercial benefits. But the degree of amelioration would be unlikely to be large. Bringing the ongoing boom in building added river-development projects substantially to a halt and vigorously pushing and expanding the now minuscule program of protecting remaining wild rivers as recreational preserves seem to embody the economically most desirable environmental policies. We will get these policies if we get them at all, however, only through a very strong and prolonged political program.

DEGRADATION OF FOREST RESOURCES

Like our inland water resources, our forest resources are a primary part of our rural recreational environment, and their protection from progressive diminution in quantity and quality over future time is essential to avert progressive environmental degradation. Moreover, because forests regulate our major watersheds, this sort of ever-continuing protection of forests is necessary to avert a progressive degradation of our inland water resources. In this sense, our forests should be "conserved" perpetually — that is, preserved against qualitative and quantitative depletion or deterioration. This imperative will be made clearer if we reject as ambiguous and indefinite in their implications two catch phrases popular among lumbermen and foresters: (1) "Conservation is wise use," and (2) "Preservation is not conservation."

Our forest resources are vast enough that there is no occasion for declaring most of them recreational preserves in which the harvesting lumber, grazing, and some mining are prohibited. Total forest land in the United States encompasses about 570 million acres (nearly 900,000 square miles), and about 200 million acres of this is public land.[9] Therefore, although much more of our forest lands should be designated as recreational preserves than are at present, preservation of good forest-based recreational environment is quite consistent with the use of a large majority of our forest lands for the careful harvesting of trees.

By careful harvesting we refer to logging practices which do not impair the natural ability of forests to reproduce themselves in undiminished quantity and quality, which do not permanently or for long periods either destroy or deface natural forest habitats (including their meadows and brooks as well as their trees and other natural vegetation), and which do not degrade the functional utility of forests as regulators of watersheds.

The environmental problem concerning us in the present part of this essay is the unacceptably widespread incidence of forest harvesting practices which, according to all the criteria just mentioned, are not "careful." That is, they do seriously impair the reproduction

[9] Marion Clawson and Jack L. Knetch, *Economics of Outdoor Recreation* (Baltimore: Johns Hopkins Press, 1965), p. 185.

of the trees removed by harvesting forest land, do destroy or permanently deface natural forest habitats, and do impose serious damage on watersheds. The general character and consequences of these logging malpractices, their extent, and the general identity of those primarily responsible for them all deserve some attention.

General Types of Logging Practices. As a preamble to discussing logging malpractices, it should be recognized that there are several distinctive principal methods of harvesting timber, each of which is appropriate for one or more types of timber stands:

1. Selective removal of older trees from uneven-aged stands of timber, with dependence on natural reproduction.

2. Thinning of overstocked stands of timber, generally those that, although merchantable, have not reached optimal maturity, again with dependence on natural reproduction.

3. Removal of an "overstory" of mature trees when underneath there is an adequate understory of younger trees which will survive overstory cutting and provide in the process of natural reproduction a new generation of trees to grow up. (This method is presently most common on the Pacific slope and some other areas.)

4. "Shelterwood" cutting of nearly all trees in a stand except for a sufficient selection of well-rooted "seed trees," which are depended on for natural reproduction. (This method is applied where seed-tree survival ability is good, and where the savable understory of young trees is unsatisfactory for reproductive purposes.)

5. Clear-cutting in a group, patch, or strip of all trees in a stand, properly followed (if there is to be adequate regeneration of the stand) by planting or seeding or both, except in the case of narrow strip cutting, where natural reproduction may be dependend on. (Artificial regeneration by planting and seeding is a must if permanent depletion of the lumber resources affected is to be avoided. Further, group and patch clear-cuts should be limited to about 25 acres apiece, to limit soil erosion and for aesthetic reasons. Subject to these severe constraints, clear-cutting may be the best method of harvesting mature stands of shade-intolerant species of trees where a savable understory of young trees is absent.)

Generally, all clear-cuts and shelterwood-seed tree cuts render the cutover land unsuitable for recreation for long periods of time, are aesthetically displeasing, and should not be used indiscriminately. Clear-cuts should not be used at all for large continuous acreages and without assurance that reseeding and replanting will follow cutting rather promptly.

With any of the tree harvesting methods just described, there are at least three critical logging processes involved. First, depending on the size of the operation, one or more "landing and loading" areas in the immediate forest must be cut clear and bulldozed bare for loading cut logs onto trucks. Second, from every landing area a logging road leading to a sawmill (or other wood-processing mill) must be constructed, cutting trees to clear a right of way and bulldozing an open path for trucks. Third, cut logs, after being stripped of branches, must be dragged or "skidded," usually with tractors, from where they fall to the nearest landing area for loading onto trucks — this process creating bare "skid tracks" from which important fractions of topsoil may be gouged out. How these three processes are conducted is crucial to the effect of logging on forest regeneration, forest habitat, and watershed.

Lumbering Practices on Privately Owned Land. How have we fared with lumbering practices in the United States in the last several decades? In general, so far as evidence is available, tolerably well in the National Forests, where all sorts of regulations of logging practices are on the books and often enforced, but rather poorly on privately owned forest land, which comprises over 60 percent of all such land and nearer 70 percent of "commercial" timberland.

Data on logging practices in privately owned forests are incomplete and sketchy, and generalizations are difficult to make. In fact, it would be hazardous to attempt to "paint with one brush" or color all or most of private lumbering practices in the country. Nonetheless there are very significant bits of indicative evidence concerning lumbering in private forests, which are consistent with the rather unfortunate earlier history of private logging in this country.

Thus, the Nader report of 1971 on *Power and Land in California*[10] suggested that most of a long list of rules or recommendations for good forestry practice were being systematically or typically violated by private owners in the redwood country of the northwestern California coast — where cutting virgin timber eons old is still prevalent — and in the inland Sierra Nevada and adjacent mountainous areas, where Douglas Fir is the principal species being exploited.

On the level of general forestry method, the most destructive practices of large and small firms exploiting private land are clear-cutting much larger areas than are consistent with erosion control and preservation of aesthetic amenities, and from inadequate to no attempts to regenerate clear-cut areas through seeding and planting. In effect, once virgin timber was clear-cut, the actual evidence of interest in replanting the forests for minor crops a century later seemed small — although one of three large redwood operators in the area has showed some improvement over this tendency.

[10] Center for the Study of Responsive Law, *Power and Land: The Ralph Nader Task Force Report on Land Use in California* (Robert C. Fellmeth, ed.), Chapter 4, pp. 43–62.

On the level of detailed logging practices, widespread typical sins of a destructive character included:

1. Failure to minimize the number of erosion-promoting skid trails.

2. Failure to conform skid trails to natural contours of terrain, further promoting erosion.

3. Failure to use light, rubber-tired tractor equipment instead of heavy, steel-cleated equipment in skidding, with consequent erosion-promoting consequences.

4. Use of tractors on steep hillsides, with similar consequences.

5. Use of stream beds for skid trails, and sometimes for stretches of logging roads.

6. Failure to minimize the number of stream crossings by skid trails and roads.

7. Failure to preserve buffer strips of uncut lumber on both sides of all streams, as a means of arresting erosion.

8. Failure to confine logging roads to one-lane design with turn-outs.

9. Failure to select gentle logging-road grades, with minimal cuts and fills.

10. Failure to confine bulldozed landing areas to minimum practicable sizes.

11. Failure to make reasonably complete disposals of slash, whether by burning or shredding.

The major consequences of breaking most or all of the rules in a "good logging practice" handbook most of the time have been propagation of extensive and intensive erosion of topsoil, greatly diminishing the reproductive capacities of the cut-over forests; destruction of natural watersheds and the augmentation of natural floods; degradation of the waters of natural small brooks and streams and of forest habitat generally. The external environmental costs of these inferior logging practices (and connected general logging methods) are visibly huge enough that, in the light of generally available information, the extra costs of lumber production with "good" methods and practices would be much smaller than resultant environmental gains. Inferior practices and methods have seldom been defended by those following them on the basis of cost savings in lumber production, but rather on the basis of the inviolability of private property rights, which in their view include the right to disregard the external social costs of their operations. We will not pause to comment on the widely recognized inadequacy of California's Forest Practice Act to impose any sort of meaningful state regulation on private lumber operators.

The phenomena discussed are by no means confined to California. In 1970 the Northwest Regional Office of the Federal Water Quality Administration published an "Industrial Waste Guide on Logging Practices," stating that there was far too much evidence of improper, low-cost logging operations resulting in streams becoming turbid and clogged with debris, their gravel-bed spawning grounds becoming covered with silt, and in stream shores being stripped of shade trees that had kept their waters cool. The report recommended design of clear-cuts to provide buffer strips along streams and building logging roads with minimal cuts and fills.

Adverse logging practices of the same or many of the sorts described appear to be common on private timberlands, though this generalization cannot be fully documented. For example, the almost model "progressive" large lumbering company, Weyerhauser, frequently makes very large clear-cuts, up to a square mile in area.

The adverse external effects of destructive logging practices on sports fisheries is predictable. For example, on the South Fork of the wild Eel River in northwestern California — which flows out of a wastershed in which redwood and other logging has been heavy — the runs of chinook salmon at a downstream counting point dropped from a fourteen-year annual average of nearly 12,000 up to 1952, to a nine-year average of about 3,700 since 1952. Similar declines have been observed on other major rivers in the same area.

Logging in the National Forests. The National Forests include about 185 million acres of forest land (about 32 percent of the national total), of which about 140 million acres supports commercial timberland.[11] Privately owned plus National Forest timberland thus accounts for all but a small fraction of that available in the United States, and for even more of that not protected from cutting in the National Parks.

Quite unlike state regulatory authorities which impose sorts of regulation on lumbering on private lands, the United States Forest Service has a comprehensive and adequate set of regulations — implemented in individual National Forests by the respective Forest Supervisors — which govern both the general methods of forest harvesting (clear-cut, overstory removal, thinning, etc.) and the detailed logging practices that may be employed by private logging companies (which can contract to conduct logging on given tracts of National Forests at given times). Among other things, the annual rate of timber cutting in National Forests is generally kept small enough — from a fraction of 1 percent to 2 percent per year — that depletion of the quantity and quality of forest land in the National Forests is not threatened.

However, it has been frequently observed that the Forest Service is lacking in manpower sufficient to enforce closely its regulations, so that independent contractors are frequently able to and do engage in some logging practices prohibited by Forest Service regulations.

The extent of low-grade or destructive logging practices in Na-

[11] Clawson and Knetch, *Outdoor Recreation.*

tional Forests generally is not known. However, instances of deviations from practices required by regulations occasionally receive publicity. One example was uncovered in a 1970 investigation of logging in the Bitterroot National Forest in western Montana, where excessive, extensive, and uneconomic clear-cutting of timber was verified, after it engendered considerable public outcry from residents of the region concerning very adverse aesthetic and other effects of large clear-cuts. Another instance involved logging in the Monongahela National Forest in West Virginia. There, a special Forest Practices Management Commission of the West Virginia legislature recently condemned past harvesting practices in that National Forest, with the result that United States Forest Service agreed to limit clear-cuts in the forest to twenty-five acres apiece — whereas some of those formerly allowed had encompassed several hundred acres.

So although the United States Forest Service and its numerous individual Forest Supervisors have an almost ideal set of logging regulations on paper, their regulation in practice evidently falls somewhat short of the ideal. Still, their general regulation is good, and logging methods and practices in National Forests are vastly superior to those on privately owned forest lands. More enforcement personnel should appreciably improve the already rather satisfactory level of logging practices in the National Forests.

Remedial Policy Measures. With respect to the federal National Forests, the problem of securing more uniformly close-to-ideal logging methods and practices seems comparatively simple. The situation being on the average quite good already, the appropriation of funds for considerably expanded enforcement of existing regulations should bring about appreciable improvements. In addition, administrative reforms in the United States Forest Service aimed generally at reducing the discretionary powers of individual Forest Supervisors in enforcing existing regulations, and also at placing greater emphasis on the enforcement function, could be comparatively easily accomplished, and should also result in securing closer-to-ideal forest management.

The problem of securing a more or less revolutionary improvement of logging methods and practices in privately owned forests is much more severe. Although a number of states have legislation providing for regulation of logging practices on private lands — such as the Forest Practice Act of 1945 in California — state regulation is almost uniformly nominal, weak, and quite insufficient to deal with the problems faced. Direct regulation by independent state authorities of private logging activities, with the aim of preventing stream and watershed damage, preserving aesthetic values, or protecting fish and other recreational resources is uniformly nominal or not provided. The motif in state legislation in this area is provision essentially for self-regulation by the private logging industry, sometimes through appointive commissions predominantly populated by representatives of logging firms and their friends. And so far as some self-regulation is secured by this route, there is typically a lack of even faintly sufficient numbers of enforcement personnel to secure general compliance with such regulation.

A simple remedy for the drastically insufficient regulation of logging on private lands might seem to involve mounting in the numerous states involved major political pressure to secure regulations of private logging practices comparable to those of the United States Forest Service, backed up by adequate enforcement personnel and stiff penalties for violations of regulations. This might be worth trying. But the political power structure in states in which logging private lands is important has, historically, appeared to be such as to make the passage and executive approval of the needed legislation highly improbable. The probability of success along this line, moreover, is lessened by the developed expertise of the private lumbering industry in producing and publicizing reams of persuasive rhetoric praising its own performance and justifying the status quo with expert selections and distortions of fact.

A more feasible approach, if possible constitutional impediments can be circumvented — as they very probably could be — would be to center political action on securing the establishment of a federal agency (independent or a branch of the existing executive structure) empowered to pass and enforce a comprehensive and adequate set of regulations of logging methods and practices, which would apply to private lumbering operations in any state. The political feasibility of this approach to the problem seems very substantially greater than the state-by-state approach because of the dilution at the federal Congressional level of the political power of private logging interests; detailed study of the character of appropriate federal legislation of the sort suggested seems to be in order. If some such action is not taken, the nation faces the prospect of a long-run and severe depletion of its forest resources and a similar degradation of its rural recreational environment.

DEFICIENCIES IN THE ACCESSIBILITY FOR RECREATION OF OUR FOREST RESOURCES

For the American citizen seeking rural recreation, there is seemingly no shortage of forested land. As suggested in the preceding section, forests in the United States cover about 570 million acres, or nearly 900,000 square miles. Moreover, government-held forest lands in the National Forests, the National Park System, and numerous state parks, include over 200 million acres, or appreciably over 300,000 square miles.[12] If nearly all, or even a tenth, of these forest resources were easily accessible to most of the population for recreational use, and if the accessible portion were of at least average quality and

---

[12] Cf., Clawson and Knetch, *ibid.*

varying in special characteristics, there would be no quantitative or qualitative scarcity, now or soon in prospect, of accessible forest resources providing recreational environment.

The problem that we face at present is some scarcity of, and some congestion in the use of, easily accessible forest land suitable for recreation. This scarcity is generally attributable to the characteristics of policies adopted by the principal federal forest-holding agencies — both the United States Forest Service and the National Park Service — and by some special Congressional actions — and failures to act. We will survey the general scope of the problem, first as it refers, in turn, to the National Park System and to the National Forests. In a preamble to this survey, however, understanding of the complex problems involved will be assisted if we describe the ongoing program of establishing on federal lands extensive preserves of "wilderness areas."

The "Wilderness Area" Movement. Under the political pressure of "conservationist" groups, there has been a recent movement in Congress and in administrative agencies to establish as federal preserves inviolate to commercial exploitation certain large "wilderness areas." Their purpose is either to provide current recreation, or simply to "be there" as parts of the virgin environment of America, for the vicarious or actual satisfaction of current and future generations. These wilderness areas are primarily forest land, though in general a minority of their acreages grow merchantable timber, reflecting an emphasis on alpine regions and other forest lands of low commercial value.

According to guidelines earlier set down by a federal commission, a true wilderness tract should be an area of public land, available for overnight recreation, of at least 100,000 acres, *with no roads useable to the public* and with no ecological disturbance — such as lumbering — except for some domestic livestock grazing in the West and some long-ago logging in the East.[13] In other words, wilderness preserves are useable mainly for limited hiking or back-packing expeditions and for more elaborate expeditions employing pack and possibly riding equine stock. Their use is heavily biased in the direction of higher-income groups, of those young or comparably endowed with stamina and good physical condition, and also those unencumbered with small children.

The National Park Service had by 1960 designated about 7 million acres of the approximately 15 million acres of the forest land under its control as either "wilderness type areas" or comparable "wild areas" of smaller size for administration and management designed to conform to the "wilderness area" standards described.[14]

[13] Outdoor Recreation Resources Review Commission, *Wilderness and Recreation — A Report on Resources, Values, and Problems*, Study Report No. 3 (Washington, D.C.: 1962), pp. 3–4.

[14] *Ibid.*, pp. 50–51.

Upon a background of United States Forest Service administrative regulations providing for 100,000-acre-plus "wilderness" tracts with no roads, no commercial logging, and no resorts or summer homes, and smaller "wild" tracts subject to the same restrictions, the federal Congress in the Wilderness Act of 1964 gave immediate statutory protection to about 9 million acres (of a total of 185 million) of National Forest lands to be designated as "wild" or "wilderness." The act also provided, though perhaps wishfully, that an added 52 million acres of public land, predominantly in the National Forests and National Park Service, should be reviewed to determine which parts thereof were suitable for inclusion in the "wilderness system." The President was instructed over a period of ten years (beginning 1964) to submit to Congress his recommendations on that part of this vast area which should be preserved as wilderness (reviewing at least one-third of this acreage by September, 1967).

The preceding descriptions of legislative and administrative actions are definitely not intended to imply judgments concerning the wisdom of the wilderness program, its adequacy or oversufficiency, or the merits or demerits of executive caution in implementing the relevant legislation. In fact, the wilderness and wild area program presents us with a dilemma and a two-edged sword.

On the one hand, something can be said for preserving a certain portion of our heretofore unexploited forest lands as an end in itself, largely for the vicarious satisfaction that many people derive from knowing that an appreciable part of our virgin forest lands are being protected more or less in perpetuity and not being cut over by loggers, overrun by hordes of recreationists, or otherwise appreciably changed from their natural state. This writer is not heavily impressed with the vicarious satisfaction argument.

More importantly, these wilderness areas can provide unique recreational experiences to a very small proportion of the population. The proportion is going to be small in part because the bulk of the population prefers alternative and less "rugged" types of recreation than wilderness areas afford, in part because a substantial proportion of the population is not physically fit enough to back-pack or mule-pack into wilderness areas, in part because wilderness areas are not very suitable for vacations of families with small children, and in part because wilderness recreation is too expensive for the bulk of the population. But even if these considerations were not decisive, we face the dilemma that a wilderness area remains a wilderness area only so long as it is very lightly or unintensively used for recreation. Accommodation of a significant proportion of recreationists in wilderness areas would (and has in some notable instances) eroded the very "wilderness" characteristics of the areas which protective legislation and regulation has been designed to preserve — with multiple camp sites, litter, and sufficient human congestion to diminish greatly the individual's satisfaction from being relatively alone in wild country. Wilderness areas can be maintained effectively as such only if their inaccessibility and terrain "automatically" ration their use to a very small part of the population, or if, failing this, governmental authorities ration their use.

"Automatic rationing" on the average has until now sufficed to deter a wilderness-destroying intensity of use of wilderness areas. For example, in 1960 all National Forest wilderness areas plus all National Park Service back country attracted less than 3 million visitor days.[15] Even if the intensity of recreational use had doubled subsequently, it would be miniscule as compared to about 300 million visitor days per year at inland reservoirs, or to the roughly 750 million visitor days per annum to National Parks, National Forests, and state parks generally.

Subject to the constraints mentioned, preserving extensive wilderness areas without question greatly improves the recreational environment of a very small minority of our population. It does so, moreover, at a relatively low opportunity cost in terms of timber production foregone, since most of the average of wilderness areas, because of alpine location or for other reasons, does not support high-grade merchantable timber. At the same time, wilderness areas, so long as they retain their distinctive characteristics, contribute very little to the provision of forested recreational habitat for almost all of our population seeking such habitat.

Two conclusions are suggested by the foregoing discussion. First, a considerable number of truly prime wilderness areas should be preserved, both because of the unique recreational environment they provide, and because many of them are in terrain too rugged to support general recreational use aside from sight seeing. In these areas, roads should be kept out and commercial exploitation of the land forbidden.

Second, there is in any forested area presently in a wilderness state implicitly a decision to be made concerning how much of it should be preserved as true wilderness and how much, if any, should be made considerably more accessible to the general vacationing public as a recreational preserve. Opening significant amounts of wilderness to more general recreational use would generally have to be implemented by installing appropriate access roads (not super highways), but would not necessarily and probably should not involve provision for intensive use based on large central, highly developed, and crowded camp grounds or trailer parks, or on extensive road networks. An attractive alternative would be to administer a previously wilderness tract as a "semiprimitive" area, with no commercial logging, severely restricted or no resort development, much more dependence on foot trails than on roads for short-distance travel, banning of all motor vehicles from motorcycles up except on

[15] *Ibid.*, pp. 119–121.

roads, and provision for very numerous small and well-dispersed camp sites with minimal sanitary and water supply facilities.[16]

Such development of extensive general recreational preserves seems attractive enough to support the suggestion that the 52 million acres of National Forest and National Park Service land that Congress has designated for consideration as possible wilderness areas should also be reviewed to determine their suitability as general recreational preserves, with relatively easy access by roads but predominant retention in a semiprimitive state, and no logging or comparable commercial exploitation.

In any event, as we will argue below, a large acreage of such easily accessible recreational preserves is needed to develop our rural recreational environment, whether or not they are cut out of tentatively designated wilderness areas.

Recreational Resources and Policies in the National Park System. The first National Park — Yellowstone — was established in 1872, followed by Yosemite National Park in 1890. Other National Parks have been added until their total number is now 36. In addition, the National Park Service — created *ex post* the establishment of the first parks — has extended its operations to the establishment and administration of about 84 National Monuments, 13 National Recreation Areas, 8 National Seashores, and 4 National Lakeshores, as well as a myriad of small historical parks, military parks, memorial parks, battlefields, historic sites, cemeteries, parkways, scenic riverways, trails, etc.

An abbreviated tabulation (on page 168) of its holdings as of the middle of 1971 shows the acreages of federal land held under various categories of National Park Service facilities.[17]

Since we are here focussing on forested land, we will neglect natural seashores and lakeshores, and all of the "all other." Only a small error is involved in neglecting the 84 National Monuments, which typically preserve as "natural wonders" in desert areas unique rock formations, unusual lava beds, and the like. The National Recreation Areas are usually broad or narrow fringes of forested land surrounding federally built reservoirs in areas with good recreational potential. The bulk of land in officially designated National Parks is forested, and the amount of nondesert forest land held by the National Park Service *in toto* is estimated very roughly at about 15 million acres or nearly 23,500 square miles. It must be remembered, of course, that about 7 million of this 15 million acres is presently re-

---

[16] We designate the sort of area described as "semiprimitive" in part because the United States Forest Service has preempted the term *primitive area* to refer to the substantial equivalent of wilderness area.

[17] National Park Service, *Areas Administered by the National Park Service* (Washington, D.C.: 1971).

National Park Service Holdings — 1971

Category	Federal acreage[a]
National Parks	14,335,000
National Recreation Areas	3,631,000
National Monuments	9,966,000
National Seashores	256,000
National Lakeshores	24,000
All other	399,000
Total	28,611,000

[a] Rounded to the nearest 1000

served as "areas of a wild or wilderness types," with difficult access and low rates of use.

The "nonwilderness" forest land of the National Park Service — about 8 million acres — would provide 4 percent of an acre apiece for a population of 200 million people — about 1,742 square feet apiece, or 35 percent of the area of a 50-by-100-foot building lot. If a tenth of the population of the United States spread itself evenly over the forested nonwilderness land of the National Park Service, there would be quite a bit of crowding. With typical camp site concentrations, a noticeably smaller fraction of the population would create severe human and automotive congestion, and the differentiation in the accessibility and popularity of different parks would selectively aggravate congestion in the more accessible and popular ones.

This is not to suggest that the National Park System represents tokenism in the provision of forested recreational habitat, but it does suggest that far more forest land than is administered by the National Park Service should be made easily accessible for recreation.

In any event, the National Park Service was not created to fullfill anything like a major or large minor proportion of the demand for forested recreational lands. The original stated objectives of creating National Parks were to preserve for present and future generations unique "natural wonders," and to make them accessible for viewing by the populace. The early executive and legislative statements concerning National Parks seemed to place a prime emphasis on the recreational values of sight seeing or "spectator" recreation, as distinct from "participatory" recreation.

The view of the mission of the National Park Service, however, has been extended as time has passed. In legislation in 1916, Congress defined the function of the service as promotion and regulation of the use of federal areas known as natural parks, monuments, and reservations — with the purpose of conserving the scenery and the natural and historic objects and the wildlife therein — to provide for the enjoyment of these in such manner and by such means as will leave them unimpaired for future generations. In 1960, Congressman Aspinall stated that, as his colleagues knew, lands in the National Park Service are generally administered under a multiuse policy, for watershed protection, outdoor recreation, fish and game habitat, and forest protection — and in some cases grazing, mining, and other purposes. And a public statement of the National Park Service in 1961 declared that multiple use of National Park Service lands established as park or recreation areas means that the lands have been classified *for the primary purpose of recreation* and managed for this primary purpose. The only way to preserve wild areas and areas of unusual scientific and historical interest, or to reserve open space for recreational purposes, is to classify our lands now for those purposes, and to manage them with the mission *not of the production of material products, but that of the preservation of land and its natural features.*

Two things stand out in these declarations and descriptions of National Park Service policy. First, it has fully evolved from the preservation of natural wonders for sightseeing purposes to the provision of a rather full range of forest-oriented recreational opportunities. Second, with respect to forests and related resources, its policy is almost strictly one of preservation without commercial exploitation by lumbering, river development, or commercial uses generally, with only minor or sporadic exceptions. Thus, the National Park Service is the guardian of our principal federal recreational preserves, inadequate in quantity as they may have become. Old hands in the United States Forest Service have been known to become vituperative about the "unconscionable waste" involved in not regularly harvesting the forest lands of the National Parks, but unharvested they remain, and probably for the public good.

Of recent years, the National Park Service has not been without its difficulties. With the explosive expansion of rural recreation activity, central areas of many of the more popular national parks (such as Yosemite) have been overloaded with visitors and have, during peak seasons, experienced severe congestion of both people and motor vehicles — and even local smog problems. These conditions not only reflect a severe inadequacy of recreational preserves, but also undoubtedly deteriorate the recreational values of the affected parks. Many of our National Parks are no longer places of escape and repose, but massive traffic jams as nerve-racking as a 5 o'clock urban rush. In our more popular National Parks (such as Yosemite, Yellowstone, and Great Smoky) the automobile is taking over. This frustrates visitors and threatens the integrity of the parks by generating ever-increasing demands for more roads, more parking areas, and more camper-trailer parks.

Some conservationists have accused the National Park Service of trying to attract swarms of visitors, playing a "numbers game." But this charge is not documented; and the basic trouble appears to be deeply seated in the scarcity of developed recreational preserves, and not alone in the scarcity of replicas of Yellowstone, Yosemite, and Great Smoky.

With respect to Yosemite National Park, plans are being studied to bar general automotive traffic in the central Yosemite Valley and some adjacent park areas, provide huge parking lots on edges of the park, and convey visitors by any of a variety of mass transit systems (monorails, minirails, tramways) designed to facilitate sight seeing. This might improve present unbearable conditions of congestion, but seems a very long way from a very satisfactory means of providing maximal recreational opportunities. It becomes increasingly clear that our National Park capacity to provide the recreational habitat demanded of it is drastically insufficient, and that much added attractive forested area should be made easily available for recreation.

Pushed by growing demand for the use of their lands, the Park Service has in some cases reacted by proposing new transmountain roads which would provide greater access to back-country or wilderness areas (as in the Great Smoky Park), but has been severely opposed by conservationist groups that place inviolability of wilderness areas above improved recreational habitat for the average vacationer. And it has been responding to congestion problems by developing task-force reports recommending expanded road systems (ecologically acceptable and aesthetically pleasing) which would, on the average, double or treble the amount of National Park lands that would be easily accessible for recreation. Thus it seems to be proceeding toward some tradeoff of underused wilderness areas for highly useable recreational areas — a step which has already been recommended above.

But whatever the Park Service does, we are going to have to turn elsewhere for greatly augmented tracts of forest that are easily accessible for recreational uses. This leads us finally to consider the resources and the policies of the United States Forest Service.

Recreational Resources and Policies in the National Forests. The National Forests provide by far our greatest federal reserve of forest land available for recreation — 185 million acres of it. However, the policy of the United States Forest Service has been to manage the National Forests primarily and predominantly for the production of timber, has accommodated livestock grazing and mining, and has made general recreation a residual claimant that does not receive a great deal of attention.

A 1962 statement by the United States Forest Service describing the official objectives of the "multiple use policy" applied in the National Forests suggests the system of priorities among uses that is actually observed. The preamble to the statement lists these objectives in the following order: production of lumber, protection of water supply, supplying grazing land, and recreational use. It is then explained that the multiple-use policy is to be applied to large areas of land, so that, on the average:

1. Lands *best adapted thereto* will be devoted to timber production.
2. Lands best adapted thereto will be opened to the grazing of livestock.
3. Other lands "perform their greatest service" when used for camping, picnicking, and other forms of public recreation, and will be made available for recreational uses subject to their compatability with paramount values.

The inference that lands supporting merchantable timber will not be developed for recreational purposes is reasonably plain.

To this it is added that alpine areas within the National Forests (marked by shallow soils, steep slopes, rugged terrains, and a general absence of merchantable timber) which are accessible by road are good candidates for recreational use of the wilderness-area type, and that logging roads tend to open up undeveloped country to recreation. The major constructive activity of the Forest Service appears to be in setting up camp-site complexes with minimal facilities and in selective removal of dead and dying logs and stumps, complete slash removal, and thinning of forest canopy to admit sunlight in existing and designated future recreation areas.

But the extent of development of recreation areas in the National Forests seems quite small. Regularly circulated statistics systematically refer, not to acreages devoted to various purposes, but to "production" measures for each forest such as annual board feet of lumber produced and the maximum number of recreational visitors that can be accommodated at any one time ("people-at-one-time"). To remedy this deficiency in data, we secured from the Forest Supervisors of five of the six large National Forests that span the extensive west slope of the great Sierra Nevada mountain range in east-central California, data on the amount of each National Forest acreage that was developed for recreation. The total acreages of these five forests range from 696,000 to 1,774,000 acres, with three above one million acres. The acreages developed for recreation in the five forests, taken individually, are 682, 859, 1,404, 1,595, and 1,541 — from 0.45 percent to 1.9 percent of the total forest acreages.

These data refer to the most accessible National Forests in a state with a huge population seeking outdoor recreation and to forest lands which, because of heavy forestation and spectacular terrain, can furnish the highest quality of recreational habitat. Though we have not assembled comparable data for National Forests in other regions, it seems improbable that recreational development in those less populous regions is any greater than found in our sample.

Having provided these token recreational preserves, the National

Forests generally do not have systems of access roads to the other 98 or 99 percent of their acreage, which would enable large numbers of vacationers to enjoy them for recreation. To be sure, hardy hikers, hunters, and fishermen can walk into underdeveloped areas, and logging roads provide selective access to some of these areas (although our experience is that it helps in using logging roads to have a four-wheel-drive vehicle and perhaps to carry a chain saw to help remove deadfall from the roads).

The primary failure in the National Forests has been a failure to provide easy access to any substantial amount of their forested lands for recreational purposes. And access is crucial. Professor Phillip O. Foss has supported this view as follows:

> Public access (i.e., access to public lands suitable for recreation) does not automatically come about . . . by the removal of prohibitions against public use. Public access can be assured only when positive measures are taken to facilitate access. In reality, the public does not have access to public recreation resources unless sufficient access roads, parking spaces, camping areas, water, and sanitary facilities are provided. Using this criterion, some federal agencies do not now provide adequate public access to recreation resources owned or created by the public. . . . If the anticipated future demand for outdoor recreation is to be satisfied, it will be necessary to construct additional, or improved, roads and parking lots . . . in the national forests, public domain, and possibly in some national parks.[18]

Writing in 1972, we concur with Professor Foss generally, suggesting however, that the need for the access developments that he proposed in 1965 is not in the future, but right now, and that the need has been acute for a number of years in many regions. The United States Forest Service, in managing the National Forests, has been unbelievably remiss in its neglect in the provision of access to adequate amounts of forest land for recreation, though it is by far the largest governmental holder of such land. The public policy issues that its performance raises, which will be discussed below, are obvious.

Privately Owned Forest Lands and Recreation. Of course, private owners control about twice as much timberland as the National Forests. It is generally agreed that these lands are predominantly used by their owners for timber production, and that some recreational by-products may be supplied when — as is typically the case — private timberlands are opened to public access. Because of destructive logging methods and practices, as well as higher-grade practices which render harvested forest lands unsuitable for recreation and

[18] "Problems in Federal Management of Natural Resources for Recreation," *National Resources Journal,* V, May, 1965, pp. 69–71.

lacking in aesthetic values, the by-product recreational habitats provided are generally of an inferior or unsatisfactory sort.

There are isolated instances in which private logging companies have modified their logging practices so as to preserve exceptional recreational resources. For example, an association of owners of timberlands in Maine through which the famed Allagash River flows have agreed to grow and harvest trees not only in accord with sound forest management, but also in such a way as to preserve the natural wilderness beauty of lands bordering the Allagash as well as other lakes and streams, to permit public use of the area for recreation, and strictly to limit building on the banks of the Allagash. This sort of policy is encouraging but distinctly atypical among private lumbering interests.

As noted, most industrial forest land is open to the public for hunting and fishing, and a few companies provide facilities for boating, camping, swimming, and so forth. But the latter sort of practice is rare, and the forested recreational habitat thus made more useable is generally inferior in quality because of past lumbering.

The general logging industry attitude with respect to recreational use of private forest lands is well summarized in an official statement of the American Forestry Association in 1962. It held (1) that multiple use of private forest land differs from such use of public lands in that more emphasis must be placed on economic returns to the owner; (2) that this implies focussing on the production of lumber as the major use of private forest land and limits the extent to which minor uses may be permitted; and (3) that recreation is the principal minor use to which private forest lands are likely to be put, but the land owners must derive some revenues from this minor use.

Under our system of laws, it seems impractical to look toward privately owned forest lands as significant additions to our rural recreational environment.

In our discussion of various holders of forest land, we have neglected to cover state parks — which contain about 5 million acres of forest land, generally as recreational preserves — because of lack of organized data concerning them. Nevertheless, their significant, if comparatively minor, contribution to providing forests for recreation should be recognized.

Remedial Public Policy Measures. The problem of a severe shortage of easily accessible rural recreational resources of forested land in the United States is simpler and more clear-cut than other rural recreational problems discussed in this essay. By the same token, it is easier to devise potentially quite adequate public policy measures to deal with the problem; our analysis of it has already implied their general character. Hopefully without being either simplistic or politically naive, we will advance here five related policy proposals:

1. *More National Parks.* A strong case can be made for increasing the number of our National Parks by enough roughly to double their present total forested acreage. The lands for the added parks could be secured, with simple legislative action and some financial support, both through the conversion of parts of National Forests into national park recreational preserves and through condemnation and purchase of privately owned tracts of forest land. In the expansion process, a disproportionately heavy, but by no means preponderant, emphasis should be given to establishing added national parks in areas reasonably accessible by automobile to the heavy concentration of population in the northeastern part of the country, where the shortage of rural recreational resources is most acute.

In the process of doubling our National Park forest preserves, National Park Service policy should be shifted away from one of insistence that eligibility of forest lands for National Park status should require that they contain "unique natural wonders," in favor of a policy of considering eligible for park status tracts with high-grade forest habitat — either virgin or mature second-growth — and with topography and other features providing significant scenic amenities.

2. *Changed Patterns of Recreational Land Use in National Parks.* Through internal changes of administrative policy, bolstered if needed by Congressional action, there should be a conversion of a very significant proportion of National Park forest lands from wilderness areas to easily accessible, semiprimitive, general recreational areas. This would require a well-planned program of building access roads into the reclassified areas and providing in a very dispersed pattern basic camping facilities of the sort appropriate to semiprimitive areas. Usual National Park land-use policies should apply to these areas. This proposal is meant to imply that a great deal of wilderness area would still be protected as such in National Parks.

3. *Revision of the General Wilderness-area Program.* Existing federal legislation should be amended to provide that the 52 million acres of forest land now designated for consideration as protected wilderness areas should be redesignated for equally strong consideration as candidate general recreational areas, primarily semiprimitive, to which easy access should be provided together with basic provisions for general recreational use. Devotion of at least half of this tentatively designated wilderness acreage to general recreational preserves is recommended.

4. *Changes in United States Forest Service Land-use Policies.* Through internal changes in the land-use policies of the United States Forest Service, bolstered again as needed by Congressional action, the effective land-use priorities now applied in managing National Forests should be revised to put recreation on a really equal footing with lumber production. This revised policy should move from paper to action initially by setting aside as general recreational

preserves at least 10 percent of the forest acreage held by the National Forests, this recreational acreage including as appropriate large tracts of merchantable timberland which offers superior recreational advantages. Adequate and easy road access to and into these preserves should be provided, together with basic facilities supporting their general recreational use.

5. *Expansion of State Parks.* Generally across the country, but in particular its eastern parts, which are undersupplied or not supplied at all with National Parks and National Forests, strong political action should be mounted to develop state programs for the acquisition of private land and dedication of public land for the creation of a vastly expanded acreage of forested state parks. It seems appropriate that some program of federal subsidization of part of the costs of creating new state parks might reasonably be developed.

Each of these proposals might be elaborated on and discussed in detail, but the preceding compressed presentation of them should suffice for present purposes.

CONCLUSION

A brief essay of this sort requires no extended recapitulation. In it, we have been concerned with three environmental problems involving inland water and forest resources suitable for rural recreation. One involves the progressive overdevelopment of our rivers for commercial purposes, with the resultant destruction or deterioration of natural stream habitat and the oversubstitution of still-water reservoirs for free-flowing streams. Another entails, largely but not entirely on privately owned forest land, destructive and short-sighted logging methods and practices that are systematically destroying the reproductive capacity of our forests, destroying watersheds by promoting erosion, and seriously defacing natural forest habitat. The third centers on the general failure of public authorities, which have under their control the resources to do otherwise, to provide easy access to anything like a sufficiency of forest-based general recreational resources to match public demands for the use of such resources, in a welter of split-jurisdiction confusion concerning diverse and conflicting aims.

These problems are all serious from an environmental standpoint, and generally interdependent. Remedial public policies are needed now — not after another ten years of special study commissions during which at least two of the problems would seriously and irreversibly worsen. Because of this, we have proposed certain remedial public policies for very early adoption. These proposals include a substantial moratorium on further river-development projects until a new environmentally oriented federal review board is created to review and make ineligible for construction added river-development projects the environmental costs of which are not very clearly outweighed by net commercial benefits. Following this course would introduce a most radical revision of federal water-development policies of the last several decades — but nothing much short of this would be efficacious.

The proposals also include the development on the federal level of comprehensive and adequate controls of lumbering methods and practices on privately owned forest lands, together with some tightening of forest harvesting regulation by the United States Forest Service. The imposition of real regulation on the private lumbering industry is as sorely needed as any new policy recommended, but also probably has the smallest chance of being attained. In this area, therefore, we should "try harder."

Finally, we have proposed a comprehensive reorientation and reform of federal policies affecting the recreational use of forest lands, aiming in the general direction of trebling or quadrupling the amount of prime forest land which is easily available for public recreation. These proposals as a whole will offend numerous established federal bureaucracies, industrial lumber interests, and the one-man-per-square mile recreational preservationists. But, at the federal level, they are not politically impossible, and could be implemented if serious cadres of the environmental protection movement could develop a bit more of consensus on prime objectives and end results to be sought.

If the preceding remarks agitate serious thought about and actual reappraisals of our policies affecting rural recreational environment, they will have accomplished their purpose.

SUPPLEMENTARY READINGS

1. Center for the Study of Responsive Law, *Power and Land: The Ralph Nader Task Force Report on Land Use in the State of California*, Robert C. Fellmeth, ed., Washington, D.C., 1971.
2. S. V. Ciriacy-Wantrup, *Resource Conservation: Economics and Politics*, Berkeley, Calif., University of California Press, 1952.
3. Marion Clawson, *The Federal Lands Since 1956: Recent Trends in Use and Management*, Baltimore, Johns Hopkins Press, 1967.
4. Marion Clawson and Jack L. Knetch, *Economics of Outdoor Recreation*, Baltimore, Johns Hopkins Press, 1965.
5. Edwin G. Dolan, *Tanstaafl: The Economic Strategy for Environmental Crisis*, New York, Holt, Rinehart, and Winston, 1969, Chapter 7 ("Preserving the Wilderness: Public Interest or Special Interest"), pp. 85–97.
6. Phillip O. Foss, "Problems in Federal Management of Natural Resources for Recreation," *Natural Resources Journal*, 5, May, 1965, pp. 62–94.
7. Charles McKinley, *Uncle Sam in the Pacific Northwest: Federal Management of Natural Resources in the Columbia River Valley*, Berkeley, Calif., University of California Press, 1952.
8. Arthur Maass, *Muddy Waters: The Army Engineers and the Nation's Rivers*, Cambridge, Mass., Harvard University Press, 1951.

9. Donald J. Morriss, "Timber Production on Recreation Areas," *Journal of Forestry*, 59, December, 1961, pp. 878–881.

10. Outdoor Recreation Resources Review Commission, *Multiple Use of Land and Water Areas*, Washington, D.C., 1962.

11. Outdoor Recreation Resources Review Commission, *Water for Recreation — Values and Opportunities*, Washington, D.C., 1962.

12. Outdoor Recreation Resources Review Commission, *Wilderness and Recreation — A Report on Sources, Values, and Problems*, Washington, D.C., 1962.

13. Edward F. Renshaw, *Toward Responsible Government: An Economic Appraisal of Federal Investment in Water Resource Programs*, Chicago, Idyia Press, 1957.

14. William Schwartz, ed., *Voices for the Wilderness*, New York, Ballantine Books, 1969.

7 The Unsatisfactory and Deteriorating Environment of Our Large Central Cities

PREAMBLE

Typically, large central cities in this country are by now the urban centers of larger metropolitan areas, frequently defined as being roughly bounded by the traditional city limits of the major cities around which extended metropolitan areas have grown. They generally are the sites of the majority of large-scale commercial activity and employment of metropolitan areas. Thus we find in them the main aggregations of large and high buildings that house the central offices of major nonfinancial and financial corporations, large law firms, big department stores, major and lesser hotels, wholesale distribution centers serving the distribution trades, and so forth. In addition, they are frequently the sites of various sorts of industrial plants, though the proportionate importance and type of those vary widely among large central cities.

Finally, they almost uniformly contain large numbers of residential housing units — ranging from hotel-type rooms through flats and apartments to single-family residences — typically providing living space for from 25 to 50 percent of the population of the metropolitan areas of which they are the centers. A significant minor part of central-city populations (generally one-third or more) ordinarily resides in residential units that are "sandwiched," or fitted into, or closely proximate to, the commercial "core" of the central city. A major proportion of this population, on the other hand, occupies outer urban rings within the central cities, and lives in flats, apartments, and (in important proportion) single-family residences.

Large central cities generally have very high population densities per residential acre in urban core areas and high densities in their outer urban rings. In addition, they tend to have very little open space proportionate to their acreages, with substantially no undeveloped land in urban cores, and from 5 to 10 percent of the land in outer urban rings undeveloped. In a word, central cities tend to be highly congested with people and with buildings.

BROAD ASPECTS OF THE COMPARATIVE INFERIORITY OF CENTRAL-CITY ENVIRONMENTS

Having defined the type of urban unit with which we are concerned, let us turn to the environment it provides for its residents. It is almost uniformly agreed in reams of publications on the subject that our central-city environments are in numerous respects bad, have been bad for a long time, and are in the midst of a process of becoming progressively worse. When we probe the meaning of this sort of environmental evaluation, we usually find that what it implies is really that these environments are viewed as distinctly inferior (and becoming more so) to actually or conceivably available alternatives, on some sort of scale running continuously from "best" to "worst."

From the individual's standpoint, the distinct (and progressive) general inferiorities of central-city environments turn out to include severe comparative disabilities in supporting physical well-being and especially in providing numerous psychic satisfactions. At the extreme, these disabilities result in undermining physiological health and in creating serious psychic dissatisfactions — and possibly a deterioration of emotional or mental well-being.

From a social standpoint, the major inferiority of central-city environments, is that (through an aggregation of impacts on individuals) they tend to engender aggressive behavior, crime, and symptoms of actual social disorganization.

OUTMIGRATION TO SUBURBS AS A SYMPTOM OF THIS COMPARATIVE INFERIORITY

Whatever the degree of inferiority of large central-city environments, some relatively simple Census statistics describing outmigration of central-city residents to suburban areas are seemingly sufficient to support the following generalization: At least a large minor fraction of previous central-city residents have evidently found the central-city environment inferior to an available suburban environment to which they had physical and economic access.

Viewing these statistics, one commentator has noted that suburbanization of residences and stores, first held in check by the great depression and World War II, then abetted by improvements in highway transportation, gathered irresistible momentum by the early

1950's.[1] This movement from central cities to the suburbs, as corroborated by Census statistics, was almost entirely by white population in the middle, upper-middle, and higher income classes — i.e., by those who could afford it.

We lack continuous and comparable statistics on this migration running from 1950. But for the single decade 1960–1970, recent Census data show that the fifteen largest central cities in the United States lost on the average (simple mean) 16.5 percent of their white population. If we omit two atypical cities, the remaining thirteen largest had an average one-decade loss of 21.3 percent of their white citizens. At the same time, the central cities generally had a relatively constant or only mildly declining total population. These migrants also evidently in large part moved to the suburbs of their metropolitan areas. In the corresponding fifteen metropolitan areas encompassing these central cities, the average one-decade increase in outside-the-central city white population was 28.6 percent from 1960 to 1970 (the outside-central-city populations having on the average approached but not reached corresponding central-city populations by 1960).

This emigration to the suburbs noted for the 1960's evidently represented an extension and acceleration of the same sort of migration that characterized the 1950's. For the two-decade period 1950–1970, net white outmigration from large central cities to suburbs probably exceeded 25 percent of the 1950 central-city white population. What of the central cities which were smaller than the fifteen largest we have so far emphasized? For the remainder of the 55 largest such areas analyzed by the 1970 Census, the percentage declines of central-city white populations from 1960 to 1970 tend to lessen with city size, but there were very substantial white-population declines in the central cities of over half of the remaining forty smaller metropolitan areas.

The data described so far tend to convince the writer that the size of the migration of white populations from large central cities to surrounding suburban areas is *prima facie* evidence that a substantial fraction of residents of central cities preferred suburban environments. And, since those who migrated were limited to those who could afford it, the percentages of central-city populations *wishing* to escape central cities were without doubt significantly larger than the percentage that actually migrated. What these people disliked about central city living is a matter we will discuss below.

BLACK INMIGRATION TO THE CENTRAL CITIES AND ITS ENVIRONMENTAL EFFECTS

Concomitant with the rapid outmigration of white population from large central cities since World War II has been a large inmigration

[1] Norton E. Long, "The City as Reservation," *The Public Interest,* Fall, 1971, No. 25, pp. 22–38.

TABLE 1

Year	Percentage of population black
1910	1.4
1920	4.3
1930	8.0
1940	9.7
1950	16.2
1960	28.7
1970	38.3

of black population to these cities. This inmigration had been proceeding slowly for a long time. But it accelerated rapidly with the beginning of World War II and has continued at a high pace ever since.

The time pattern of growth of Negro population in large central cities is fairly well represented by the pattern for the central city of Cleveland, Ohio — here defined as the area lying officially within unchanging city limits. The percentages of its population which were black, at decade intervals beginning in 1910, are given in Table 1.

We observe here a fairly typical pattern for central cities of gradual growth of the percentage of blacks in the population from negligible at the turn of the century to appreciable but quite moderate until the involvement of the United States in World War II. Then, in the 1940's, the black-population percentage rose sharply, largely because of the migration of black people into the central cities to ease the labor shortage created by peak production of munitions in a major war — this migration often resulting from industrial recruitment of labor force.

The black-population percentage in the central cities might have peaked before 1950, but it certainly didn't. One hypothesis is that the black people who had been recruited into industrial employment during World War II preferred for the time being the environments they found in large central cities to those they had left, and "wrote home" encouraging others of their race to follow them. Whatever the reason, the black migration to the central cities has continued at a high rate ever since. It has been estimated that from 1950 to 1960, the Negro population of all principal central cities increased from 6.5 to 9.7 million, or by about 50 percent.[2] Picking up more detailed Census statistics beginning in 1960, we find that between 1960 and 1970, the black population of the fifteen largest central cities rose on the average from 22.9 to 31.8 percent of the total populations of those cities — reflecting a nearly 40 percent increase in black population in one decade. The trend of black migration may be finally tapering off,

[2] Anthony Downs, "Alternative Futures for the American Ghetto," *Daedalus*, 97, Fall, 1968, p. 1332.

but not by much so far; and the modal large central city by now has a population that is around one-third black.

Environmental Impacts of Black Inmigration — Economic Tendencies. When we consider the outmigration from large central cities to suburbs of much of the more affluent white population of metropolitan areas in conjunction with the concomitant inmigration of black populations to the central cities, we observe two related phenomena: First, beginning around 1940, very large numbers of black people, amounting by 1970 to about 20 percent of central-city populations, immigrated into new and frequently unfamiliar economic and social environments. Second, the ethnic and socioeconomic composition of the large central cities experienced a drastic change, as the black immigrants effectively replaced a comparable number of the more affluent white population. On the level of socioeconomic change, there tended to be a "downward homogenization" of central-city populations.

The environmental consequences of these two phenomena have been many, complicated, highly interrelated, and too numerous to consider all at once. To begin somewhere, let us first center directly on their impacts on the economic status of the black inmigrants, and indirectly on the effects of this economic status on their immediate environments.

It is generally agreed that their economic status, as measured by rate of continuous employment and by individual or family income, has been *on the average* poor, though dispersed among individual cases all the way from regularly employed at good wages to chronically unemployed. A first reason for this poor average showing has been that at least a substantial minority of able-bodied inmigrant black adults could supply only semiskilled or unskilled labor, and that there has been a short demand for this sort of labor within the generally nongrowing central cities.

A second reason is that the total demand for semiskilled labor in the central cities has progressively declined as the outmigration to the suburbs of the more affluent part of the white population proceeded. This has resulted mostly from the fact that companies in the distributive trades (including department stores and specialty shops) and in the service trades have followed their best customers to the suburbs by establishing branch outlets in various suburban shopping centers, shifting major portions of their sales volumes and of their demand for labor from the central cities to the suburbs. (A distinctly lesser tendency of this sort has been observed in the movement of corporate headquarters and of industrial plants.) Consequently, a central city of relatively constant population has tended to offer significantly fewer employment opportunities as large parts of its relatively affluent white population moved to the suburbs and were replaced by black inmigrants.

Third, metropolitan labor markets are typically so segmented and poorly organized that central-city black residents in general have not had effective access to the jobs that followed the white migration to the suburbs. Blacks who might secure relatively low-income jobs in the suburbs are deterred from doing so by the cost of commuting to reach them. And they are generally unable to secure suburban housing close to those jobs because they cannot afford it and because of numerous institutional barriers to racial integration of the suburbs.

Fourth, at least a part of the major labor unions in central cities — and particularly building-trade unions — have been unwilling to admit to membership more than token fractions of the inmigrant black populations and have thus excluded the great majority of eligible black workers from numerous types of central-city employment.

Fifth, inmigrant black populations either brought with them or have developed a minority of fatherless families with children, headed by mothers who have been deserted by their husbands or who have borne illegitimate children. This minority has been disproportionately large as compared to that for the entire central-city population. In these families, the employability of the mothers is generally low, and problems of child care deter them from accepting employment. In consequence, they are very frequently supported by governmental welfare payments, which means that in general that they have very low incomes.

As a result of all the circumstances just enumerated, substantial minorities of central-city black people earn either low or "poverty" incomes, or earn no incomes and are supported by poverty-level welfare payments.

So much for the economic status of central-city black populations as measured by income. Let us now turn to the effects of this economic status on their immediate environments.[3] The substantial minority of them who have very low incomes cannot afford reasonably high-grade, well-maintained housing, and could not even if *de facto* segregation within central cities did not effectively limit their housing opportunities to highly segregated areas. When we add the fact that their effective housing opportunities are rather systematically confined to rather well-defined racial ghettos, their plight is worsened. For these ghetto areas typically supply out-of-date and poorly maintained or decaying housing — sometimes in the form of single-family residences, but more frequently in the form of residential units which are fractions of old houses broken up into a number of flats by their landlords. Thus, to the decrepitude of the housing is added small floor spaces per person or family unit, and residential crowding or

[3] A part of these effects stem from the misallocation of residential land among users, particularly between black and white users. In this instance, the misallocation has its main roots in unbalanced personal income distribution and in racial prejudice.

congestion. Moreover, given its need for housing and the limitations on the supply available, the poor minority of the central-city black population has often been forced to pay relatively high prices for quantity plus quality of housing rented.

We will turn in a subsequent section to the broader environmental consequences of *de facto* racial segregation into ghettos and of the development of true slums within these ghettos. For the moment, let us focus on the fact that a substantial minority of central-city black people, because of the circumstances described, have very poor housing environments because of the low quality of the buildings they occupy, insufficiency of housing space, and human congestion in their residential buildings and neighborhoods. Their housing environments, moreover, are usually distinctly poorer than those of the central-city white people whose earnings are not above the middle-income level. A corollary of this is that the housing environments of central cities have *on the average* worsened for their whole populations as a result of the change in the racial composition of these populations.[4] Unfortunately, we lack data revealing whether or not the housing environment that inmigrant blacks encountered in the central city was viewed as better or worse than the ones they left.

Environmental disadvantages other than those connected with housing, of course, also go with the low incomes of the central city's minority black group. Important among these is an effective lack of economic access to open country, to rural vacation trips, and to other

---

[4] Some incomplete indications of the degree of inferiority of housing in the poorer Negro ghettos is provided by some 1970 Census data for the City of Cleveland, which makes the following comparison of housing among (1) the outer urban ring of the central city, which is predominantly white; (2) the major poverty area of the inner urban ring, designated as Hough, which is predominantly black; and (3) the central slum area within the Hough poverty area:

	Population per residential acre	*Percentage of housing units without plumbing*	*Percentage of housing units with more than 1 person per room*
Outer urban ring	31.6	1.31	3.61
Hough poverty area of inner urban ring	59.0	6.47	11.01
Central slum within Hough poverty area	77.2	7.07	14.21

These data tell us only a little bit about differences in housing quality among the areas, and nothing about differences in state of maintenance. Also some very pertinent data are lacking — namely those which would refer to the average number of persons per room in housing units with more than one person per room in each of the three areas. United States Bureau of the Census, Census of Housing, *1970 Block Statistics, Final Report HC(3)-178, Cleveland, Ohio, Urbanized Area* (Washington, D.C., 1971).

avenues of temporary escape from ghettos. Consideration of such disadvantages more or less automatically leads us to turn to environmental consequences of black inmigrations of a more sociological sort.

Environmental Effects of Black Inmigration — Sociological Tendencies. There have been a number of sociological results of the large inmigration of black population to central cities. Most of them seem to stem in considerable part, however, from the fact that the black population which emigrated to the central city (largely after 1940) became predominantly *de facto* segregated into racial ghettos.

This pattern of segregation seems to be fairly represented in 1970 Census statistics for Cleveland, as follows:

1. In the inner urban ring of the central city (its core), of 115 Census tracts:
   a. Twenty-six had 85 percent or more black population (usually more than 95 percent).
   b. Fifty-two had 88 percent or more white population, and of these, 33 tracts were all white.
   c. The remaining 37 tracts were unsegregated or mixed in varying degrees.
2. In the outer urban ring of the central city, of four separately incorporated municipalities and 27 Census tracts:
   a. One tract had a 97 percent black population.
   b. Three municipalities and 23 tracts were over 91 percent white, and of these, two municipalities and 16 tracts were all white.
   c. One municipality and 3 tracts had relatively balanced black-white integration.
3. In the inner suburban ring of the metropolitan area, of thirteen separate municipalities and 74 Census tracts:
   a. Thirteen municipalities and 38 tracts had populations that were 93 percent or more white, and of these, eight municipalities and 31 tracts were all white.
   b. Twenty-five tracts were 85 percent or more black.
   c. Eleven tracts were significantly integrated.
4. In the outer suburban ring, of 35 Census tracts:
   a. Thirty-three were 92 percent or more white, of which 25 were all white.
   b. Two were integrated at about a 30 percent black population level.

The general pattern of segregation of most of the black population into predominantly black ghettos and of keeping the preponderance of the remaining neighborhoods either lily-white or close to it is fairly clear. Similarly clear is the pattern of concentrating the great bulk of the black population into parts of the inner urban ring and the substantial absence of black population in the outer suburban ring. A variant pattern is that, whereas the outer urban ring was predominantly white, the inner suburban ring had a significant minority of black population, reflecting perhaps in part a lesser degree of racial discrimination in the somewhat higher socioeconomic groups that populate inner suburbia than in the lower such groups that live in the outer urban ring.

Overall, however, confinement of the black population to a number of racial ghettos is the motif, and it is a disturbing one. Such extreme racial segregation as is reflected in the data just described is generally associated with social disorganization or a breakdown in established social organization. Drastic racial differences among neighborhoods or larger areas have demonstrably increased bifurcation of urban communities, exaggerations of racial biases and hatreds, and — especially in influential segments of the black community — disrespect of established local governments, of law enforcement, and especially of the urban police. These tendencies tend to surface in dramatic increases in aggressive behavior in black sections and in serious social disorders that have in recent years been reflected in dangerous riots. The resultant general tendency toward social disorganization, together with its numerous manifestations, has probably done more than anything else to degrade the general environments of central cities.

Some of these manifestations are indeed severe. There seems to be ample evidence that, as the proportions of black people in central cities became large, crime rates increased greatly — with an emphasis on armed robbery in the streets ("mugging"), aggravated assault, rape, and crimes of violence generally. We will not cite such statistics as are available on increases in the rates of various types of crimes, either for whole central-city populations or for their black components because of the notorious unreliability of police statistics on crime. Given some "true" overall crime rate and some "true" black crime rate, the reported crime rates can and do vary widely with the intensity of law enforcement, with the bases of grounds for arrests, with the proportion of arrested persons who are booked, with the degree of inequality of police practice in arresting or booking white and black people, and so forth. As evidence of greatly increased central-city crime rates, we are more impressed with many apparently reliable journalistic reports concerning the reluctance of many black and white residents of central cities to be alone on the streets at night, with reports that in various areas of large cities, apartment dwellers are afraid to use the parking lots provided to them, that in such areas many male adults venture forth at night only if armed with baseball bats or lead pipes, that mothers do not allow their children to play outdoors, and so forth. Increased central-city crime rates — generally, but especially in or near racial ghettos — of course stem in part from poverty and from a growing drug culture. But more broadly they reflect social disorganization in the ghettos, coupled with a rejection by a significant number of black people of the rules and mores of the going social organization of the white "establishment." Needless to say, high crime rates do deteriorate the environments of central cities.

Another manifestation of environmental deterioration in central cities is the widely reported substantial increase in sanitation problems in poverty areas due to large accumulations of uncollected garbage — noxious in itself, but also resulting in large increases in the population of rats, especially in cities bordering on oceanic water or on large lakes. This phenomenon apparently has a number of causes. One is poverty, which induces or forces people not to pay for municipal garbage collection services and instead to dump their garbage in any convenient place, such as gutters, vacant lots, and public trash cans. Another, in some cases, is the inadequacy of municipal garbage collection systems, in terms of coverage and of insufficiently frequent pickups of garbage, especially in densely populated areas. Still another, unfortunately, is the failure of inmigrant minority populations to acquire "citified" attitudes toward garbage disposal, and thus to "join the system" of having their garbage regularly carted away — instead relying on gutters, vacant lots, and so forth.

Possible "Snowballing" of the White Migration to the Suburbs. Without citing other sorts of central-city environmental deterioration that are linked to large inmigrations of black people and to their *de facto* confinement in ghettos, let us consider a possible further effect of black inmigrations on central-city environments.

We have noted that there was a large outmigration of the more affluent whites to the suburbs in the 1950's and that this migration continued and accelerated between 1960 and 1970. We have also suggested as a principal explanation of this white outmigration that the migrants felt that the environment of the central city was distinctly inferior to the alternative environment of the suburbs. They had generally felt this way at least as far back as the 1930's, when the black populations of large central cities were quite small, typically not reaching 10 percent of total central-city populations. An inference that may be drawn from this suggestion is that large numbers of whites left the cities because of general deficiencies in their environments, and not because of the presence of large percentages of black people in the population. Thus, they left for the suburbs without being "pushed" by a black inmigration to central cities; contrariwise, they just left, and in the process created a central-city "vacuum" of redundant housing that was progressively filled by inmigrating blacks.

This explanation of the process of the turnover in the racial composition of central cities seems extremely plausible as applied to the earlier stages of the white migration to the suburbs — perhaps generally through the 1950's. Thereafter, we should stop and reconsider. A believable hypothesis — unproven, of course — is that as black populations rose (to around 23 percent of large central-city populations by 1960), and as their inmigration and ghetto-ization induced deterioration of centray-city environments, a great deal of white out-migration to suburbs was induced in one way or another by the presence in central-city populations of really important fractions of black people.

The possible motivations of whites who left central cities to escape from the blacks could have been several. First, plain old racial prejudice may have made them uncomfortable living in a city with a large minority — threatening even to become a majority — of its population black. Such prejudice is widely deplored, but it certainly exists. Second, the general deterioration of the central-city environment that was induced by large black inmigrations and the *de facto* settlement of blacks in racial ghettos may have swung the environmental preferences of many white citizens from the central cities to the suburbs. Finally, but by no means least important, may have been the federally supported enforcement of racial desegregation or integration of the public schools — by various means, including extensive "bussing" of children to schools outside their neighborhoods. This move began progressively to break the link between *de facto* segregation of blacks into isolated ghettos and *de facto* segregation of black children into predominantly black schools. Whatever the merits of school desegregation, large fractions of the white populations of central cities evidently opposed it. And whatever the merits of implementing school desegregation by bussing, even larger proportions of whites very evidently opposed that.

Given this variety of possible motivations, it is quite possible that a large part of the later white outmigration to the suburbs has been motivated by the presence of large fractions of black people in large central-city populations, together with school and other desegregation policies of the federal and other governments.

If this hypothesis is correct, the black inmigration to the central cities since 1940, at some stage, began to have "snowballing" effects in the directions of progressively increasing proportions of blacks in the populations of these cities, of downward homogenization of central-city populations in terms of socioeconomic status, and of general deterioration of central-city environments. Moreover — again if the hypothesis is correct — this process of change in the racial composition of central cities and of the environmental deterioration that it induces has by no means run its course. It is hard to predict at what point it will dwindle and central cities will reach relatively "stable states."

GENERAL DEFICIENCIES OF THE CENTRAL-CITY ENVIRONMENT

So far, our discussion of central-city environments has centered on the most dramatic dynamic process of social change that has affected them in the last twenty-five or thirty years. Thus, we have focussed on the large black inmigration into (and white outmigration from) central cities; on the deficiencies of housing and neighborhood environments that inmigrant blacks found in the central cities; and on the deterioration of central-city environments that followed their arrival, together with their segregation in ghettos.

A broader problem, however, concerns the major deficiencies of central-city environments that are more or less unconnected with blacks in the population; and in this section we will consider them. As a preamble to this discussion, it should be emphasized that a sensible inquiry should not center on "what was the matter to begin with" — e.g., before the rapid turnover in the racial composition of central cities, or from the outset of the emergence of large urban centers. Almost, if not quite, all of the deficiencies of central-city environments have for a long time been in the process of dynamic change — generally for the worse — so that most of them are best viewed as processes rather than steady states. This has been true particularly since the great suburbanization movement began after World War II. Therefore, our discussion must concern not only how deficient various aspects of the central-city environment are now, but also how these deficiencies have developed and where they are moving.

Pollution in Central Cities. A major deficiency of central-city environments is found in several types of pollution to which they are subject. Construing the term *pollution* not too broadly, in cities its principal sorts are air pollution, water pollution, and noise pollution. Large central cities are affected with by far the highest concentrations of these types of pollution of any residential areas in the country.

AIR POLLUTION. The most important of them is probably air pollution, because everyone, perforce, breathes the air around him. And the air mantles over large central cities are typically very significantly polluted with photochemical smog, carbon monoxide, sulfur dioxide, hydrogen sulfide, particulate matter of various sorts, and a number of other lesser air pollutants. This phenomenon, and its adverse effects on human health and plant life, as well as its undesirable aesthetic and other consequences, have been discussed in Chapter 5, pp. 112–113.

Air pollution in central cities, and almost as much in the inner suburban rings of their metropolitan areas, has become increasingly severe since the later 1940's, largely because of the increasing intensity of photochemical smog. In spite of ameliorative technological changes that have substantially reduced the pollutant emissions of motor vehicles per vehicle mile of driving, the increase in human population in metropolitan areas and the greater increase in the per capita usage of automobiles have resulted in more and more smog. It is notable that this increase in central-city air pollution is very largely attributable to the shift in the composition of metropolitan populations that we have already noted.

That is, the outmigration of the relatively affluent white population from the central cities to the suburbs has been matched about proportionately by an increase of automotive commuter traffic to the central cities and back to the suburbs. In large part, the suburbanized white populations have kept their jobs in the central cities and commuted to and from the suburbs in individual automobiles, generating more photochemical smog both en route and in the central cities. Statistics on the burgeoning of commuter traffic between suburbs and central cities clearly belie those easy and drastically inaccurate generalizations that by and large the outmigrants to suburbs took their jobs to the suburbs with them. Although some commerce — especially in the distributive trades — followed them to the suburbs along with the jobs which that commerce provided, a preponderance of the metropolitan economic activity and of the jobs it provided have remained in central cities. Thus, the migration to the suburbs has created a burgeoning population of drive-it-yourself commuters, which has been increasing faster than we can add and widen metropolitan freeways and highways.

There is no other plausible way of explaining the greatly increased use of automobiles and the congested traffic problems of the central cities. It is thus clear that the large outmigration to the suburbs from 1950 to 1970 created, as an external environmental cost, a large addition to the air pollution of central cities and immediately adjacent areas. (It is also clear that the outmigrants to the suburbs took a considerable part of central-city air pollution to the suburbs with them, thus defeating in part one of the objectives of their migration.)

WATER POLLUTION. Almost all of our major metropolitan areas, and with them their central cities, are adjacent to or fringe upon oceanic bays or inlets, large inland rivers, estuaries of rivers approaching the sea, or parts of the Great Lakes system on the northern border of the east-central United States. And these waters are by now almost uniformly heavily polluted. The pollution arises in greatest proportion from the discharge into these waters or the rivers feeding them of pollutant effluents by private industrial concerns, which have generally viewed these waters as nature's free sewers. The effluents consist of chemicals or the fluid residuals of chemical and other processes, of organic materials that are waste by-products of production, and of other sorts of industrial sewage. Another important contribution to water pollution consists of incompletely treated or raw muncipal sewage. And in some areas, the return flow of irrigation water to river channels introduces a complex of pollutants including mud, fertilizers, pesticides, and whatever else has been added to irrigated agricultural land — this all proceeding toward central-city regions. The typical result is that the open waters adjacent to central cities are, from heavily to unbelievably, saturated with a bouillabaisse of pollutants. This sort of situation is found in the river and ocean bay waters adjacent to Boston, New York City, and

Philadelphia, in the Allegheny River next to Pittsburgh, and in cities downstream on the Ohio River, in Great Lakes waters adjacent to Buffalo, Cleveland, Detroit, and Chicago, in the San Francisco Bay and its river estuaries, and so on.

This water pollution problem has not been responsible for unsafe or contaminated municipal water supplies in cities generally, although in many areas the sources from which these supplies are drawn are polluted enough that heavily treated and chemically disinfected municipal tap water does not rate high on the scale of palatability. However, waters adjacent to central cities are sufficiently polluted that they are severely limited in their natural functions of providing sites for recreation to city dwellers. They range from, at worst, being repulsive and odoriferous public nuisances to, at best, being suitable only for recreation not involving water contact, such as boating and, occasionally, fishing. In these ways, water pollution has degraded the total environments of central cities.

NOISE POLLUTION. The large central city is a rather noisy place in the daytime, and not especially quiet at night, though the intensity of noise within it varies from place to place. Here we will confine ourselves to the general noise to which the urban populace is more or less automatically exposed (excluding consideration of occupational noise from which workers in selected occupations suffer, because this is not a general environmental phenomenon and not primarily characteristic of large central cities).

The relative importance of principal sources of noise perceived by urban residents is suggested by the compiled results of field studies conducted by the Department of Housing and Urban Development in the central cities and inner suburban rings of Los Angeles, Boston, and New York City, which drew on large and representative samples of the populations of these areas.[5] For these three cities combined, a rank ordering of conscious noise sources was developed, in which the most noticeable noise source was assigned a rating of 10.0, and other noise sources were assigned ratings indicating their importance relative to the most noticeable source of noise (Table 2).

The top rating of traffic as a source of perceived noise is unsurprising. Central cities today tend to be crisscrossed with freeways and their on- and off-ramps, and numerous other traffic arteries — all of which carry heavy general automotive traffic, commuter traffic, and a complex of truck traffic that includes everything from local delivery trucks to huge intercity tractor-truck and double-truck combinations. It is generally agreed that the noise generated is primarily tire noise and motor noise and that heavy trucks generate a high proportion of total traffic noise. In addition, the whole web of downtown streets is

[5] United States Federal Housing Administration, *Noise in Urban and Suburban Areas: Results of Field Studies* (Washington, D.C.: 1967), pp. 21–24.

TABLE 2

Noise source	Noticeability rating
Traffic	10.0
Children/neighbors	6.9
Planes	2.3
Industry	2.3
Other	1.9
Animals	1.9
Sirens/horns	1.7
Passers-by	0.9
Sonic boom	0.8
Motorcycles	0.8
Trains	0.5

afflicted with noisy, heavy traffic. This is not a persistent source of annoyance to the bulk of central-city residents when at home, but the downtown working force is continuously exposed to it on working days.

The high average rating of children and neighbors as sources of noticeable noise evidently reflects fairly dense or congested building of residential units of all sorts and the high incidence of living in apartments or flats — generally the absence or insufficiency of open spaces separating residential units. The relatively low rating assigned to planes even in sample cities that have major commercial airport developments seems attributable to the location of major airports on or outside the fringes of central cities and on the commercial airlines' usual selection of landing and takeoff paths to pass over water or over thinly populated areas.

It is evident that central-city residents not only notice urban noise, but are bothered by it in varying degrees. To the extent that they are bothered, noise imposes an external environmental cost and deteriorates the central-city environment. We have no data on intensities of bother or annoyance with city noise or its general psychological consequences. However, the Federal Housing Administration studies of noise in Los Angeles, Boston, and New York, cited above,[6] recorded for the three cities combined the percentages of the population sampled which indicated that they were "bothered" by specific sources of noise. The results are given in Table 3.

Comparison of this noise-annoyance rating with the previous rating of noticeability of noises suggests that the quality and intensity of noises is more closely related to their ability to bother people than the frequency or persistence with which they are perceived.

The statistics presented suggest that noise in central cities does in-

[6] *Ibid.*

TABLE 3

Source of bothering noise	Percentage of population indicating bother
Traffic	15.4
Children/neighbors	13.9
Other	6.2
Planes	5.4
Animals	5.0
Sirens/horns	3.9
Industry	2.7
Sonic boom	2.3
Motorcycles	2.3
Passers-by	2.3
Trains	0.8
Not bothered by noise	39.8

deed appreciably degrade their environments, but that its impact is much less widespread and probably much less serious than air pollution. Still it deserves attention in any environmental program.

Two Matters Related to Pollution. SOLID WASTE DISPOSAL. Considerable concern has been expressed by some students of urban environmental problems about the burgeoning volume of solid wastes generated in central cities — encompassing trash and garbage, worn-out or wrecked automobiles, industrial solid wastes, etc. — that have to be disposed of somewhere, preferably in some way that is not environmentally detrimental to the recipient areas. The question generally posed is where can and where should we deposit the ever-accumulating body of such wastes, and whether or not the lack of acceptable solutions to this problem portends another subvariety of environmental crises.

It would appear that up to now solid wastes have not been the basis for a serious environmental problem. Except for the results of the failure of some central-city residents to avail themselves of regular municipal garbage collection — thus propagating accumulations of uncollected garbage in city gutters and vacant lots — solid waste is being regularly disposed of in a manner which does not create a pollution or sanitation or other environmental problem. Advanced techniques of sanitary landfill in vacant areas around cities — sometimes preceded by high-temperature incineration to reduce the bulk of solid waste (though except under advanced techniques this may contribute to air pollution) — is by now generally successful in compacting and covering solid wastes in a manner that does not generate sanitation or pollution problems. Moreover, the land areas used for sanitary landfills have so far seldom been located and managed in such a way as to result in aesthetic disfigurement of the landscape; and very frequently the usefulness and economic values of the recipient areas have been enhanced by landfills.

As time passes, however, more and more additional land which is currently vacant is needed for sanitary landfill disposal of solid wastes; and we are probably approaching through time a point at which some aesthetic disfigurement of rural landscapes — an environmental loss — will be the price paid for disposing of our garbage. This sort of disfigurement may occur, for example, as undeveloped canyons are filled up with compacted and covered solid waste, or other nonproductive rural lands are similarly used. Using the oceans as recipients of solid waste does not appear to be an environmentally sound procedure. We may thus face in the foreseeable future an environmental dilemma revolving around solid waste disposal, and some technological breakthroughs in waste-disposal methods are sorely needed. At the present date, however, we would not rank solid waste disposal as a serious environmental problem of the central cities.

The waste-disposal problem created by the regularly increasing numbers of motor vehicles that are ready for the scrap heap each year is a rather special one. Some students of urban environments have pointed to the aesthetic degradation of city environments by the proliferation of unsightly automobile junk yards and also of the appreciable incidence of defunct automobiles abandoned on city streets. These developments do tend to degrade central-city environments, but in the long run they do not need to. Automobiles are made primarily of metal, and there is a virtually insatiable demand for the scrap metal that worn-out or wrecked automobiles can provide, and regularly have been providing — in addition to providing used parts for currently operating motor vehicles.

The reason for some special waste-disposal involving defunct automobiles is largely that this sort of waste disposal has not been incorporated into and made an integral part of muncipal waste disposal systems, but instead has been left to fairly disorganized aggregations of private enterprises that collect defunct automobiles, strip them of salable parts, and eventually direct them toward enterprises organized to reduce them to salable scrap metal. This way of doing things does create some unsightly messes. An obvious remedy is to incorporate the collection of worn-out and wrecked vehicles into municipal waste-disposal programs designed to haul the vehicles to out-of-the-way centralized collection points and to license high-grade operations adjacent to collection points which will expertly strip them of reusable parts and compact them into scrap metal for ready sale. Auto scrapping would thus become a centralized industrial operation of economic value, no more objectionable than many other industrial operations. And the bulk of aesthetic blights now associated with the disposal of old automobiles would be largely removed. This part of the solid waste-disposal process thus should not in the long run create any serious environmental problem.

AESTHETIC DEGRADATION OF URBAN LANDSCAPES. Urban planners of the architectural persuasion have long complained that the heights, bulks, designs, and locations of buildings in the downtown areas of central cities are not such as to provide aesthetic amenities, but rather tend to wall off vistas and views and to create on ground levels monotonous outlooks and auras of confinement in canyons of large buildings. This sort of development is interconnected with failures to preserve within such areas sufficient areas of open space or to pay heed to the preservation of natural scenic views. Much of their complaint seems true, though in some central cities urban redevelopment plans have substantially lessened these environmental deficiencies.

Similarly, dense and continuous building of residences in outer urban rings, coupled with a failure to preserve adequate open spaces, have had comparable consequences. Thus, most large central cities, both downtown and in their densely built residential areas, have tended to be ugly and monotonous and also to induce impressions of confinement without visible routes of escape. Of course, terrain makes a difference, and it is harder to avoid a lack of scenic amenities in central cities built on flat plains than in those with hilly terrains. But even in a city like San Francisco, with a hilly terrain and surrounding bay and ocean waters to provide vistas from the hills, there has, in recent years, been increasing public outcry against the erection of numerous new high-rise buildings which screen off natural vistas and destroy the natural scenic amenities of the very hilly landscape. We will terminate this discussion here simply by noting that central-city environments generally have become aesthetically inferior because of the sorts of development described.

There is one other sort of central-city aesthetic blight, however, which has resulted from extensive suburbanization of metropolitan populations, and which is manifested in the typical accumulation in central cities of webs of massive freeways, the building of which has both induced and been induced by the huge volume of automobiles that carry commuters to and from the central cities. These freeway systems — and especially the elevated ones, which are most common — are generally massive concrete ribbon patterns, ugly in themselves, that shut off views or vistas and frequently bifurcate natural neighborhoods through which they pass. In general, they are a source of serious and pervasive aesthetic blight, degrading the central-city environment. Because they often occupy a fifth or more of the land space of central cities, their mere construction tends to bring with it the untoward aesthetic consequences mentioned. But these consequences have been worsened by their design. The ruling engineering mentality in highway departments, which is strongly influenced by the proposition that a straight line is the shortest distance between two points, has resulted in urban freeway designs that tend to maximize their aesthetic disamenities. It would not be much of an exaggeration to say that, on the average, aesthetic considerations have had very little to do with the designs of our modern urban freeways.

Of course, these freeways as used for commuting have been responsible for creating a large surplus demand for downtown parking structures and lots, both large users of scarce urban land. It has been estimated, for example, that in the extreme case of Los Angeles, about half of the central-city area is by now devoted to freeways and parking facilities. This tendency points in the direction of paving over the bulk of central-city areas — hardly an environmental advantage. Generally, the congestion of central cities with automobiles, roads to carry them, and places to park them is in many places approaching crisis proportions; drastic remedial measures are called for.

Psychological Effects of High Urban-Population Densities. In the appraisal of the environment of large central cities, a remaining important question concerns the extent to which congested housing and working conditions in these cities have adverse psychological effects on their residents, and also on their nonresident working populations. Such congestion-induced effects may range from nervous tension or general nervousness, through feelings of confinement and frustration, through neurotic tendencies and neuroses, to psychotic illness (severe mental derangement).

We have already touched on this issue in part in discussing above the psychological reactions of individuals and minority groups within inmigrant black populations in central cities, when they are residentially located in racial ghettos — noting the exaggerated incidence of aggressive behavior and of dissociation from established and other social organization. But whatever we found there did not give a clear picture of the effects of urban congestion per se, because of the obvious concomitant influences of recent inmigration and of residential ghetto-ization. What we seek now is any general relationship of central-city congestion to the psychological well-being of its residents and nonresident workers, aside from phenomena particular to black inmigrations and *de facto* segregation of black people in ghettos.

DEGREES OF CENTRAL-CITY CONGESTION. As a preamble to this inquiry, some indication of the degrees of congestion in large central cities seems in order. Here, we should first distinguish residential congestion from the congestion encountered in downtown city streets.

The latter sort of congestion is typically severe, involving persistent crowding of individuals (with periodic daily peaks) and continual work-day crowding of motor vehicles. This downtown congestion affects whatever population works in and/or resides in downtown areas of central cities. The intensity of this sort of congestion has not

TABLE 4

	Population	Percentage of acreage residential	Population per residential acre	Square feet of residential land per person
Inner urban ring	324,839	30	55.7	780
(Poverty area)	(39,400)	(52)	(59.0)	(740)
(Central slum)	(5,037)	(52)	(77.2)	(560)
Outer urban ring	526,598	48	31.6	1,380

been systematically measured, but is readily visible to residents of or visitors to our large cities.

As to residential congestion,[7] which is seemingly of equal or greater importance, experts generally agree that it should be measured in two dimensions of different significance: number of residents per acre or other area of residential land; and density of the occupation of individual residential units, as measured by resident persons per room or square footage of floor space per resident. Though these two measures of residential density are significantly intercorrelated, efforts have been made to distinguish between the effects of the two sorts of congestion.

What degrees of intensity of residential congestion are found in central cities? To get some up-to-date notion of this, we have drawn on 1970 Census statistics for the central city of Cleveland, which was about the thirteenth most populous in the United States in that year and has numerous important characteristics typical of most large central cities. Cleveland was the first large city for which fairly complete 1970 Census statistical data were made available.

The statistics below compare residential densities per unit of land area for the inner urban ring and the outer urban ring of central-city Cleveland in 1970, and also such densities for those parts of the inner urban ring identified as the main poverty area (Hough) and the central slum section of the Hough poverty area (Table 4).

Clearly, there is a distinctly greater residential density per unit of land area in the inner urban than in the outer urban ring, and much greater density than anywhere else in the central slum area. To develop a better notion of these varying densities, we may note that the density in the inner urban ring as a whole and in its poverty area corresponds to *an average* of about 3.8 to 4 persons per 30-by-100-foot residential lot, which represents noticeable but not severe crowding. The density in the central slum area corresponds to an average of

---

[7] A part of the residential congestion problem, involving the misallocation of urban residential land among uses and users, has been a subject for abstract analysis on pp. 28–36 of Chapter 1.

about 3.6 persons per 20-by-100-foot residential lot, which represents fairly severe crowding. The residential density in the outer urban ring, on the other hand, corresponds on the average to about 3.6 persons per 50-by-100-foot residential lot, and represents very moderate urban population density.

Of course, the "density impacts" of these ratios of residents to residential land areas are intensified by the fact that there is more or less continuous and uninterrupted building of one sort or another (residential, commercial, industrial, institutional) in both the inner and outer urban rings. There is no undeveloped land in the inner urban ring, and in the outer urban ring only 7 percent of all land is undeveloped. Moreover, comparatively miniscule areas are devoted to public parks and other open-space development in either ring. Thus, in the inner urban ring, there is not much open space available in the usual residential area, other than city streets and sidewalks. Gardens or yards surrounding residential units are absent or minimal in size, especially after allowance is made for driveways and garages or other parking places. In the outer urban ring, residential density per unit of land area is such as on the average to afford residents private space in moderate-sized yards or gardens, in addition to space associated with the city streets. But the land of the whole ring is pretty completely occupied by buildings, so that open spaces such as vacant lots are scarce.

We have been citing, of course, average residential population densities mainly for two large areas — the inner and outer suburban rings of Cleveland. Within each area, densities vary considerably among tracts and among blocks, so that given the mean densities, we encounter in various neighborhoods both much lighter and much heavier residential densities than indicated by the area means. The substantial incidence of neighborhoods of considerably higher than average residential density in the inner urban ring is perhaps a matter for particular concern.

Let us now turn to statistics on central-city congestion within residential units. These perhaps deserve especial attention because social psychologists and sociologically oriented psychiatrists have placed considerable emphasis on the importance to adult individuals of "a room of one's own," where a person can secure privacy when desired and include some and exclude others at will.

Some Census statistics cited in n. 4, p. 184 for Cleveland in 1970 actually reveal very little, and implicitly conceal a good deal, about the incidence of crowding in central-city residential units. On such crowding per se, they indicate only the percentages of residential units in various areas that have 1.01 or more persons per room. These percentages were for Cleveland's inner urban ring 8.51; for its outer urban ring 3.61; for the Hough poverty area 11.01; and for the central slum 14.21. But the above and below 1.01 persons per room dichotomy is unrevealing and quite insufficient.

First, it tells us nothing about the average number of persons per room in residential units with 1.01 or more persons per room. But simple deduction tells us, for example, that a three-room residential unit in this class must have *at least* four residents (three rooms for four people), a four-room residential unit must have at least five residents (four rooms for five people), and so forth. These are *minimum* congestions in residential units classed as having 1.01 or more persons per room. The average congestion as measured in terms of persons per room unquestionably exceeds these logically necessary minima, although by unmeasured amounts.

Second, use of the ratio of the number of people per residential unit to its gross number of rooms is misleading if we are looking for indicators of the incidence of crowding which is destructive of individual privacy. From any total number of rooms in a residential unit — whether three, four, or more — we need generally to deduct at least one general-purpose room that is no individual's private preserve — namely, a kitchen — and perhaps, in addition, a sitting room which, although it may house a bed or more, is again the private preserve of no one. If deductions of these general-purpose rooms were made from rooms available in residential units, the Census statistical showings and actual measures of in-residence crowding would be significantly revised. First, the percentage of residential units with 1.01 or more persons per "nongeneral-purpose" room would rise very significantly. Second, the average number of persons per "nongeneral-purpose" room would rise correspondingly. And, without pursuing the argument further, it is plain that the in-residence "congestion index" is much larger than Census statistics might indicate. Our general conclusion is that destructive crowding within individual residences is a much more pervasive phenomenon than Census statistics indicate, that it is probably quite pervasive in the inner urban rings of central cities, and that it is very much so in poverty areas.

POSSIBLE PSYCHOLOGICAL EFFECTS OF URBAN CONGESTION. It is difficult to support very many generalizations about the psychological effects of urban residential congestion for two main reasons. First, the bulk of research attention of social psychologists and sociologically oriented psychiatrists has centered, in the mental health area, on the relationship of residential density to the incidence of psychoses (severe mental derangements). And the incidence of psychoses is slight enough that it could not be rated as a dominant aspect of the urban mental health picture. (In downtown areas of central cities, where the incidence of psychoses is generally the highest, the annual incidence of discovered psychosis is only in the neighborhood of 150 to 200 cases per 100,000 population.) Second, the research experts in question have developed little data on the incidence of conditions of psychological stress or of neuroses, and practically no relationships between the frequencies of these slighter and more common psychological disturbances and the frequencies of psychoses. Thus, we are unable to infer from a finding that psychoses are positively associated with residential urban density (increasing as density becomes greater) the hypothesis that the same positive correlation exists between residential density and the incidence of psychological stress, neuroses, and other relatively minor forms of mental disturbance. Some hypotheses of this sort have been offered by various sociologists and social psychologists, but they generally lack documentation or are weakly supported by research evidence.

Given this state of affairs, let us refer first to evidence on the relationship of psychoses to urban residential congestion, and subsequently turn to hypotheses concerning much less severe psychological effects of central-city population density.

A study by Faris and Durham, first published in 1939, but sufficiently respected that it was reprinted as late as 1960, produced some basic findings on the relationship of the incidence of psychoses to urban residential population density.[8] Studying this relationship for Chicago in 1930–31, the authors found a strong positive correlation of residential population density per unit of land (also probably per residential room) to the annual rate of psychotic disorders per 100,000 population. The rate was highest in residences in the central business district, and declined progressively as one moved outward from this center to locations progressively further from the central business district to the periphery of the city — in any direction (which excepted one or two) in which population density decreased progressively with increasing distance from the city center. The magnitude of decrease in incidence of psychoses was from about 140 cases per 100,000 population in the central-city area to about 50 per 100,000 annually on the periphery of the city.

Subsequent research, referring not only to American cities but also to Hong Kong and to London, has tended to confirm their general finding; but a number of experts have concluded that the incidence of psychoses is much more directly related to crowding *within residential units* than to the density of population per unit area of residential land (although, of course, the two sorts of crowding are fairly highly intercorrelated). The explanation offered for this more specific relation of in-residence crowding to psychoses is that most or at any rate very many people individually require regular access to a room or "space bubble" where each can secure absolute privacy, and which is "his own" in the sense that he can exclude others with whom he does not want contact and selectively invite in still others with whom he desires association. This sort of privacy plus the opportunity for the individual to "escape" residential crowding that is unpleasant to him is held indispensable to the reasonably full mental health of many people. The result of constant trespass is aggression

---

[8] Robert E. L. Faris and H. Warren Durham, *Mental Disorders in Urban Areas* (first printing, 1939; reprinted, New York: Hafner, 1960).

and also, evidently, a higher incidence of psychotic behavior. These findings have been substantiated in part by research findings that as more children are put into a classroom of the same size, the incidence both of aggression and of psychological "withdrawal" increases.[9]

Let us now turn from the relationship of residential density to psychoses to its relationship to psychological stress and neuroses. It has been noted that high densities of residential buildings on lands is by no means always accompanied by comparably high population densities per unit area of land, or by crowding within residential units. That is, within regions of central cities of generally high population densities, there are areas in which individuals or families occupy uncrowded residential units, most frequently in the form of flats and apartments. Under these residential conditions, it has been noted that the effect of high density housing on human social behavior is much more that of loneliness than of crowding, and that the most common behavioral symptoms are those associated with psychological withdrawal. One study indicated that in London, other circumstances and influences being equal, the incidence of some sort of psychological illness was 63 percent higher among residents of flats or apartments than among residents of single-family houses.[10] These general average tendencies, of course, should not conceal the fact that there are wide differences among individuals in their reactions to various housing and living conditions. The big city tends to be a comparatively lonely place, but extroverted, outgoing, and gregarious souls are likely to find pleasant acquaintances and develop friends anywhere that other people are. Nevertheless, we observe in the average tendencies cited one indication of the relationship of psychological stress or neuroses to congested living conditions, and one significant environmental cost of central-city congestion.

Behaviorally oriented sociologists and others have offered some plausible hypotheses also bearing on the psychological effects of urban congestion. One is that the frequent stimulation and interaction concomitant with dense living engender psychological and even physiological strain and tension.[11] Pertinent especially to psychological stress imposed on people who work downtown, as well as those that live there, is an hypothesis advanced by Marion Clawson.[12] He suggests that people abroad in the streets of downtown areas "feel crowded" because the typical individual is exposed to a larger number

[9] Gerhard Rosenberg, "High Population Densities in Relation to Social Behavior," *Ekistics*, XXV, June, 1968, pp. 425–427.

[10] *Ibid.*

[11] Halliman H. Winsborough, "The Social Consequences of High Population Density," *Law and Contemporary Problems*, XXX, Winter, 1915, pp. 120–125.

[12] "Open (Uncovered) Space as a New Urban Resource," in H. Perloff (ed.), *The Quality of the Urban Environment* (Washington, D.C.: Resources for the Future, Inc., 1969), pp. 139–204.

of sensations, primarily visual, than he is prepared to absorb. More people and objects force themselves on his attention than his perceptive ability is able to cope with. Anyone who seeks to comprehend the whole or major portions of downtown urban scenes finds himself overwhelmed with visual, auditory, and perhaps olfactory sensations. Faced with the great complexity of the normal street scene, the viewer either suffers *feelings of crowding*, or retreats into a self-imposed selection of only a small part of it.

The accumulation of findings of organized studies and of prolonged more casual observation by qualified people seems sufficient to support the general hypothesis that both residential congestion and out-of-doors downtown congestion are significantly conducive to psychological stress on a broad scale, and to neurotic symptoms and neuroses on a probably somewhat lesser scale. What the evidence has not so far told us is whether these psychological effects are largely confined to downtown areas or inner urban rings, or whether the effects are also felt in reduced degree in outer urban rings. Considering the factors usually identified as causing stress and neuroses, we would expect these psychological complaints to have a distinctly lower but no means zero incidence in outer urban rings, and a still lower incidence in suburbs. However this may be, the psychological effects of central-city congestion appear to impose a very significant environmental cost.

PUBLIC POLICIES TO IMPROVE CENTRAL-CITY ENVIRONMENTS

Devising public-policy remedies to alleviate or cure the ailments of central-city urban environments is not an easy task. The ills are both numerous and variegated in character and require different types of policy treatment. In particular, only a minority of them are subject to cure by waving the magic wand of technological change. Many of them seem remediable only by inducing or forcing a reallocation of the uses of privately owned land, together with a relocation of people; and remedies of this sort are not necessarily feasible politically. Therefore, it seems appropriate to consider both urban environmental problems and corresponding public-policy remedies in a somewhat piecemeal fashion, proceeding from the simpler to the more difficult.

Urban Problems of Pollution and Aesthetic Degradation. AIR AND WATER POLLUTION. Central-city problems of air pollution and water pollution can be and are being attacked by various direct means. Prospects for success are good. Means include direct regulations, administered in various ways, of the design of products that emit air pollutants or cause water pollution, like automobiles and detergents. They also include imposing taxes or other penalties on pollution-gen-

erating products or processes, providing incentives for pollution-reducing technological changes; and public subsidization of product
and process changes which will greatly diminish the volume of pollutants reaching air mantles and streams or bodies of water. Water
pollution may also be combated by public enterprise activities designed to regenerate, augment, and aerate streamflows. Because such
policies have already been discussed in Chapters 4 and 5, we will not
expand our discussion of them here.

NOISE POLLUTION. Annoying urban noise is much more difficult to
abate, except in very modest degree by the regulation of truck and
automobile designs in order to obtain vehicles which will travel more
quietly.

Another policy measure might involve regulations which required
the routing of through highway trucking well around cities on an
expanded system of peripheral freeways, and even insisting that
major loading and unloading facilities for heavy trucking destined
for central cities be located adjacent to such peripheral roads, substituting quieter means of shuttling cargoes to their ultimate destinations.

A more drastic measure, which is being widely considered and has
been or is being implemented in some American cities, would involve
the large-scale substitution of relatively quiet mass transit systems
(subway or underground within the central cities) for private automobiles as the mode of transport that carries suburban commuters
to and from central cities. However, it is not clear at this point that
provision of even very good and fast mass transit systems would induce any mass shift away from the automobile by commuters, unless
their use of autos for commuting were rather heavily taxed, and such
taxation might very well not be politically feasible.

Urban noise from most other sources (for example, neighbors and
children) is not readily abated. In selected instances, direct regulations might accomplish something. For example, jet airlines might be
required under threat of penalty to develop and use less noisy jet
engines, and feasible revisions in take-off and landing paths at airports might be sought to reduce the extent to which departing and
arriving aircraft pass over populous areas.

AESTHETIC DEGRADATION OF URBAN LANDSCAPES. Existing degradation of urban landscapes by commercial building heights, bulks, and
locational patterns, and by webs of urban freeways, are hard to undo,
at least in the short or medium term.

It is clear that public efforts should be organized to secure much
more attention than heretofore to aesthetic considerations in further
urban freeway routing and construction. Also, as existing downtown
commercial and public buildings are progressively replaced with new
ones, and as more large buildings are added, political pressures should
be organized to secure improved zoning and building codes oriented

to well-conceived master plans for the improvement of scenic values and for the provision of more light, air, and open space in downtown areas.

This is easily recommended, and most large cities do have central land-use planning authorities to the recommendations of which zoning and building permit agencies are supposed to be responsive. But really implementing urban master plans that are intended to control central building locations, heights, bulks, and densities in downtown areas is especially difficult because of the political power of opposing commercial interests, and of building-trade unions which want to maximize construction employment.

We have already mentioned the desirability of incorporating into municipal waste-disposal systems the collection and centralization of scrapping of defunct automobiles.

Downtown Residential Population Densities. It is agreed by many that the adverse social and other environmental effects of high residential population densities in inner urban rings have not been significantly mitigated by substituting for old and decrepit housing new low-cost (and generally subsidized) housing in large clusters of apartments also located in the inner urban areas. This appears to be so whether or not the supplying of new low-cost housing of this sort is accompanied by clearing blighted or slum residential areas for development to support expensive apartment houses or new commercial buildings.

The inner urban congestion problem is not much alleviated by this sort of policy, and the adverse sociological tendencies associated with such congestion seem to follow the rehoused residents to the neighborhoods of their new and improved living quarters. That is, the policy shows distinct signs of tending, within medium time intervals, simply to relocate poverty areas and slums within inner urban rings, and not of coping with the basic congestion problem. Moreover, razing an old residential neighborhood to prepare its land for "urban redevelopment," and relocating its previous residents in new low-cost housing elsewhere, may be worse since it may disrupt a well-organized, "self-policing" neighborhood, and substitute for it one that is poorly organized and not adequately "self-policing."

If rehousing is to be an instrument of policy for improving the environments of inner urban rings, and also of the people who have been living in them, it should be linked with a very substantial geographical dispersion of city-core residents into much less crowded areas, where residential densities will be significantly lower. Densities no higher than are typical of outer urban rings should be sought.

THE LINKAGE BETWEEN HIGH POPULATION DENSITIES AND PROBLEMS OF LARGE BLACK POPULATIONS IN INNER CITIES. Problems of excessive residential density in inner urban rings are solidly linked to the excessive and dense populations of recently inmigrant black people in the same areas. And the policy solution of substantial geographical dispersion of city-core populations is one that would very heavily involve, and perhaps should emphasize, such dispersion of black populations. Such an emphasis seems appropriate because central-city black populations, in addition to living in degraded environments, generally are in severe economic difficulties resulting from the shortage of central-city demands for the largely unskilled or semi-skilled labor that they can supply.

Therefore, our further discussion of proposals for relieving congestion in the inner urban rings of central cities will focus heavily on proposals for the geographical dispersion of black urban populations. Such dispersion has the rationale (for the white urban poor as well as for the blacks) of relieving economic distress in central cities, as well as the rationale of relieving undesirable psychological and social conditions.

Proposals for Geographic Dispersion of Urban Black Populations. Nearly all of the authorities whose work we have read in academic journals and in periodical media directed at the intelligentsia propose some plan for or form of massive geographical dispersion of urban black populations, by moving them to locations distinctly outside central cities.

One economic rationale for this policy has been suggested by Anthony Downs.[13] He suggests that, given unemployment and poverty in black central-city ghettos as well as among poor urban whites, most new employment opportunities are being created in the suburbs of our metropolitan areas, not anywhere near to central-city ghettos. If we are going to provide jobs for the rapidly expanding ghetto population, particularly jobs that do not call for high levels of skills, we must somehow bring these potential workers closer to the locations of new employment opportunities. This can be done in three ways: by creating better transportation between the ghettos and surburban job locations; by moving job locations to the ghettos; or by moving ghetto residents to the suburbs.

A preponderance of informed opinion seems to choose the last-named alternative as the most possible, or perhaps only feasible, one. The improved transport solution seems unpromising, especially since we have been unsuccessful in providing rapid and inexpensive transportation of suburban white commuters to and from central cities. Not only distributive trade retailers, but also in lesser degree industrial plants and central corporate offices, have been moving outward to the suburbs at various rates and are unlikely to reverse this trend, because of higher taxes and higher land costs in central cities. This leaves us with the solution of moving ghetto residents to the suburbs, and as noted the bulk of experts favor some version of this solution, both on economic and sociological grounds.

[13] Downs, "Alternative Futures," pp. 1331–1377.

Let us review several of the more prominent proposals that have been made.

Kain and Persky[14] propose subsituting for conventional urban renewal and public housing programs a program designed drastically to increase the supply of low-income housing in the suburbs, with governmental subsidization as necessary, to induce the transfer of a large portion of central-city ghetto residents to the suburbs. This would remove the geographical limitations on the opportunities (which the authors say exist) for the employment of blacks in the suburbs. This program, as they conceive it, would not necessarily incorporate racial integration in suburban neighborhoods. But it could provide smaller and less densely populated black communities, with corresponding environmental advantages.

L. and P. Davidoff and Gold[15] preface their proposal with the observation that there is a superfluity of unoccupied or thinly occupied good building land in suburban areas surrounding metropolitan areas — that even along the Boston-Washington megalopolitan corridor, about 80 percent of the good building land is substantially unoccupied. They specifically propose a shifting, engendered by governmentally planned and financed rehousing and relocations, of black and other economically surplus central-city residents to developed and previously undeveloped suburban areas. As to low-income housing in the suburbs, they propose emphasis on row housing and garden apartments (erection of which would require substantial revision of typical suburban zoning and building regulations). Such low-cost housing would, preferably, be built in small developments in old or new towns, in a context where the towns could and should assure the preservation of large amounts of open space, through "cluster zoning" and "planned unit development." This would result in a combination of high densities in parts of tracts with set-asides of substantial acreages for recreational use. Thus, prospectively, no suburban slums and no "sluburbian" sprawl. Like other authors mentioned, these hold (without documentation) that the metropolitan job market has already decentralized toward the suburbs, and would decentralize more to provide jobs for the suburbanized black and poor former residents of central cities.

Before proceeding to a more extreme proposal, we would like to interject one major reservation concerning the sorts of suggestion so far described. Each one is viable only on the generally undocumented premise that there has been a quantity and quality of decentralization of metropolitan job markets — resulting from outmigra-

---

[14] John F. Kain and Joseph J. Persky, "Alternatives to the Gilded Ghetto," *The Public Interest,* No. 14, Winter, 1969, pp. 74–87.

[15] Linda Davidoff, Paul Davidoff, and Neil M. Gold, "The Suburbs Have to Open Their Gates," *The New York Times Magazine,* Nov. 7, 1971, pp. 46–59.

tions to suburbs of retail stores, service trades, industry, and corporate central offices — that is sufficient to create an unfulfilled demand for unskilled and semiskilled labor anywhere nearly large enough to absorb masses of suburbanized blacks and others who are supposed to be moved from the central cities. We have not seen statistics that document this premise, though a time when we are nearing the end of over two years of generally depressed business conditions is perhaps not a fair time to count open jobs. Before people push further for the adoption of the sort of proposal reviewed, conditions in suburban job markets should be extensively and intensively examined.

Another alternative proposal to solve problems of central-city congestion is that of "conurbation" — the development of an aggregation of *separate* urban communities around each very large central city, securing some degree of population dispersal and some escape from undue residential concentrations in central cities. Some observers of this sort of development around London, both native and visitors, have been very favorably impressed by this sort of development there. In the London area, of course, the development was greatly assisted by the bombing out of central London during World War II. Many informed observers do not believe that conurbation is a feasible or especially attractive alternative for the United States. It could be pointed out, however, that relocation of central-city residents in numerous suburban towns, especially if these towns were in the outer suburban rings of metropolitan areas, could *nolens volens* be a stepping stone toward conurbation.

A much more extreme proposal for urban decentralization has been advanced by Spilhaus,[16] as by others. He bases his proposal on a categorical denial of the argument that we cannot, even if we would, dismantle our central cities. And his proposal is indeed to dismantle them, developing instead a system of *dispersed cities of controlled size*, surrounded by open areas of land. He would wish to retain cities as the major loci of residence and industry, big enough to offer the advantages of city living, but small enough not to be subject to unplanned overgrowth. Cities with populations of about 250,000 apiece are mentioned as illustrative of the city sizes he would seek. In such cities, he alleges, we would not have pollution, traffic congestion, riots, and other ills that develop as cities become too large. Such cities, he feels, would be attractive enough to induce people to move to them from wherever they had been. His suggested gradualistic approach to this revolution in city living would begin with one model experimental city, very well planned and managed.

This is of course a somewhat Utopian scheme, and could conceivably be implemented economically only through a long evolutionary

[16] A. Spilhaus, "The Experimental City," *Science*, 159, February, 1968, pp. 710–715.

process (if accomplished by revolution, it would bankrupt the revolution). We do not feel it to be feasible in the foreseeable future, and, like any reader, can only speculate about its many probable disadvantages, as well as about the probability that it would not be a panacea for urban ills.

Our general conclusions about the prospects for improving central-city environments are, as suggested in this essay, about as follows. First, some aspects of these environments — like those involving pollution of various sorts — can be very appreciably improved by economically and politically feasible public policies; and these sorts of improvements are at least under way. Second, the more severe environmental problems — revolving around central-city congestion, the rising proportions of unskilled or semiskilled blacks in central-city populations, and their *de facto* residential ghetto-ization — are not going to be easily remedied. The policies proposed for widespread suburbanization of black and other central-city residents seem to have greater putative merit than those focussed on central-city renewal, but they are untested and the probability of their success is very difficult to assess. Nonetheless, these problems, which are worsening, are sufficiently severe that we should do something — and something different than we have tried before. Rapid movement toward the implementation of sizeable pilot programs for dispersal of black and other central-city populations into the suburbs of metropolitan areas should probably be made, because this dispersal policy holds forth enough promise that it should be tried.

SUPPLEMENTARY READINGS

1. Linda and Paul Davidoff and Neil M. Gold, "The Suburbs Have to Open Their Gates," *The New York Times Magazine*, November 7, 1971, pp. 46–59.
2. Anthony Downs, "Alternative Futures for the American Ghetto," *Daedalus*, 97, Fall, 1968, pp. 1331–1377.
3. Robert E. L. Faris and H. Warren Durham, *Mental Disorders in Urban Areas*, New York, Hafner, 1960.
4. Harold J. Haskins, "A Strategy for the Ghetto: The Philadelphia Story," in *Agenda for Survival: The Environmental Crisis — 2*, Harold W. Helfrich, Jr., ed., New Haven, Yale University Press, 1970, pp. 71–83.
5. John F. Kain and Joseph J. Persky, "Alternatives to the Gilded Ghetto," *Public Interest*, No. 14, Winter, 1969, pp. 74–87.
6. Norton E. Long, "The City as a Reservation," *Public Interest*, No. 27, Fall, 1971, pp. 22–38.
7. Harvey S. Perloff, ed., *The Quality of the Urban Environment: Essays on "New Resources" in an Urban Age*, Baltimore, Johns Hopkins Press, 1969.
8. Jerome Rothenberg, *Economic Evaluation of Urban Renewal*, Washington, D.C., The Brookings Institution, 1967, especially Chapters III and IV.

9. Alvin A. Schorr, *Slums and Social Insecurity,* Washington, D.C., U.S. Department of Health, Education, and Welfare, 1963.
10. A. Spilhaus, "The Experimental City," *Science,* 159, February, 1968, pp. 710–715.
11. U.S. Federal Housing Administration, *Noise in Urban and Suburban Areas: Results of Field Studies,* Washington, D.C., 1967.
12. Halliman H. Wainsborough, "The Social Consequences of High Population Density," *Law and Contemporary Problems,* 30, Winter, 1965, pp. 120–125.

8 Some Environmental Impacts of Our Freeway and Airline Transportation Systems

In the last two decades, and especially since 1960, there has been a mounting public concern in this country over the adverse environmental impacts of our highways and of our airline transportation systems. The time at which such concern began to assume serious proportions is related dually to dramatic technological developments in commercial aircraft design and to the institution of a massive federal program for the building nationwide of a comprehensive network of limited-access rural and metropolitan freeways.

As regards airlines, the strategic technological breakthrough involved the development, and introduction in 1959, of the jet-powered subsonic airliners. These revolutionized air travel by reducing air travel times between relatively distant points by from a half to three-fifths — for example, reducing transcontinental flight time from twelve or more to five or six hours, and halving flight times over routes as short as a few hundred miles. As the major airlines rapidly converted to jet-powered equipment, their use for medium- and long-distance travel increased progressively and dramatically (and is still rising rapidly), so that they are in the process of becoming — except for rather short distance trips — the major mode of passenger travel other than the private automobile, outstripping railroads and buses combined. In addition, they have become a significant minor carrier of freight (selectively according to its value relative to its weight and bulk). By now, therefore, airliner flights into and out of the airports of major cities have become so numerous that they are generating distinct environmental impacts in these main areas of their departures and arrivals.

210

As regards freeways, the federal government in 1956 launched — and has since proceeded very rapidly with — a program of supplying the nation with a "whole new set" of rural and metropolitan super roads. They are generally characterized by having access to and egress from them limited to on ramps and off ramps, eliminating cross traffic from intersecting roads. They are generally of multilane construction in each direction, with opposite moving lanes separated by dividing strips. Their designation as freeways derives from the fact that their use is not subject to charges or tolls.

The resulting Interstate Highway System is planned to provide (and it is approaching completion) 35,000 miles of rural freeways that will connect 90 percent of all United States cities of over 50,000 population, and 6,000 miles of freeways or super highways in metropolitan areas. Ninety percent of the cost of the Interstate Highway System (IHS) is borne by the federal government (10 percent by the states), with federal financing from a Highway Trust Fund automatically fed by federal taxes on gasoline and automotive repair items. The currently estimated total cost of the system is about $70 billion. Thus, it has been justly characterized as both the greatest public works program in history and the largest political pork barrel. The environmental impacts of the construction of the IHS have been important, numerous, and varied — especially in metropolitan areas.

Let us discuss in turn the major environmental impacts first of present airline transportation systems and second of our recently created massive system of freeways. Both involve principally the external environmental costs of the side effects of the provision of goods and their services, of the general sort analyzed on an abstract level on pp. 11–20 for Chapter 1.

AIRLINE TRANSPORTATION SYSTEMS

A full evaluation of the environmental impact of any transportation system must take account of the impact first of the operation of the transport vehicles, second of the roadways (or airways) they travel, and third of connected facilities essential to their effective operation. In the case of commercial airlines, attention has usually centered on the vehicle, the jet-powered airliner.

The "roads" that commercial airliners travel are bands of open atmosphere — typically air corridors between 25,000 and 35,000 feet in altitude — plus lower altitude take-off and landing air corridors originating or terminating at ground level. These do not per se impose environmental problems, although air space is becoming crowded enough that fairly complex flight-control regulations, applying both en route and at landings and take-offs, have had to be imposed by federal regulatory authorities in order to keep individual aircraft systematically and safely separated at all points. Included among these are queuing systems for aircraft about to take off or about to land, and instrument landing-control systems for low-visibility conditions, depending heavily on ground-based radar installations.

The third major component of airline transportation systems of course consists of airports, from and at which airliners must take off and land, in order to pick up and deliver passengers and other cargo. These airports also serve as service and repair stations for aircraft and as fueling points. They are the origin of an environmental problem probably as important as any generated by airline operation.

There are three major environmental impacts of airline operations that deserve emphasis. These are (not in order of importance) pollution of the air in metropolitan areas; creation there of noise nuisance or pollution; and traffic and parking congestion engendered by ground travel to and from major airports, in smaller part by airline passengers and in larger part by persons employed in these airports and in the noncentral urban districts that tend to grow up around them. Let us consider these in turn.

Air Pollution. Because airliners have huge engines that consume fuel at very high rates, and visibly emit smoke on take off, there has been some general concern about their contribution to air pollution in metropolitan areas. The principal airline sources of air pollution (other than attracted ground traffic) are evidently exhaust emissions of departing and landing planes, jettisoning on take off of some unburnt jet fuel that accumulates in on-plane sumps, and exhaust from testing engines on the ground in the course of servicing operations. In spite of some unsupported and unbelievably wild guesses concerning the resultant airliner contribution to air pollution, it seems to be comparatively small.

Data prepared by official sources for the San Francisco Bay Area — which is not badly atypical in any obviously relevant respect of most metropolitan areas — sustain this impression.[1] In 1970, the three major commercial airports in the nine-county San Francisco Bay Area that were equipped to and did handle nonmilitary airliners were San Francisco International Airport, Oakland International Airport, and San Jose Municipal Airport. In that year, they together served an average of about 1,380 commercial aircraft "operations" (landings plus take offs) per day, or about 690 airliners per day "in and out." The area airliner traffic was thus "in the major league" of metropolitan areas.

The percentages of the total tonnages of major air pollutants emitted into the air of the nine-county Bay Area in 1970 on the average day which came from commercial air carriers are shown in the first row of Table 1. It is evident that commercial airliners contributed

[1] Bay Area Air Pollution Control District, *Aviation Effects on Air Quality in the Bay Region* (San Francisco: 1971), pp. II-2, V-7, V-9.

TABLE 1

		Air Pollutant			
	Partic.[a]	*CO*[a]	*NO$_x$*[a]	*HC's*[a]	*SO$_x$*[a]
Percentage emitted by commercial air carriers	4.5	0.5	0.7	0.8	0.7
Percentage emitted by all aircraft	6.7	1.1	1.3	1.5	1.2

[a] Partic. = particulate matter; CO is carbon monoxide; NO_x covers nitrogen oxides; HC's represent uncombusted hydrocarbons; SO_x covers sulfuric oxides.

negligibly to air pollution in the area as a whole and that the only appreciable (but still small) contribution was in the form of carbon particulates in smoke.

All aviation in the area (including private general and military aviation as well as commercial) also contributed negligibly to air pollution — the contribution of the noncommercial aviation ranging roughly from 50 to 100 percent of that of commercial aviation. The percentage, but not the absolute-tonnage contributions of aviation to air pollution, were greater in the outer ring of the nine-county area, where pollution from automotive sources was smaller. The source of these data, the Bay Area Pollution Control District, estimates the contributions of both commercial and total aviation to air pollution in the Bay Area in 1980 as on the average less than double those of 1970 in absolute terms, and still negligible in percentage terms. This is in spite of the expectation of somewhat reduced overall nonaircraft air pollution, and of substantially increased commercial airline and other aviation traffic. Our conclusion is that aside from local ground concentrations of air pollutants at airports, commercial aviation does not now present or in the near future promise to present a serious air pollution problem.

Noise Pollution. Commercial airliners arriving at and departing from metropolitan airports undoubtedly create considerable noise pollution or nuisance within metropolitan areas. (In addition, airports themselves generate the most intense relatively unconfined noise in urban areas, as taxiing of planes and ground testing of aircraft engines are added to landings and take offs of planes, but the resulting noise nuisance is rather highly localized.) Some commentators have held that, unless checked, aircraft will probably become the most pervasive and disturbing source of urban noise in the future, even if the shift to larger planes results in the number of airliner operations growing more slowly than the number of airline passengers.

At present, they definitely are not. Data cited in Chapter 7 above (pp. 192 and 193), referring to the noticeability and "bothersomeness" of noise from different sources in the central cities and inner suburban rings of Boston, Washington, D.C., and Los Angeles in 1966 or 1967, suggest that in terms of noticeability, noise from aircraft rated a poor third or fourth behind traffic noise and noise of children and neighbors.

There appear to be several related reasons for the relatively low incidence of noticeability and irritability of aircraft noise, and especially of commercial airliner noise, in metropolitan areas. First, metropolitan airports, needing large areas of open space for take offlanding runways, are typically located well away from central cities, generally within outer suburban rings — at distances from city cores of from fifteen to twenty-five or more miles. Thus, they tend to be placed in areas of low density of residential population. Second, commercial airliners do not make either landing approaches to or take offs from major airports equally from or to all points of the compass.

Instead, a typical airport will have two sets of runways, with each set having a different directional axis — e.g., a roughly north-south and a roughly east-west set of runways — to facilitate the ability of planes to land and take off approximately against the wind under different typical wind-directional conditions. (Usually one general wind direction is dominant, and another secondary.) Further, the approach routes of arriving airliners and take-off routes of departing ones are generally parallel to and centered on the axes of the two sets of runways. Thus, there are relatively narrow air corridors, each aligned with a set of runways, through which airliners pass in approaching and leaving the airport — corridors generally a very few miles in width. With a wind predominantly from the north, commercial aircraft will make landing approaches in an air corridor running from south to north (to use the runways with that directional axis), and will also take off from south to north. Then, air traffic in general will traverse a well-defined and fairly narrow south-to-north air corridor extending from a number of miles south of to a number of miles north of the airport. With a westerly wind, comparably, landing and departing aircraft will traverse another east-to-west air corridor extending from a number of miles east to a number of miles west of the airport.

This procedure tends to "canalize" intense aircraft noise perceived at ground level at any one time to a moderately narrow band of underlying land or water, with the perceived noise level dropping off progressively and substantially as one moves laterally away from the long sides of the air corridor. Thus, in a large metropolitan area, only a small fraction of the land area is either regularly or periodically affected by commercial aircraft noise of 100 decibels intensity or more (compared to 95 decibels for heavy trucks at a distance of twenty feet), and a very small part of that to noise of 115 decibels or more. (The "pain" threshold for noise is generally set at 135 to 140 decibels.)

Moreover, the resulting environmental impact on people is lessened by the fact that large parts of the air corridors used for landings or take offs in metropolitan areas very frequently pass over water (with no residents below to be bothered), or pass over land areas of low residential population density.

There are two factors, however, that tend to aggravate the airliner noise problem in some degree. First, at peak hours for aircraft landings — especially in poor weather — queues of circling planes often accumulate, waiting for their turns to land, and fly over large areas of land around airports for periods as long as a quarter to a half hour per plane, temporarily spreading higher noise levels as perceived on the ground quite widely. This effect, on the other hand, is mitigated considerably by the fact that the "holding" altitudes of queued planes are generally three or four times those of landing and departing planes.

Second, if a metropolitan area becomes large enough to support a fair number of major airports (let us say five or six or more), and if these airports are quite disparately located, the number of landing-take-off air corridors in the metropolitan area increases, and larger fractions of the land in the area are subjected to intense aircraft noise. It is this sort of possible widespread development, based on anticipation of greatly increased volumes of commercial air traffic, upon which various commentators have evidently based their predictions that, in the future, aircraft are likely to become the most pervasive and disturbing source of urban noise.

The commercial aircraft noise that we now have apparently exacts some environmental cost in metropolitan areas, although this cost is difficult to measure. One as yet unpublished and pioneering statistical study˙gives us some sort of indicator of this cost by calculating the effects of increasing aircraft noise on the sales value of residential land.[2] This study centered on the San Francisco International Airport, which has the largest traffic volume in the San Francisco Bay Area and a high concentration of commercial jet aircraft. The airport is located about fifteen miles south of the San Francisco central business district, in San Mateo County. Residential values in that county only were considered, because all of the commercial aircraft noise there is generated in the air corridors approaching and leaving that airport.

The assessed values per square foot of land was the independent variable — measured for a random sample of residential lots (ex-buildings) in each of various Census tracts in that part of San Mateo County most affected. It was used in a series of multiple regressions of several functional forms. The independent variables used included

[2] Paul K. Dygert and David B. Sanders, "On Measuring the Cost of Noise from Subsonic Aircraft," paper presented to the Western Regional Science Association, Santa Barbara, Calif., February 1971.

TABLE 2

Tract No.	Sales Value-Noise Elasticities by Equation Numbers			
	6'	8'	9'	10'
12	−.54	−.56	−.46	−.48
56	−.72	−.73	−.70	−.69
64	−.81	−.84	−.76	−.79
39	−1.18	−1.16	−.93	−1.17
24	−1.17	−1.18	−1.10	−1.10

the Composite Noise Ratings (CNR, based dually on intensity and frequency of aircraft noise) of the sample lots, and variables reflecting site character, accessibility, and neighborhood characteristics. We will not undertake to trace here all of the alternative functional forms and specifications of equations used, or report on numerous interesting intermediate results.

The end findings of the experiment (arrived at after much winnowing out of statistically insignificant results) refer to the partial elasticity of the sales value of residential land with respect to differences in its aircraft-generated CNR. This elasticity is $e_n = \frac{\delta V}{\delta N} \cdot \frac{V_i}{N_i}$, where V refers to assessed value of residential land per square foot, N refers to aircraft noise level (CNR), and i refers to a Census tract.

The land-price to noise partial elasticities calculated by the four most productive equations for five Census tracts are shown in successive columns in Table 2.[3]

This experiment — though based on just one area and one airport — suggests that residential land values are negatively related to the level of aircraft noise, although the values of the land-price to noise elasticities must be viewed as quite tentative. Moreover, the decline of land values with the increase of aircraft noise is a not always reliable proxy measure of the environmental losses imposed by given increases of aircraft noise levels, as is suggested by the analysis on pp. 28–36 of Chapter 1. But there is a fairly strong indication that aircraft noise does impose appreciable environmental costs on residents living under landing and take-off air corridors. The aggregate environmental cost of commercial aircraft noise could be very sizeable.

Traffic and Parking Congestion. Some of the more serious environmental problems generated by the intensive use of commercial air carriers for long-distance transportation involve substantially increased traffic congestion on freeways and other highways which are major routes of ground approach to and departure from airports, and the creation of massive automobile parking problems at airports.

[3] In all of these equations, aircraft noise was significant at the .05 level.

Because major airports are typically located on the outer edges of metropolitan areas, the average outgoing or incoming air passenger has to travel on the ground distances in the range of from fifteen to twenty-five miles between his airport and his local point of origin or destination. A large airport like the San Francisco International Airport has about 700 commercial airliner departures per 24-hour day, and the same number of daily airliner landings. At the largest airports, like John F. Kennedy International Airport in New York, O'Hare Airport in Chicago, and Los Angeles International Airport, the commercial airliner traffic volume will exceed by various amounts 1,000 arrivals and 1,000 departures daily.

In addition, there is generally severe peaking of both departures and arrivals within a few hours of the day. Thus, an airport with 700 airliner departures per day will in an interval prior to the beginning of the departure peak hour generate ground travel to the airport by from 20,000 to 30,000 passengers per hour on an average day, and in an interval after the beginning of the arrival peak hour generate ground travel per hour away from the airport of a comparable number of passengers. (The daily peak-hour ground traffic volume of course fluctuates appreciably around these averages according to the day of the week.)

In the typical case, passengers will approach an airport from several directions and by several different routes, but the bulk of their ground travel will be canalized on a very few major traffic arteries, including urban freeways and other super highways, with one major route usually dominant. Thus, air passengers travelling on the ground to and from airports tend to create or add to traffic congestion. They do so more importantly than they otherwise would because their peak hours of ground travel generally coincide with, overlap, or are close to the peak hours of commuter travel using the same highways.

Their large addition to traffic congestion results, of course, from the fact that nearly all air passengers (other than those using helicopter services) perforce approach and leave airports in motor vehicles, and the addition is larger the greater the percentage of them who arrive in private automobiles or taxis. The proportion of passengers using "public transportation" — i.e., busses or "limousines" that run from central-city points to airports and back — apparently varies considerably among major airports. For example, 73 percent of all air passengers using San Francisco International Airport arrive and depart by private automobile, and this percentage is undoubtedly even higher for Los Angeles International Airport. On the other hand, 50 percent of the air passengers travelling from the Chicago Loop area to O'Hare Airport use public transport, though they account for only one-fourth of the air passengers using the airport. The air passengers travelling from Manhattan to Kennedy Airport are evidently at least as dependent on busses, though again only a fraction of Kennedy air passengers depart from Manhattan. It would appear in general that, at practically all major airports, at least two-thirds of air passengers

make their ground arrivals and departures by either private automobiles or taxis, with private automobiles dominant.

Thus, on routes approaching airports in metropolitan areas, automotive traffic congestion (otherwise already heavy) is made severe to
critical by the ground travel of airline passengers to and from the
airports — especially during peak or near-peak commuting hours.
This imposes a cost in travel time and annoyance on commuters, and
also a cost on the air passengers involved. If, in order to take a flight
of an hour or less from New York to Washington or from Los Angeles
to San Francisco, the peak-time air traveller needs to spend an equal
amount of time reaching the airport, he suffers a distinct time and
annoyance cost, along with the commuter with whom he is competing
for road space. (The proportionate importance of this cost, of course,
dwindles as flights are longer, although it is still appreciable for transcontinental flights, if ground travel on both ends of such flights is
considered.)

Actually, in centering attention on air passenger ground travel
fitted to peaks in airliner take offs and arrivals, we have not yet
touched on the major source of traffic congestion connected with airports. The typical major airport has developed and is further developing into the core of a noncentral business district, which includes
hotels, business and professional centers, retail shopping centers, and
large industrial parks — which together daily employ far more persons than there are air passengers using the major airports.[4] As a
result, only about one-fourth of daily trips to and from airports are
made by air passengers. Three-fourths, on the average, are made by
employees of the airports, more importantly by employees of the
commercial and industrial establishments surrounding the airports,
and by visitors.

Moreover, nearly all (about 80 or 90 percent) of these nonair-
traveller workers in or near, and visitors to, airports travel by private
automobile. The magnitude of the total automotive congestion problem created by air passengers is thus less than a fourth of that
generated by major airports as a whole — and the total congestion is
approaching the unbearable. The future problem looms larger. Estimates place total commercial air passenger trips per year at 280 million by 1975, as compared with 115 million in 1967. With growing
passenger volume there will probably be a comparable growth in the
size of the noncentral business districts surrounding airports.

As a frosting on the cake, major metropolitan airports have developed truly massive automobile parking problems — created in part
by air passengers who leave their autos at the airport from the time
they leave by air to the time they return, and in part by the daily
parking of employees in the airports or in their surrounding noncen-

[4] David K. Whiteford, "Airports and Assessibility," *Traffic Quarterly,*
XXIII, April, 1969, pp. 275–283.

tral business districts. Walking distances from parked autos to airports typically range out to a half mile or mile, imposing added burdens on air passengers, and have become severe enough at some airports that shuttle busses are supplied to carry passengers from their parked vehicles to the airport central buildings. These massive parking lots (and structures), moreover, are generally aesthetic blights, to which more attention should be given.

The traffic congestion problem, however, is primary, and endeavors to remedy or ameliorate it are sorely needed.

Ameliorative Public Policy Measures. The environmental impacts of airline transportation systems that we have emphasized above all involve metropolitan areas and include air pollution, noise pollution, and ground traffic congestion generated around airports and on main highways connecting them with principal areas of origin or destination of airline passengers. Let us consider, in turn for each of these environmental problems, possible remedial or ameliorative public policies.

It is fortunate that airlines do not now, or in the near future promise to, contribute significantly to the overall air pollution problems of metropolitan areas. Big as their engines are, a thousand planes landing and taking off daily from a large metropolitan area can hardly compete with two million automobiles as sources of air pollutants, especially since the airliners spend tiny fractions of their flying times within metropolitan air mantles.

This circumstance is fortunate because effective means of appreciably reducing air-pollutant emissions of aircraft jet engines have not in general been suggested as yet, much less developed. Airliners are in a particular sort of "bind" here, comparable to that encountered with automobile engines. That is, exhaust-emission suppressant systems are also generally power reducing systems. And whereas the average motorist may be displeased only in a minor way because his emission-controlled automobile has less power, acceleration, and speed than a 1970 model, operating airliners cannot afford to sacrifice peak take-off power or power generally, if adequate performance and safety are to be maintained.

On the horizon or in the process of implementation at the present time are jet-engine modifications that should reduce substantially the volume of particulate (smoke) emissions from jet aircraft taking off, but very modest if any improvements are in prospect which would much reduce the emission of the full range of other air pollutants mentioned above. Moreover, major research attention is unlikely to be given to these other aircraft emissions because of their nearly negligible proportionate importance in metropolitan air pollution. Thus, the reduction of the particulates in jet-engine smoke is likely to produce mainly a cosmetic improvement in our air mantles.

There are more ideas in circulation concerning the abatement of commercial aircraft noise in metropolitan areas. Federal regulatory authorities have already imposed regulations requiring faster or steeper take offs of airliners from major airports, within limits of safety and aircraft capability, in order to minimize the ground distances over which the aircraft are at low enough altitudes to create noise nuisances below them. Further movement along this line seems to be in the offing. (Unfortunately, safety considerations place severe constraints on steeper landing paths.) Furthermore, feasible silencing devices are in the process of development for the exhaust ports of turbojet engines, although feasible ones have not been developed for other jet engine designs. Finally, serious consideration is being given to mounting jet engine nacelles above instead of below aircraft wings, in order to use the wings as sound buffers between the engines and the ground. The promise of this tactic cannot be assessed at this time.

Some other routes to ameliorating aircraft noise problems would involve moderately realigning aircraft approach and take-off air corridors to and from airports (and perhaps runways with them) in order to have these corridors pass over less heavily as contrasted to more heavily populated areas. In the first months of 1972, for example, something of an indignant citizens' movement arose in suburban Beverly Hills (north of the Los Angeles International Airport by about twelve or fifteen air miles), concerning the airport's use of a northbound take-off corridor that passes directly over Beverly Hills (and residential property closer to the airport on the same line). This corridor seems to honor the shortest-distance-between-two-points principle as applied to Los Angeles–San Francisco flights, and conditions of wind and terrain would seem to permit shifting it westerly somewhat more oceanward, to reduce the amount of residential area under the take-off corridor for northbound planes. A systematic reexamination of the routes of approach and take-off corridors to and from metropolitan airports — with noise pollution considerations strongly in mind — seems to be needed, with feasible ameliorative revisions to be required by the federal government as indicated.

Feasible methods of dealing with problems of acute traffic congestion on main highways leading to and from metropolitan airports and in the vicinity of airports are more difficult to come by. Whiteford, in the article cited above,[5] proposes the selection of new or alternative metropolitan airport locations with an eye to ground transportation capabilities. This seems a sensible notion at first glance, but we encounter two difficulties. Maximal ground transportation capabilities in metropolitan areas are now ordinarily provided by major metropolitan freeways that already carry congested commuting traffic between suburban areas and central cities. It would hardly be the counsel of wisdom to locate airports adjacent to such freeways, be-

[5] *Ibid.*

cause they would only aggravate already serious problems of commuter traffic congestion. The result of this sort of airport location strategy is beautifully illustrated by the location of the San Francisco International Airport on the edge of the only major urban freeway that is used by a multitude of suburbanites south of San Francisco for commuting — a road that seemingly never can be made wide enough to avert severe peak-hour congestion.

Contrariwise, finding an airport location which is *not* near freeways of major transportation capabilities, and would not much increase traffic on them, will usually be difficult. So far as such locations can be found, the indicated prescription is that a metropolitan airport needs several access routes (long routes, not offshoots from major freeways) of its own, which will not be heavily travelled by general metropolitan traffic. Assuming that locations of this sort could be found, however — not a foregone conclusion — these new airport access routes would tend on the average to attract suburban development adjacent to them and commuter traffic on them, thus ultimately defeating their initial purpose. The general conclusion toward which we are forced is that any metropolitan airport really needs a few "private" major access routes, not open to general traffic. Such routes might be highways restricted to airport-oriented traffic, or high-speed and attractive mass transit systems. There are not many in-betweens, but we can hardly afford to let the ground traffic congestion problem centered on metropolitan airports just "grow like Topsy" as it has up to now.

One palliative that has been suggested is the development, for at least several miles in several directions from any metropolitan airport, of immediate-access highways of vastly expanded capacity, to handle the aggregated traffic of several main routes converging on the airport. This may seem a minor measure, but certainly a good one; we are unable to assess its impact on general traffic congestion related to airports.

FREEWAY SYSTEMS

As was pointed out above in the case of airlines, any transportation system has as essential components the transport vehicles it uses, the roadways or airways it travels, and any connected facilities essential to its operation. This is true of freeway systems in general. The major components of such a system include primarily the highways on which motor vehicles travel and the vehicles that travel on them. (We will neglect separate consideration of supporting service stations and maintenance and repair facilities required by the vehicles.) The vehicles travelling on freeways are for some relevant purposes conveniently classified as passenger automobiles, light local-use delivery trucks, and heavy freight trucks used mostly for relatively long-distance interurban transportation.

This distinction among the main components of freeway systems may be important to recall in the succeeding discussion. This is so because, of the environmental costs imposed by these systems, some are necessarily shared by vehicles and freeways; some are primarily attributable to the vehicles; and some primarily to freeways per se. And knowledge of the primary sources of specific types of environmental costs is useful in guiding the formation of remedial public policies.

Examples of the "asignment of responsibility" of environmental costs between freeways and the vehicles that use them will be developed in the following discussion. In this discussion, the environmental impacts of metropolitan freeway systems will be discussed more or less separately from those of rural freeway systems because of the differing character and importance of the two sorts of impact. Let us begin by considering metropolitan-urban freeway systems, hereafter referred to for brevity simply as urban freeway systems.

ENVIRONMENTAL IMPACTS OF URBAN
FREEWAY SYSTEMS

An urban freeway system will be considered to include, in terms of roads, freeways within a metropolitan area which connect the suburban ring of the metropolis with the central city and which, further, traverse the central city in some sort of network to facilitate the movement of motor vehicle traffic generated within the central city and the delivery and return of suburban commuter vehicles to and from their central-city points of destination.

The environmental costs of urban freeway systems include those arising generally from heavy traffic congestion in central cities and inner suburban rings and from central-city parking congestion, those attributable mainly to freeway routing and design, and those attributable mainly to the types and designs of vehicles that use the freeways.

Central-City Traffic Congestion. Severe motor vehicle traffic congestion in the central cities of metropolitan areas (and also in merging inner suburban rings) is an almost universal phenomenon in large American metropolitan areas. This congestion develops not only on freeways, but also on city streets and secondary highways within cities. In addition to adding greatly to the costs of travel in terms of time and of annoyance to motor vehicle drivers and passengers, it is the source of various specific environmental costs to central-city residents — notably serious ground level air pollution and annoying levels of traffic noise.

The apportionment of the blame for such traffic congestion among specific sources is not easy. The vehicles that travel to, from, and in the central city share the blame with the freeways that they travel on. More precisely, the blame falls on an unduly high amount of motor traffic in ratio to the transportation capabilities of freeway systems, particularly at peak commuting hours. Because commuter traffic from and back to the suburbs is critical in engendering central-city traffic congestion, a fuller explanation of this congestion involves: (a) the large and increasing outmigration of comparatively affluent whites to suburbs as places of residence, coupled with their commuting (largely in private automobiles) to jobs in the central cities; (b) the provision of massive urban freeways to facilitate and, hopefully, to speed large volumes of commuting trips; and (c) the expansion of the automobile population sufficiently to provide an amplitude of vehicles for the commuting in question. In this explanatory system, it is interesting to note that suburbanization promotes the building of more and wider freeways, and that more freeways promote more suburbanization by increasing the accessibility of suburban land.

Some estimate of the proportion of the blame for central-city traffic congestion attributable to urban freeway systems could be made if we were able to estimate the amount of additional freeway traffic that their provision has generated. That is, if we could estimate the volume of commuter and related traffic there would be now in any metropolitan area if, let us say, IHS urban freeways had never been built, we could compare that volume with the present volume to determine how much added metropolitan traffic the IHS urban freeways have generated. Data are not available to support quantitative estimates of urban freeway-generated traffic, but it is probably quite substantial. If it is, urban freeways have imposed some corresponding environmental loss on central cities, though this may be offset in part or even wholly by the improvements in living environment that "freeway-pulled" outmigrants to the suburbs have gained.

In summary, suburbanization and metropolitan freeway building have combined to impose a severe environmental cost of traffic congestion.

Environmental Impacts of Urban Freeway Routing and Design. As urban freeways enter a central city, they generally radiate to form a relatively dense network of individual freeways aimed at various destination areas, massive and complex interchange structures, where one freeway crosses another or where freeways join, and numerous off and on ramps by which vehicles can leave or enter freeways. With freeway systems typically occupying around 10 percent of central-city land, and with elevated construction of them within central cities being the rule, they inescapably create a great deal of aesthetic blight, regardless of their specific routing. In addition, urban freeway systems have been most frequently routed with little consideration for their external environmental costs to the central city of their routing. The adverse environmental consequences stemming from freeway-generated aesthetic blight and from freeway routing have been discussed on pp. 195–196 of Chapter 7.

Noise and Air Pollution. The facts that freeways bring into central cities, as concomitants of highly congested traffic, general air pollution, severe ground-level air pollution in certain areas, and a great deal of traffic noise have already been discussed in Chapter 7 (pp. 189–190 and 191–193). We will not reconsider here these significant environmental costs of urban freeways — attributable in large part to the types and designs of the vehicles involved. It may be worthwhile to reiterate that findings of a study of Boston, Washington, D.C., and Los Angeles showed automotive traffic to be the most noticeable source of noise in these central cities and also the most bothersome.

ENVIRONMENTAL IMPACTS OF RURAL FREEWAY SYSTEMS

Thirty-five thousand miles of multiple-lane, divided, rural freeways crisscrossing the contiguous 48 states of our country from coast to coast and border to border sound like an amazing amount of rural super roads. But the country is very wide and long, and the IHS rural system seems in no danger of paving over more than an insignificant fraction of our countryside. Cassandra predictions that the IHS, financed by a limitless fund of earmarked taxes, will ultimately bring fast, paved roads to every nook and cranny of our rural areas are sheer conjectures — and not very plausible ones at that. At present, rural freeways do not seem generally to constitute blights on the landscape, and have probably improved the environments of urban and rural residents alike by expanding the areas which are readily accessible to them by automobile and making highway travel safer. (They have also, of course, provided a substantial subsidy to the intercity and interstate heavy trucking industry, the resultant cost savings of which have helped bring the rural IHS system close to the margin of economic feasibility.)

The rural freeways, moreover, are, from the standpoint of their users, considerably superior to their immediate antecedents, which were either two-lane or multiple-lane paved rural roads. The latter generally passed through the centers or fringes of the numerous towns on their routes — slowing travel and generating periodic traffic problems — whereas the freeways typically by-pass all towns, leaving the traveller options as to whether or not to drive through towns en route to his destinations. Further, the antecedent roads, which typically were "open access" and fringed by land on which commercial building was uninhibited, tended to become axes for roadside "ribbon developments" of drive-in eating facilities, auto service facilities, merchandise establishments, and used-car lots and auto junkyards which extended along highways for considerable distances outside of the towns through which the roads passed. This produced a particular sort of ugly small-town sprawl, interfered with better land uses, and created dangerous traffic problems. The closed-access freeway which by-passes towns and adjacent to which building is prohibited, has aborted this undesirable sort of ribbon development along main highways.

There are some problems, however, connected with freeways as they affect commercial developments in or near towns or small cities in areas of low-density population which are generally in the paths of the freeways. Because commercial building is generally forbidden along the sides of the closed-access freeways, commercial developments oriented to freeway travel are typically developing in series of off-freeway "nodes" created by the intersections of freeways with local "feeder" roads leading into adjacent towns — and are usually being located close to the freeways on these feeder roads (generally accessible to the freeway by off ramps and on ramps between feeder road and freeway).[6]

Ideally, the feeder road would, for freeway travellers, connect the freeway with the central business district of a town, but it is really not doing this. After the installation of the freeway and the feeder-road interchange, the earliest developments are typically those of service stations, cafes, and other retail establishments designed to cater to the freeway motorist — close to the interchange. Thereafter, these establishments tend to be joined by business establishments directed to serving the needs of the local rural community, though they are some distance from its center. These commercial operations tend to concentrate along the feeder road, with residences some distance from it. Thus, in countless rural communities, the freeways are encouraging a town sprawl in its worst possible form. Measures to abate this tendency and secure different sorts of freeway-oriented commercial development will be considered below.

AMELIORATIVE PUBLIC POLICY MEASURES

The environmental problems associated with urban freeways that we have discussed above are those primarily of central-city traffic congestion generally, freeway routings and designs within central cities, and connected noise and air pollution. The major problem involving rural freeways involve rural town sprawl at rural feeder-road interchanges. What to do?

The general traffic congestion problem in central cities — linked to suburbanization and massive commuting — is, from a practical stand-

---

[6] Barrie B. Greenvie, "Interchange Planning Rural Areas," *Traffic Quarterly*, XXIV, April, 1970, pp. 265–269.

point, the most difficult to cope with. It is easy to propose that metropolitan areas build extensive rapid mass transit systems, and induce commuters to use them on a broad scale — thus speeding their trips to and from work and effectively abating central-city automotive traffic congestion problems. But systems possibly elegant enough and reliable and fast enough to wean large proportions of commuters away from their automobiles are terrifically expensive to build and operate (especially if central-city subway routes are used to avert an extreme noise problem), and take a long time to build. And after they are built, there is anything but a guarantee — perhaps not even a 50 percent probability — that they would ease the automotive traffic problem appreciably. Of course, steep charges or tolls for the use of freeways by automobiles at commuting hours might be combined with rapid transit systems to coerce the shift of commuters from their autos to new fast trains, but this tactic seems to rate low in political feasibility.

A less drastic policy measure would involve continued dependence on freeways for commuting traffic, but would selectively ration their use at commuting peak hours. This could be done by changing urban freeways to controlled toll roads, and charging sufficiently steep tolls during peak commuting hours to discourage nearly all motorists but commuters from travelling on freeways except at low-toll, off-peak hours. If this sort of measure were combined with closing freeways to all heavy and practically all light trucking traffic during two peak morning and two peak evening hours — imposing a not very severe economic penalty on truckers — the peak traffic congestion problem might be considerably ameliorated. Shunting the "through" traffic of heavy trucking around cities on peripheral roads should assist in this endeavor.

A more basic remedy to central-city traffic congestion would emerge from progressive promotion of dispersal of commerce and industry away from central cities and into outer suburban areas — perhaps developing conurbation — but the feasibility of this sort of revolutionary move is distinctly in doubt.

A second problem involves freeway routing and design in central-city areas. The multiple errors that have already been made in this regard have been recounted above, and because freeways are very durable structures with high initial capital costs, we are likely to be a long time in reversing the errors already committed. As freeways are replaced, or new freeway systems are built in additional urban areas, however, the counsel of urban planners who have been educated by our record of past mistakes should be followed. Briefly, new urban transport planning should be guided by a total environmental approach, which emphasizes social and community values on an equal footing with commercial transportation considerations. Freeway design and routing should be made subject to strong environmental requisites and constraints and to rational system configuration requirements, with much greater responsiveness of freeway network geometry and alignment to environmental considerations.[7]

With specific reference to the noise problem created by urban freeways, a number of ameliorative measures have been suggested. These include the installation parallel to elevated or ground-level freeways of sound walls or barriers. It is noted that a five-foot masonry wall can reduce traffic noise by 5 decibels or more, and that more substantial results can be had with higher and thicker walls. For ground-level freeways, reasonably deep and dense landscape planting of buffer strips on the edges of freeways can secure comparable noise-suppression results, in addition to adding aesthetic value. Further, conversion of ground-level freeways to cut sections (the road level being below ground level), with planted slopes and embankments, may be even more effective in traffic-noise suppression. Most of these ameliorative measures seem capable of implementation without rebuilding freeway systems entirely.[8]

Some equally promising proposals include the following: use of quiet road surfaces on freeways; requirement of adequate mufflers on large trucks; and a similar requirement for them of noise-damping engine housings. The heavy trucking industry, with its highway-borne locomotives and freight cars, has been running with the bit in its teeth for much too long with an externalities-be-damned attitude.

Concerning the rural town sprawl problem that has been developing around freeway interchanges, the preferable remedy would seem to involve town zoning and building codes and town planning, to provide for freeway-oriented commercial enterprises and slow-speed circulation routes entirely off main feeder highways in the general areas of interchanges — with specified setbacks from the main freeway. These would be designed to permit commercial development on both sides of any such circulation route, and thus encourage the maintenance of commercial buildings at their rears as well as at their fronts, because the rears of half of such buildings would be visible from the freeway. They would also facilitate parking and landscaping, and permit optimal development of interior lots as well as feeder-road frontage lots.

This alternative is considered generally superior to "frontage road" developments parallel to freeways, which generally are faced only toward the freeway — thus wasting land — and often are dangerously confusing to motorists. There are alternative devices for improvement, such as local-planned unit development programs, implemented by appropriate zoning ordinances, which could achieve comparable or better results. However they are dealt with, the developing unsightly freeway interchange clusters of commercial development, inefficiently aligned along feeder routes in a sprawl

[7] Herbert S. Levinson, "Transportation and Conservation," *Traffic Quarterly*, XXIII, January, 1969, pp. 45–57.

[8] Burton H. Sexton, "Traffic Noise," *Traffic Quarterly*, XXIII, July, 1969, pp. 427–439.

pattern, should be positively discouraged and rectified as possible where they have already developed.[9] The writer has observed a number of instances on interstate freeways — usually between towns — where the desired economic and aesthetic results of commercial development have been nicely achieved.

As the preceding discussion has suggested, traffic congestion and other problems engendered by metropolitan freeways are not among the most tractable serious environmental problems that we encounter. In the realm of public policy, somewhat deficient ameliorative measures together with some more extreme experimental measures seem to be the order of the day. In this regard, urban freeway problems are comparable to those of central-city residential congestion and disproportionate black populations. We are undersupplied with magic wands to wave away some of our more severe environmental problems and are faced with the necessity of ingeniously muddling through as best we can.

SUPPLEMENTARY READINGS

1. Bay Area Pollution Control District, *Aviation Effects on Air Quality in the Bay Region*, San Francisco, 1971.
2. Ann Fetter Friedlaender, *The Interstate Highway System: A Study in Public Investment*, Amsterdam, New Holland, 1965.
3. Barrie B. Greenvie, "Interchange Planning in Rural Areas," *Traffic Quarterly*, 24, April, 1970, pp. 265–269.
4. Helen Leavitt, *Superhighway, Superhoax*, New York, Doubleday, 1970.
5. Herbert S. Levinson, "Transportation and Conservation," *Traffic Quarterly*, 23, January, 1969, pp. 45–57.
6. A. Q. Mowbrary, *Road to Ruin*, New York, Lippincott, 1969.
7. Jeremiah D. O'Leary, Jr., "Evaluating the Environmental Impact of the Urban Expressway," *Traffic Quarterly*, 23, June, 1969, pp. 341–351.
8. Burton H. Sexton, "Traffic Noise," *Traffic Quarterly*, 23, July, 1969, pp. 427–439.
9. U.S. Bureau of Public Roads, *Highways and Economic and Social Changes*, Washington, D.C., 1964.
10. U.S. Urban Advisors to the Federal Highway Administration, *The Freeway in the City*, John Simonds, author, Washington, D.C., May, 1968.
11. David K. Whiteford, "Airports and Accessibility," *Traffic Quarterly*, 23, April, 1969, pp. 275–283.

[9] Barrie B. Greenvie, "Interchange Planning."

9 Summary and Conclusions

In our general analysis of environmental degradation and its management in Chapters 1 and 2, we suggested a general dichotomy of sources of this degradation into: (1) "pollution" (by-product wastes and side effects of production and consumption) and (2) misallocations of lands and waters among uses and users. After considering in Chapter 3 the essay by Anthony Downs on the socioeconomic, sociological, and political aspects of the recently popular "environmental-preservation" movement, we turned in Chapters 4 through 8 to five specific environmental problems, analyzing in each case their detailed characteristics and the public policy measures available for dealing with them. As indicated in the last section of Chapter 2 (pp. 56–57), Chapters 4, 5, and 8 dealt primarily with problems of pollution (including side effects) and with public policies for their abatement. We noted there also that both Chapters 6 and 7 dealt in part with environmental problems — and possible remedies for them — attributable to misallocations of lands and waters among uses and users, stemming from a variety of sources, and in part with external environmental costs either of production or of misallocations of lands among urban users.

DIFFERING CHARACTERISTICS OF DIFFERENT ENVIRONMENTAL PROBLEMS

A comparison of the different specific environmental problems discussed in Chapters 4 through 8 makes it clear that in matters of detail they have very essential differences, which are not revealed by a generalized theoretical analysis of all such problems. A few of these detailed differences deserve mention.

First, some specific environmental problems have very complex technical or technological origins, as do those of air and water pollution and of aircraft noise. Their technological origins must be rather fully understood as one essential basis for evaluating proposed policies for remedying them. This, however, may, overall, be an advantage, because environmental problems with complex technological origins are most likely to be remediable by technological progress — a sort of cure which may tend to be easier to attain than superficially simpler remedies.

On the other hand, some other specific environmental problems have no complex technological origin, being traceable mostly to human decisions made by governmental agencies or private individuals. These include problems which arise from misallocations of lands and waters among uses and from the choice of destructive production techniques by private concerns engaged in exploiting certain natural resources. Most environmental problems in this category are susceptible to rather simple remedies taking the form of moderate to severe changes in public policies governing the allocation of natural resources among uses or regulating the production techniques of those exploiting certain natural resources. Rather obvious remedies of this sort, however, may frequently be difficult to secure because they are not politically feasible, given the alignment of the power of special interests which would suffer from them and thus oppose them — often quite effectively.

Still other specific environmental problems — represented among those we have discussed by problems of central cities — involve, in addition to allocational or technological origins, intricate sociological origins. These may tend to be the most difficult to remedy — may even seem to defy remedy. In addition, they are problems the remedies for which will probably have to be fashioned by drawing on much more than economic analysis.

However this may be, every important environmental problem has its own essential peculiarities, which must be understood in detail before reliable judgments can be made concerning appropriate remedial policies.

RELATIONSHIP OF GENERAL ANALYTICAL AND SPECIFIC CASE FINDINGS CONCERNING ENVIRONMENTAL ILLS: DIAGNOSIS AND PRESCRIPTION

Allowing for the unique characteristics of any specific environmental problem, a significant question still remains. To what extent is there an integrated relationship between the diagnoses of and remedial prescriptions for environmental problems that emerge respectively from general economic analysis and from studies of specific environmental problems?

This question can be answered most effectively by distinguishing two functions that both general economic analysis and specific case studies generally perform with respect to environmental problems. The first is the diagnosis of the sources and the symptoms of particular environmental problems. The second is the selective prescription of public policy remedies for specific environmental ailments. Let us consider the relationship of general economic analysis to specific case studies separately with respect to diagnosis and prescription.

General Theorizing and Specific Case Studies: Diagnosis. Diagnosis of any environmental problem, broadly construed, generally embraces an identification of the sources of the ailment, an analysis of how these sources produce the ailment, and a description of its manifestations. Chapter 1 was devoted to a general theoretical analysis of such sources, linkages of sources to environmental deterioration, and prognosis of the characteristics of this deterioration. Chapters 4 through 8, in the earlier parts of their main sections, were generally devoted to the same three tasks, in each chapter as applied to a specific environmental problem.

A first question thus concerns the extent of relationship of the general diagnoses of environmental ills in Chapter 1 to the diagnoses of specific ills in Chapters 4 through 8. For example, did the general diagnoses of Chapter 1 provide meaningful guides to diagnoses of specific environmental problems in Chapters 4 through 8? And, conversely, were the specific diagnoses in those latter specific chapters adequately anticipated in the general diagnoses of Chapter 1?

With minor exceptions, the general theoretical and the specific problem analyses referred to were, *on a qualitative level*, highly reciprocal. For example, the general diagnoses of the sources, operative mechanisms, and results of environmental problems involving pollution broadly construed — as based on Figures 1 through 3 in Chapter 1 — proved to be generally applicable to specific problems of water pollution, air pollution, aircraft and freeway noise pollution, traffic congestion and aesthetic blight generated by freeways and airports, and degradation of forest lands by private owners. The theoretical formulation of the results of producers disregarding external social costs of their operations fitted all of these cases well, and provided a general rationalization for them.

Similarly, the general theoretical analyses of the sources and consequences of misallocations of lands and waters among uses (either rural or urban) provided — again on a qualitative level — a rational basis for approaching specific problems such as the allocation of rural water and forest resources between commercial and recreational uses. And the relevant general theoretical concepts were employed in discussing specific resource allocation problems.

The major deficiency in the general theoretical diagnoses of environmental problems appeared in the explanation of deteriorations in central-city environments. Here, the general theoretical economics of optimal allocation of land among users was useful but insufficient. The treatment of the specific case of degradation of urban environments clearly must draw not only on general economic theory, but also on theoretical constructs traditionally left to the realm of sociology.

General Theorizing and Specific Case Studies: Prescriptions. Prescription of the remedy for any specific environmental problem, given its diagnosis, ideally involves first an indication of the sort of remedy which should be most efficacious. Thus, we should hope to indicate whether a pollution tax or a subsidy to producers would have the preferable effect on the end environmental pollution, or whether another alternative — such as imposing governmental rules limiting the pollutant emissions potential of a product or process which could be sold — would be preferable under some circumstances. Or we should wish to indicate whether a reallocation of rural land and water resources from commercial to recreational uses should be approached by governmental fiat or by levying differential charges for recreational and commercial use of given bodies of natural resources. (The latter decision is likely to be heavily constrained by institutional custom and by law applying to the use of public lands.)

Such a prescription ideally involves second, given the sort of remedy chosen, a specification of how severe the remedy chosen should be. If we are to impose a pollution tax on producers emitting pollutants into a stream, how high per unit of pollutant emission of given quality should the tax be? If some public forest resources are to be transferred from logging use to recreational preserves, how much of the available forest resources should be transferred?

General *a priori* economic analysis is especially good at answering the second sort of question, because it assumes, for example, that the external environmental costs of a given amount of water pollution are measurable in monetary terms, in which event it is easy to argue that any pollution tax on water-pollutant effluents should equal their known environmental costs. Similarly, it assumes that the change in aggregate economic welfare that results from any incremental transfer of forest resources from commercial to recreational use is known (because it assumes that the increment in recreational welfare as well as the decrement in commercial welfare are known), and can thus tell us just how much transfer from one use to another will add to aggregate economic welfare.

Unfortunately, practically none of the *quantitative* prescriptions of general economic theory can be applied, and this for one simple reason. As pointed out on pp. 52–55 of Chapter 2, the environmental costs of almost any type of environmental degradation, or the reductions or increases of these costs that would result in given decreases or increases of this degradation, are not measurable in monetary terms: "We don't know their dollar costs." Consequently, they are not commensurable with the costs of abating them, and we are left without a guide as to how much (from a welfare standpoint) it is worth spending to accomplish a reduction of x percent in the unvalued physical pollutants present in an air mantle or a stream of water. Similarly, we lack any precise guide as to the amount of a pollution tax per unit of pollutant which would be equal to the environmental costs of the pollution per unit. In the same vein, we have very far from a precise notion how large the net environmental benefits of reallocating any appreciable amount of forest land from commercial to recreational use would be, and thus (knowing the costs of removing such land from commercial use) have at best only the vaguest idea of how much forest land should be so transferred.

For public policy purposes, we are thus left without enough information to arrive at even roughly approximate optimal decisions on how much should be spent on abatement of various types of pollution, or how much land or water should be reserved for one use or another. This fundamental disability of practitioners in environmental fields shows through in every one of the preceding five chapters (4 through 8), since in each case either the recommended severity of the remedy supported has from an economic standpoint been arbitrarily chosen (as in the case of emissions standards for automobiles), or put forth in qualitative terms (as in the cases of recommending "some" water pollution taxes, some degree of modification of aircraft take-off and landing corridors, some revisions of routing and design of freeways, and so forth).

Fortunately, however — as discussions of specific environmental problems in Chapters 4 through 8 indicate — general economic analysis has not left us entirely bereft of guidance in prescribing remedies for these specific ailments, even if we cannot derive monetary measures of their environmental costs.

Strictly *a priori* and essentially qualitative analyses of measures to remedy environmental ills tell us at least three things about remedies for specific pollution problems. First, although some means of reducing the use of pollution-generating products like automobiles — especially their intensive use in small and confined areas — is probably indicated, the major thrust of remedial policy should be to induce or force technological changes in these products that will reduce, as much as seems desirable when costs of these technological changes are reckoned, their pollution-producing potential. The same applies to pollution-producing production processes, like many that emit pollutants into air mantles or into streams. Curtailment of their use may be an initial remedial step, but the end goal should be to induce or force technological changes in these processes that will reduce their pollutant effects, down to any level that seems justified in view of the costs of making the connected technological changes.

This rule holds whether these technical changes are induced by pollution taxes or are forced by setting arbitrary permissible limits on the pollutant emissions or effluents of culprit products or processes.

Second, if a choice is to be made on the one hand between taxes on pollution generated by products or processes and on the other subsidies to producers to finance ameliorative "treatment" of pollutant emissions, the remedy of choice is, with great uniformity, pollution taxes. This is because such taxes do, and subsidies do not, provide incentives for producers to devise technological changes which will reduce the pollution-generating capacities of their products or processes. (This rule, of course, does not preclude the alternative policy of setting arbitrary permissible limits on the pollution generated by products or processes, with an eye to the costs of conforming to these limits.)

Both of these rules, derived essentially from *a priori* economic analysis, are applied in Chapters 4 and 8, and in the middle part of Chapter 6, in evaluating public policy measures for abating water pollution, aircraft and automotive traffic noise, and deleterious logging practices. A conclusion is that the "magic wand" of technological change should be invoked as a basic remedy for environmental ills whenever existing technology is responsible for them.

Third, general *a priori* analysis suggests strongly that the makers rather than the users of pollution-producing products should be taxed or regulated in order to bring about needed technological changes. The tax or regulation will generally have a stronger, less diluted, or more direct impact if applied to the producers. Also, the producers are ordinarily the parties best equipped to introduce remedial technological product changes. This rule has been closely adhered to in the analysis of policy measures dealing specifically with pollution problems involving both motor vehicles and urban freeways.

When we turn to environmental problems involving the allocation of lands and waters among uses and users — in the usual context wherein the monetary value of a tract of land or stream of water in at least one of its alternative uses is not measurable — *a priori* economic analysis is really not of much assistance in formulating remedial prescriptions. The essential qualification of the "doctor" here is the possession of "common sense" in this case, a detailed knowledge of the governmental and other institutional complex which has made, makes, and can alter decisions concerning the allocation of natural resources among uses and users. Thus, for example, in devising prescriptions for remedying misallocations of rural lands and waters between commercial and recreational uses, one needs to be thoroughly acquainted with the identities, legal powers, and interrelationships of the various federal and other governmental agencies that make the crucial allocative decisions in question.

In this area in particular, the knowledge of the person recommending environmental policies needs to extend far beyond the limits of pure economics, because of the crucial role of complex governmental institutions. His knowledge should also comprehend a great deal of technical information relevant to the specific allocative problem in question. The preceding becomes especially clear in the discussion of allocative problems in Chapters 6 and 7. It should be emphasized, however, that as long as we lack monetary evaluations of so many critical environmental costs and benefits, the quantitative aspects of the prescription of a wizard concerning proper land and water allocations are likely to be based on pure guesswork, and that the most that he really does is to suggest desirable directions of remedial movements.

When we encounter a problem — like deteriorated central-city environments — which embraces important socioeconomic, ethnic, and sociological components, we have a tiger by the tail, and the most broadly trained economist-sociologist-political scientist is hard put to devise predictably efficacious prescriptions for remedying the ailment. In this area, therefore, there is understandably a maze of conflicting counsel.

One purpose of this combination of text and readings has been to acquaint students both with the economic nature of environmental problems generally and with the detailed character of some salient specific environmental problems. Another has been to encourage him to examine and think about the present extent of our abilities to formulate useful and feasible public policies aimed at arresting environmental deterioration and improving our environment in some measure. The serious student of environmental problems should proceed from here to a reading of a rapidly burgeoning literature, especially in both long-established and newly introduced journals and periodicals, that is rapidly developing knowledge concerning a wide variety of environmental issues.

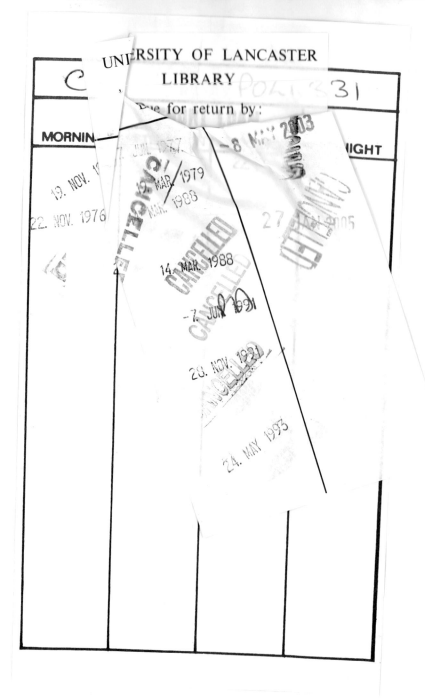